"Ron Leonard has done a masterful job communicating truth in a world riddled with deception. He capsulizes timeless truths and make them applicable to real life! The book is theologically accurate and intellectually stimulating. It's a must-read and I highly recommend it!"

~Steve Hutchison, Speaker and Author of *"Me Tarzan, You Jane!"*

"Ron Leonard has written a book that can readily assist all of us to live better lives by improving our critical thinking skills. With clarity, humility, stimulating case studies and stories, and helpful doses of humor, Ron addresses how we can discern truth, which after all, should be one of everyone's primary concerns. Covering a broad range of topics, the author sets up a journey of discovery to develop a framework for wise and fruitful living, regardless of the reader's age, status, or background. He uses the best selling Book of all time as a mirror to the soul, and masterfully arranges a conversation to help us find truth and live according to it."

~Mike Olejarz, National Training Staff and former East Coast Director of Chi Alpha Christian Ministries

DISCERNING TRUTH IN A WORLD FILLED WITH LIES

Ron Leonard

DISCERNING TRUTH IN A WORLD FILLED WITH LIES.

Copyright © 2014 by Ron Leonard, P.C.C. Published by Truth or Counseling Publishing. 7950 Chagrin Road Chagrin Falls, OH 44023.

All rights reserved. Printed in the United States of America. Published by Truth or Counseling Publishing. Copyright under Berne Copyright Convention, Universal Copyright Convention, and Pan-American Copyright Convention. No part of this book may be reproduced, stored in a retrieval system, or transmitted in any form, or by any means, electronic, mechanical, photocopying, recording or otherwise, without prior permission of the author except in the case of brief quotations embodied in critical articles and reviews.

Scripture quotations marked (NIV) are taken from the Holy Bible, New International Version®, NIV®. Copyright © 1973, 1978, 1984, 2011 by Biblica, Inc.™ Used by permission of Zondervan. All rights reserved worldwide. www.zondervan.com The "NIV" and "New International Version" are trademarks registered in the United States Patent and Trademark Office by Biblica, Inc.™
Scripture quotations taken from the New American Standard Bible®, Copyright © 1960, 1962, 1963, 1968, 1971, 1972, 1973, 1975, 1977, 1995 by The Lockman Foundation. Used by permission. (www.Lockman.org).
Scriptures marked (KJV) are taken from the King James Version of the Bible. Public domain.

Library of Congress Control Number: 2014946439

ISBN 978-0-9905670-0-4

Cover by Raphy Decipeda

Learn more at: www.truthorcounseling.com

To those who've been lied to.

TABLE OF CONTENTS

Foreword

I am so glad that you have picked up this important book. If you allow it to, you will be the wiser for reading it. This book has been in the background of most of our marriage of 25 years, but especially the last few.

Truth has been a pursuit of Ron's since he was 15 years old. The following pages are the gems uncovered along the way. Ron is someone who will go back to the store if he discover that he was undercharged 50 cents. He would not tell our children about Santa or the Easter Bunny because "that would be lying to them." He helped me to learn that even telling truth in a way that is misleading is still a lie. I know you will be inspired by "Discerning Truth."

Lori Leonard, D.O.

Acknowledgements

"I prefer to make up my own quotes and attribute them to very smart people, so that I can use them to win arguments."
~Albert Einstein

I've read a lot of books, and I've always been confused by the acknowledgements. I figured a book involved the author, the editor, and hopefully a supportive spouse. I've always wondered why the author thanks dozens of people. Is he trying to score brownie points by mentioning them? Does the author go around saying things like, "If you let me borrow your car, I'll mention you in my book"?

Having gone through the process, I now understand all too well why acknowledgments look the way they do. Instead of the one direct contributor I originally anticipated, there were more than half a dozen. Just as important was the dozens of people whose enthusiasm and excitement created the momentum for me to keep writing and to break out of my five pages a year slump.

Specifically, thanks to Joe Revesz for your detailed and untiring correction of my manuscripts. It's a whole different book because of you. What Joe contributed in detail work, Marty Bartels contributed in concept proofreading. Thank you Marty. Thanks to Dan Tillett for providing spiritual oversight and giving your honest feedback on the tougher chapters. Thanks to my wife for providing the female perspective so I didn't offend half my readers. My thanks to the authors who came before me; Greg Wasinski and Steve

Hutchinson, for showing me it can be done and for answering innumerable questions.

Further thanks to Jon Davis for his input and mostly for his Barnabus-like encouragement when I started to drag. Thanks to Raphy Decipeda for an awesome cover. Thanks also to Terry Tung for innumerable favors, great and small--I am still plotting ways to pay them back when you're not looking. Thanks to Estelle Brown for numerous suggestions and encouragements.

In the junior division, thank you Luke and Abbie for not complaining once, for all the hours the book took your father away from you. Thanks also to Simeon Brown for opening up for me the mysterious mind of the teenager.

Finally, thanks to the dozens of people who told me my book idea was great. You made me believe it too. I hope it's everything you thought it would be.

Thank you Jesus. For Everything.

Chapter 1

Some Words about the Author and His Intentions

"All truth is God's truth."
~Augustine

I love the truth so much it hurts. That's what this book is about. All the rest is details.

Why am I writing this book?

Thirty-some years ago at age 15, I determined that I had to know what truth was. I knew there had to be more to life than revisiting last night's sitcoms with my classmates. My soul was dusty and dry; so empty and lifeless I could taste it. That hollowness gnawed away at my insides.

I became desperately determined in my heart to find THE TRUTH. I was totally committed to paying whatever price to find it. It was my all-consuming desire. It still is. So, among many other lesser adventures, it was not long before I discovered Truth's name.

Jesus.

I had already decided in my soul that I had to have truth at any cost. So, when I heard a true and clear account of Jesus, I flew to him like an iron filing does to a magnet. Of Him, "even the whole world would not have room for the books that would be written" (John 21:25b NIV). Countless others of greater talent have written of that Truth. This book is largely concerned with truth with a small t. I write of it, not because it is of equal importance, but because it appears to be oft overlooked. Also, even small truths reflect on Truth, as we shall discover.

Let me explain as best I can. I love truth. I love it so much it hurts. I've had to train myself to not become visibly upset at the slightest truth infraction. Sometimes I treat the breaching of truth as though it were the puncturing of my own skin. As you can guess, I find living in today's world difficult. The greatest grief I feel is not the lies that the world tells. Lying is its job and I'm no longer surprised by it. No, the greatest grief I feel is when the Church of Jesus Christ, to whom is entrusted Big Truth, is unable or unwilling to correctly handle smaller truths.

To what am I referring? I am speaking of the Church's clumsiness in handling truth in the scientific realm. I am speaking of how you can find the Christian radio channels in an area by simply surfing and listening for the bee pollen and other questionable nutrition ads. I am speaking of how the average Christian seems to be little better than the average person at discerning between truth in everyday things, whether they be in human relations, economics or politics.

I am not just writing because they are painful. I am writing this because the non-Christian world is watching us. Post-modernism aside, they are watching us and judging whether or not we have the Truth as we claim. If they see that our ability to handle the small truths is no better or worse than their own; won't they conclude that our ability to lead them to The Truth is suspect? There are millions of non-Christians to whom truth is very important. There are many others that are actively seeking after Truth as I was. That is why I am writing this book.

Who is writing this book?

An important means of discerning truth is understanding the person who is trying to impart it to you. Truth doesn't come in a box, it comes in people. Whether you are getting your truth from a textbook, a pamphlet, a broadcast, or a conversation, they all start with a person. The better you know that person, the better you can filter out that person's intentional and unintentional distortions of the truth. Toward that end, I'm providing some personal background to help you in evaluating the things I have to say.

Everyone has various filters that we view reality through. We call these many things: predilections, prejudices, experience, schemas, core beliefs, etc. The following are some of mine. Educationally, I have the following background: a Bachelor's in Psychology, an Associate's in Computer Science, a Master's in Business Administration, and a Master's in Pastoral Clinical Counseling. These influence how I view life as well as much of the topic selection in this book.

Personally, I grew up the middle child of three boys and had a father who habitually lied to get what he wanted. I'm sure that this last has a lot to do with my lifelong truth quest. I am married with two children. My wife is a physician and we have been together for 25 years. I am a therapist working in an assortment of outpatient and inpatient settings. Before being a therapist, I worked in manufacturing, and before that, as you can see from the above, I was a professional student. There were several interim periods, where I delivered pizzas, loaded diapers onto trucks, and counted garbage trucks. I'm also a member of Mensa, if you care about such things.

Theologically, I am a mixed bag. I was brought up Catholic, was in the Assemblies of God for a long time, was a janitor at a Lutheran church and went to a Brethren Seminary. I worked for three years at a Catholic hospital, worked eight years at a Lutheran family service agency and four years at a non-denominational Christian Counseling agency. Presently I attend a Christian and Missionary Alliance Church. Like many of you, I have not found the perfect church, but God continues to mold my life anyway. If I had to use only one word to describe my theological position it would be: “evangelical.”

I have had the privilege of seeing the body of Christ from a number of points of view. This has laid waste to many of my notions of what was “wrong” with other denominations. It has also made me even warier of one-size fits all answers to complex theological questions.

Politically, I am a card-carrying member of the Christian right. Yes, there is no such organization and I have no actual card. But if there were, I would have that card. I am more Conservative than I am Republican. Ultimate truth cannot be found in politics, but Conservatism has been a more useful tool for me to discern truth with than has Liberalism.

In regards to temperament, I am a type B. When I was first writing this book, it took me two years to write the first ten pages. That this book was finished is evidence that God still does miracles.

Above most of these things, I am a skeptic. Truthfully, this sometimes borders on the openly distrustful. I still, however, repeatedly find myself to have not been distrustful enough. Being skeptical of my <u>own</u> good nature and honesty in dealing with the truth has been priceless for me. I discover more things by distrusting and examining my own motives than by any other means.

Who is this book written for?

This book is written from a Christian perspective, but I wrote it with the intention that it be useful for persons of all faiths. So long as you're interested in truth, join right in.

So, who is this book written for? This book is written for the teenager who is trying to sort out the cloud of noise and lies that she is exposed to every day. This book is for the person who always finds himself one step behind everyone else. It is for the housewife trying to determine if she should believe the talking heads on her TV. It is for the businessman who is wary of the usual offerings of the self-help world, both personal and professional. It is for the person who is good at catching lies, but worried about the ones he hasn't caught yet. It is for the person who believes that the real truth is deeper and richer than what they've seen so far.

It is written for you.

Chapter 2

What is Truth?

~Pontius Pilate

When I was 14, I had a secret notebook. It was long and brown and sat in a base with a pen holder attached. It didn't have much paper in it, so I reserved the very best of my teenage insights for it. Right around the middle page, I wrote the following: "The truth is that nobody knows what it is." When I was 15, and I had met the author of truth, I amended it to read: "I was 100% totally wrong, baby!" Yes, I still have the notebook. That particular page was entitled, "The Truth." Call it a life-long obsession.

The dictionary states (you knew that was coming, didn't you?) that truth is:

1. Conformity to knowledge, fact, actuality, or logic.
2. Fidelity to an original or standard.
3. Reality; actuality.
4. A statement proven to be or accepted as true.
5. Sincerity; integrity; honesty.[1]

We have many different views of what truth is. Here is my belief about truth boiled down to one sentence:

I believe that truth is what God says it is.

Let's see how this corresponds with our dictionary definitions. Definition one is not contradictory, but it is an incomplete attempt to capture the Truth of God. I like definition two, as God is the standard that all truth needs to be compared to. Definition three works as God is reality and has created reality. God's reality, however, is much deeper than what we refer to as reality. We grab a table and we say that the table is *real* because we can touch and see it. God often feels less real than a table or because we can't perceive Him with our five senses. A thousand years from now, however, the table will have been burned in a fire or decomposed to dust in a landfill. The properties that made it so real to us will have totally disappeared. God, however, will be exactly the same a thousand years from now. He will not have changed in the least. The reality of God underlies the "reality" of all those other things we like to cling to.

Definition four reminds us of God's Word. Definition five tells us about God's nature. We cannot really see truth through man's sincerity, integrity, and honesty as those are all blemished and imperfect. Only God perfectly models these things for us. The statement that I began this section with I believe to be a profound one, so I will repeat it:

Truth is what God says it is.

They say that $E=mc^2$ is truth. Why is it true? Some would say that it is true because scientific observation and analysis have determined it to be true. This is only true at a very surface level. $E=mc^2$ only because God says it is. You cannot understand science unless you understand this. $E=mc^2$, only because God made it that way. If God wished, he could make E not equal to mc^2. The same for the speed of light, Plank's constant, or the number of days it takes the Earth to rotate around the sun. These things are only true because God made them that way.

Let us take a look at a common misconception. People will often speak about my truth and your truth and our shared truth. For instance, you might say it is my truth that you should be faithful to your wife, but it is your truth that sex outside of marriage is an enriching thing for everyone.

You might say in this case that there are two truths. This is wrong. There is one truth and one lie. One statement agrees with God. It is truth. One statement disagrees with God. It is a lie. Many people say that their truth is *true for them.* This is a lie. What they mean when they say this is that their "truth" *is appealing* to them.

Is the above analysis *always* true? Allow me a little nitpicking. I can say that my truth is that I hate pickles and love sausage. But, you have a different truth and love pickles but hate sausage. How does that square with the statement, "Truth is what God says it is"? Aren't we, at least in this limited case, making our own truth?

No.

Who invented DNA? Who invented food? Who made both of us? That's right, God. So, it is true that you and I love and hate opposite foods. This is only the case, however, because God determined that it was going to be that way. I'm overstating my case to make a point, of course. We do have free will, but we truly have very little room to plant our own little makeshift flags and declare ownership of our own unique truths.

This ties into one of the most important principles of discernment: One of our biggest barriers to seeing truth clearly is our desire for truth to be *what we want it to be.* We don't want people we love or admire to be wrong or incompetent. Conversely, we don't want people we dislike or consider to be of low character to be right about anything. One of the most fruitful places you can learn is from people that disagree with you. People we think of as bad or self-serving are still often right. It's maddening, I know.

We also don't want things that illustrate our shortcomings to be true. It's intensely embarrassing and painful to admit that we hurt someone due to our own selfishness. For truth to grow, pride must die.

How Do we Know Truth?

What are some of the ways we know truth? Here are nine of the most important ways.

1) Logic

When I was getting my undergraduate degree, I was tempted to minor in philosophy simply on the strength of the enjoyment I got from the logic classes. It was immensely satisfying to puzzle through a confusing pile of facts and come up with the correct answer by applying some structured rules. I had more than enough confusion at that age and having a tool to straighten out my thinking felt wonderful. I would highly recommend that everyone take a logic class at some time in their life.

Sometimes you will hear people talking of using *dispassionate* logic to solve things. That is, taking the emotions out of a decision and using only logic. But, how does one become dispassionate? How do you know if you really are? If you take out the emotions, how do you know you took out the right ones? Isn't there something besides logic involved in choosing which problems to care about in the first place?

Also, simply using logic does not address the issues of assumptions. We all have assumptions, some of them learned at an early age. Some of these assumptions are not easily reducible through logic. For instance, how about the assumption, "It is good to use logic." How do you judge that with the use of logic?

It is very important to understand assumptions, both yours and those of others. It is common to find yourself in an argument where you are both using the same basic facts, but reaching different conclusions. This is a sign that you are really fighting over basic assumptions.

2) Deductive, Inductive and Abductive Logic

Deductive Logic

Deductive logic, like Sherlock Holmes, attempts to deduce what is unknown from what is known. The formal approach to deductive logic is sometimes called *syllogistic* logic. A syllogism contains three required parts, a Major premise, a Minor premise, and a Conclusion. It looks something like this:

Major Premise: All cats in Venice eat gray mice.
Minor Premise: Seymour is a cat in Venice.
Conclusion: Seymour eats gray mice.

It's a handy tool if you keep in mind that your conclusions are only as solid as your premises are. If one or both of your premises are wrong, your conclusion will probably (though not necessarily) be dead wrong as well. Also, a good argument is phrased in a way that if your premises are true, your conclusion *must* be true. Here is an argument that does <u>not</u> do that:

Major Premise: All Socialists are human.
Minor Premise: I am a Socialist.
Conclusion: I only eat oranges.

Even if both premises are true in this case, the conclusion has no logical relationship to them and the conclusion is false.

It is one thing, of course, to puzzle through and deduce that Seymour the cat only eats gray mice. There is no emotional or personal investment in that. After all, he's not *your* cat. It is quite another to apply logic to things in your life you care deeply about. After all, you really *want* Johnny to care for you and love you because then your life would be so happy. After all, weren't you meant to be happy?

You want Senator Finkelberry to be virtuous. He said he would fight for those things you care deeply about. He spoke movingly about them and he votes just the way you want him to. Those accusations *must* be made up.

As you can see, logic alone is not sufficient in many cases.

Inductive Logic

Inductive Logic is similar to Deductive Logic. In deductive logic, the premises drive us inexorably to our conclusion. In Inductive Logic, our premises show that our conclusion is *probably* true. Inductive Logic attempts to derive general principles from a collection of specific examples. Our faith in the truth of our conclusion can be weak or strong depending on the strength of our observations and the strength of their relationship to the conclusion. While this sounds much less desirable than the certainty of deductive logic, it's a kind of logic we use more often.

A strong inductive argument would look like this:

Premise 1: All the dogs that I know bark.
Premise 2: Everyone I've asked about dogs say that all the dogs they know bark as well.
Conclusion: All dogs probably bark.

A weak inductive argument would look like this:

Premise 1: The women in my family can't read maps.
Conclusion: Women probably can't read maps.

When discerning truth, it is important to know which sort of an argument is being made. It is also important to understand that deductive conclusions can be wrong and that inductive conclusions can be wrong more often.

Abductive Logic

Abductive logic is a more "common" kind of logic. Deductive and Inductive logic involve problems where the information on the issue is fully or very largely known. Abductive logic usually involves working with limited or incomplete information. Using abductive logic, a doctor can reason that a child with an elevated temperature and sore throat has either a cold or strep. If you've watched the TV show, "House" you know it could also conceivably be plague or some other exotic illness. The vast majority of the time, however, the doctor will be correct even with her limited information. Abductive logic is much better than simple guessing and can be applied much faster. Concluding that your driveway is wet because it rained last night can be done much more quickly than pausing to consider all the possible causes of wet driveways.

3) Reputation

As mentioned earlier, truth largely comes to us through persons. When a person tells us something is the truth, there are several questions we must consider. First, does this person have the *expertise* to have the correct answer on this? For instance, we generally don't take a five- year-old's word on anything that doesn't relate to Sponge Bob. Why? They don't have the knowledge base, experience, or skills to give us useful information. If the problem is car related, we're much more likely to believe a car mechanic than our spouse.

We're also much more likely to believe that a scientist can predict global warming effects if they work in climatology as opposed to chemistry. That's why it is important to ask, "Which scientists?" when you're told "scientists say." There is certainly no lack of people with opinions on important topics. While all people have opinions, most opinions are better when backed by actual knowledge.

The second question you need to address is the person's *character*. Let's revisit the broken car. A car mechanic should, by virtue of his training and experience, be better at diagnosing a suspicious engine noise. Some car mechanics, however, are dishonest and invent imaginary problems which they can then fix for a hefty fee. So, even though they have the necessary expertise, they are actually a less reliable source of information because of their poor character.

The third question concerns the person's *objectivity*. What if they have the necessary expertise and the needed character? That is a good start, but their conclusions may be colored by their heartfelt opinions on the topic. What would happen if you asked a washer salesman if Splash-O Washers are superior to Suds-O Washers? Even an essentially honest salesman will tend to prefer Splash-O Washers if those are the ones he has in the store. His objectivity may be even worse if he earns a commission when he sells Splash-O Washers.

The Rush Limbaugh show is another good example. Rush has criticized both Republican and Democratic presidents in the past. But, is he likely to give *exactly* as much scrutiny to a Republican president as a Democratic one? So, even though he has the necessary expertise and inside knowledge on presidents, you may want to look to other sources if you are interested in the failings of Republican presidents.

The fourth factor is *reliability*. Some people refer to this as a person's "track record." In high school, I had a friend named Tim. Tim didn't lie for personal gain. But, he loved giving out information in *very certain tones*. This information was always wrong. "The meeting is at 10 o'clock," he would tell me authoritatively, when it was actually at 2 o'clock on a different day, and I would end up missing the event. Tim didn't gain anything from this. He was my friend and wasn't interested in making me look bad and ruining my life. He just loved giving out information. He was in a position to know and was objective, but his facts were simply not reliable.

In summary, here are some questions to ask yourself when you evaluate someone's *reputation*. 1) Does this person have enough background in this field to know what they're talking about? 2) Is this person trustworthy enough to give me accurate information? 3) Do they have the character to question their own assumptions about life if the evidence requires it? 4) Will this person's spiritual, moral, and political outlook on life color their perceptions on this issue? 5) Does this person have something to gain from convincing me of this (i.e. money, self-gratification, fame)? 6) Have they been reliable in the past?

4) Direct Experience

Direct experience is something you witnessed firsthand. You saw, heard, tasted, touched, and/or smelled it yourself. We often refer to this as firsthand experience or simply *knowing*. I have heard it said that, "The man who has had an experience, is not at the mercy of a man with an argument."

While direct experience is a powerful way to experience truth, it is not 100% accurate. Why? Because part of our perception is based upon the *meaning* that we assign to that event. For example, in the Rodney King trials, both the defense *and* prosecution made extensive use of the tape recording of the beating. Both sides viewed the same recorded experience, but drew opposite conclusions. They assigned a different meaning to what was being seen and tried to convince the jury of their meaning and their "truth." In politics, this is often called, "spin," as both sides are trying to assign a different significance to the same event.

Also, our perception of an event is not the total understanding of the event. In the famous parable of the five blind men and the elephant, the five blind men all directly experienced the elephant, but came to different conclusions as each one experienced only part of the full reality. This happens repeatedly in courtroom trials. Multiple direct witnesses to an event habitually give conflicting evidence. This is because their points of view, both spatially and cognitively, are quite different.

Finally, direct experience is clouded as it is filtered by our ability to recall. Once the event is past, our memories are incomplete. One detail that stands out in your memory may have been forgotten in a second person's, and grossly distorted in the mind of a third.

5) Secondhand Experience

Secondhand experience is what you learn from watching others. I didn't have much dating experience in high school. Nevertheless, I learned many things about dating (for instance that it was potentially dangerous and unpleasant) from watching the experiences of others.

6) Intuition

Intuition is what we call knowing things without really knowing why. Intuition is suspecting your significant other is hiding something without having a real reason why. People that study these things believe it results from a collection of perceptions that are known to the sub-conscious mind and percolate their way into our consciousness as impressions or ideas. Some people are very intuitive, while others don't seem to know there is such a thing. I have found that it should not be fully trusted, but that it should never, ever be ignored.

7) Scientific Analysis

Scientific analysis is like secondhand experience, only done by scientists. Scientific analysis is often reported to us through a third party, such as the media or John Tesh. The more parties that have processed scientific knowledge before it gets to us, the more questions we should ask of it. This will be discussed at full length in the chapter on Science and Truth.

8) Divine Revelation

Divine revelation is often difficult to assess, especially if you are getting it secondhand. In my experience, there are a great deal more false prophets than real ones. In this area I am a great fan of the superiority of first hand experience. Even this can be highly suspect as we humans are very creative people, and can imagine that any unique experience is a sign of divine favor. One of the hallmarks of divine revelation is that it is reveals information that we could not have obtained through any other method. Divine revelation is more confidently discerned when the answer you receive is not the one you were looking for.

9) Personal Relationship

This is related to number eight above. In John 14:6 (NIV) we find these words: "Jesus answered, 'I am the way and the truth and the life. No one comes to the Father except through me.'" If Jesus is THE Truth, it follows then that if we know Jesus personally, we know Truth personally as well.

*****

Truth comes to us in a person, persons or in a Person. We'd all prefer that truth be about what we want, but it stubbornly refuses to care about our feelings. In a short space we've examined some methods to help us sort out truth from error, or truth from bald-faced lies. To help us know why lies happen, our next chapter discusses why people lie, and lie repeatedly.

Chapter 3

Why People Lie to Us

"There is beauty in truth, even if it's painful. Those who lie, twist life so that it looks tasty to the lazy, brilliant to the ignorant, and powerful to the weak. But lies only strengthen our defects. They don't teach anything, help anything, fix anything or cure anything. Nor do they develop one's character, one's mind, one's heart or one's soul."

~José N. Harris

"The worst part about being lied to is knowing you weren't worth the truth."

~Jean-Paul Sartre

To best discern truth, we need to confront the fact that the people we see every day, who smile at us and tell us nice things and upon whom we rely for financial and emotional support----lie to us. We all hate being lied to, that's probably why you're reading this book. If you want to know <u>when</u> you're being lied to, you need to know <u>why</u> you're being lied to.

Why do people lie to us?

That's a great question. You would think it would be so much simpler to tell the truth. As I've often been told, "When you lie, you have to keep two sets of books." And yet, liars are ubiquitous. Some do it rarely, many lie to us often, and a few lie to us compulsively. What motivates these people anyway? For purposes of discussion, I've separated them into two rough types. Type I is the well-intentioned liar and Type II is the malignant liar. These are, of course, rough groupings and there is not always a clear line between the two.

Type I liars tell us untruths with the honest belief that their lies are more helpful than hurtful. This does not mean that the Type I's lies can't devastate us and our relationships. They certainly can, and often do. It is the fact of their basic trustworthiness that allows us to become vulnerable to them in the first place. Their methodology, however, is quite different from that of the malignant liar.

Type I liars wish us well. If they lie, it is typically for reasons of self-protection or out of a desire to protect us. If they tell a self-serving lie that hurts us, they feel bad about it. They may even feel bad about a self-serving lie that doesn't hurt us. Their conscience is still quite active and hinders their worse behavior.

Many people assert that some lies are good, as they protect other's feelings. I say that even these lies are destructive. These lies destroy the opportunity for closer relationships. By lying about their true thoughts and feelings, Type I liars distance themselves from those around them. If they told the truth lovingly and respectfully instead, there would be an opportunity to learn something new and very important, both about themselves and others.

It is usually after these "crises" of sharing unpleasant feelings that a relationship really deepens. When we learn that we can both speak and hear unpleasant things about each other, while still being loved and honored, we grow closer and less fearful of each other. On the other hand, when we tell white lies to each other we destroy those opportunities, and our relationships remain at the same shallow levels they were before. When people are lied to, they are usually aware at some level that they are not being told the whole truth. This makes them both wary and uncertain of the liar.

As mentioned earlier, Type I liars will most often lie to protect themselves. They lie quite often to avoid embarrassment. It might be the embarrassment of the moment over a misplaced word or deep shame over their horrible behavior. Husbands who have hit their wives routinely lie to me about the extent of their past violence.

Type I liars also lie to avoid discovery by others. Everyone has things that they would like to conceal, and lying is an obvious tactic. It keeps others from getting too close to the truth. People commonly wear masks and project false fronts for a reason. They fear that you won't like who they really are. Lying protects them from this horrible fear.

People also lie to avoid self-discovery. To make themselves comfortable, they lie to themselves to maintain their self-image. This is driven by fear. Very few things go well in life when they are motivated by fear. 1 John 4:18 (NIV) sums this up well: "There is no fear in love. But perfect love drives out fear, because fear has to do with punishment. The one who fears is not made perfect in love."

The second type of liars is the Type II or malignant liars. They lie primarily for self-gain. The worst of these are known colloquially as sociopaths. These are the con-men, career criminals, and all-around takers among us. The official psychological term for sociopaths is *Anti-Social Personality Disorder* (ASPD). Through some combination of genetics, horrific background, and free will, they have become incapable of empathy. Let us examine the main part of the official definition from the *DSM-IV-TR*, the authoritative psychological handbook. Perhaps you will recognize someone you know in these descriptions.
On page 706 the following (partial) criteria are listed:

> A) there is a pervasive pattern of disregard for and violation of the rights
> of others occurring since age 15 years, as indicated by three (or more) of the following:

1) failure to conform to social norms with respect to lawful behaviors as indicated by repeatedly performing acts that are grounds for arrest

2) deceitfulness, as indicated by repeated lying, use of aliases, or conning others for personal profit or pleasure

3) impulsivity or failure to plan ahead

4) irritability and aggressiveness, as indicated by repeated physical fights or assaults

5) reckless disregard for safety of self or others

6) consistent irresponsibility, as indicated by repeated failure to sustain consistent work behavior or honor financial obligations

7) lack of remorse, as indicated by being indifferent to or rationalizing having hurt, mistreated, or stolen from another[2]

The way that sociopaths lie is qualitatively different. They do not lie primarily to avoid social embarrassment. They lie primarily for financial, material, sexual, or other gain. Sometimes they will lie to you just for the joy of seeing you confused and cheated.

The betrayal from these miscreants may catch you totally unprepared. We expect that people around us will behave in certain "correct" ways. We might expect harm from a stranger, but not from someone we have been friendly with and for whom we have done thoughtful favors. When people do us wrong, we expect that they will be remorseful when confronted. Sociopaths don't follow any of these rules.

They are aware of societal norms, but instead of following them, they use them to further exploit others. The sociopath sees these rules as other people's "weaknesses" and pounces on them gleefully. In contrast to the Type I liars, the sociopath's lack of empathy allows him to tell atrocious lies without fear of reprisal from his non-existent conscience.

Sociopaths usually have a very natural charm. They have made a careful study of others and have a well crafted exterior of likeability and sensitivity. They know that this presentation puts others at ease. This meticulously cultivated sense of sincerity allows them to exploit others. Ted Bundy, a famous sociopath, honed his social skills so keenly he could charm young woman the very first time he met them. He used this ability to talk women into his car or home where he then murdered them.

Self-awareness is very important when dealing with these people. That quiet little voice inside of us can alert us when we are dealing with a sociopath. The feelings that are stirred up inside you can be a powerful clue to the nature of others.* If you notice yourself trusting far too quickly, this is a great indication you are being conned. Spontaneous and deeply-felt belief in someone you don't know well is a good sign you are being manipulated.

Application of the Preceding to International Relations

It is a common, often reflexive notion in international relations that other countries would be more cooperative and like us more if we could only show them that we mean them no harm. After all, isn't that how we deal with our neighbors and how we expect others to deal with us? When we speak to another country's leader harshly, isn't that just mean? Who would want to work with a mean country? Wouldn't being talked to rudely make <u>us</u> irritated? Of course it would. So,

---

* This is an important tool for the therapist. We are very commonly required to evaluate people who are strangers to us. The feelings aroused in us by the people we are interviewing is a very helpful tool in diagnosing and treating them.

why shouldn't we use the same approach with our foreign neighbors?

The false assumption in all this is that *foreign leaders are just like our neighbors.* Fortunately, our neighbors are not sociopaths, but the leaders of other nations very often are. I'm not talking in the main about the leaders of democratically elected countries (though I'm sure there are exceptions). I'm talking about the leaders of countries that are run by single-party dictatorships. I'd think it would be very difficult to become the leader of one of these countries *without* being a sociopath. Having empathy for your fellow man would be an intolerable hindrance to obtaining power in a dictatorship.

So, trying to reason with a sociopathic leader as you would with your neighbor can only lead to failure. Sociopaths don't care if you are well intentioned toward them. They are not interested in repaying you for your loving behavior. They are only interested in how much personal gain they can obtain from you. If you are unilaterally nice to them, they see this as a weakness they can take advantage of.

The Addict as Liar

Addicts lie. They also abuse various substances. Spend any time with them though, and you'll find that the same empty cavern that never stops craving more drugs is the same wellspring that spews forth an ocean of lies.

Alcohol is the substance most often used by addicts and its victims are commonly called alcoholics. There are 16.8 million persons that either abuse or are dependent upon alcohol in the US. An estimated five persons live with each alcoholic. This adds up to an additional 67.2 million family members who are affected by alcohol, roughly 21 percent of the U.S. population.[3] In addition, there are millions more individuals who are addicted to cocaine, heroin, hallucinogens, methamphetamines and other street drugs. Still millions more are enslaved by prescription drugs and these drug addicts have many millions more family members who are deeply impacted by their behavior.[4] These addicts live in widely varying circumstances and acquire and consume their respective substances in a variety of fashions. What they all have in common, is that they lie like a rug.

At the hospital-based behavioral health job I work in, calls from addicts are the most dreaded. It's hard to talk to someone who has been using. Their ability to hear and reason while under the influence makes communication difficult. Also, they will tell the most outrageous lies in order to get treatment. Most irritatingly of all, they are not even good lies. They're either obviously false or easily disproven. The addicts will claim that they've already been approved to come in (our department arranges the approvals), they have a bed waiting for them, or they are personal friends with the psychiatrist.

It is startling to realize that addicts are so caught up in their pathetic lies that they don't realize how obvious these lies are to others. One study found that family members realized alcoholics had a drinking problem an average of seven years before the alcoholic sought help.[5] Addicts honestly believe that their lies are effective. One reason for this is the debilitating effect of drugs on the brain. Another reason is that we are <u>not</u> a confrontative society. As a consequence, alcoholics are often not challenged on their lies and poor behavior. We are all too "polite" and don't want to make people angry by setting them straight.

Addicts don't learn to lie so lavishly right after their first drink or their first hit. They grow into it. They begin by lying to themselves: "I'm different; <u>I</u> won't become addicted," or "I can handle it and I'm not hurting anyone," progressing to the infamous, "I can take it or I can leave it alone."* Their ability to lie at will results from lying over and over to themselves first.

When addicts lie to you, it isn't to harm you personally. Most often, it's to protect themselves from facing up to the

---

* In my early twenties I was at a rehab facility to apply for a job. In the 30 seconds it took for me to go from the front door to the office, I overheard a lady tell a third person, "I can take it or I can leave it alone." She seemed totally oblivious to the silliness of announcing this while she was in rehab.

shame that threatens to swallow them up. The amount of shame that addicts carry is a well kept secret. Looking at them, you wouldn't know they were feeling any pain at all. In reality, they are filled to the brim with self-loathing.

When you're an addict, your wants only grow in intensity and immediacy. Alcoholics are especially notorious for this. Alcohol works very quickly and effectively in calming the nerves of the alcoholic. As a result of these repeated stress and quick-relief cycles, alcoholics begin to expect that all of their problems should be resolved just as quickly. Getting a detox bed from a hospital or a favor from a friend the normal way is a huge stress to their low frustration tolerance. So, they revert to lying as a faster and easier way of getting what they want.

Teenagers and Truthfulness

Another "special category" of liars is teenagers. Teenagers lie frequently, but usually for different reasons than mature adults.* One reason they lie is fear. Teens often do not feel the same solid connection to their parents that they had previously. Friendships with their peers have become more complex and tentative as well. Newly forming romantic relationships are both exciting---and terrifying. Due to these new feelings of instability, teenagers often fear that their relationships may be easily damaged or destroyed. They lie out of fear of this destruction. Your teen may need to be reassured that your relationship as a parent to them is not as fragile as it feels. They also need to be held accountable for their lies.

Teenagers also lie when they feel caught between trying to please their parents and their peers.[6] Sometimes what will please the teen's parents will simultaneously offend his friends. This threatens to damage the teen's ever-fragile social standing. Teens often find the easiest way out of this double-bind is to lie. They lack the experience that tells them that lies only make things worse. Giving them that

---

* Yes, teenagers and *immature* adults do often lie for the same reasons.

experience by telling them how their lies hurt us and break our trust is part of our job as parents.

Teens also lie out of pragmatism. They lack the necessary skills to handle conflict the hard way. These include such skills as explaining their side, compromising, or graciously accepting things they don't like. Lying seemingly "solves" these difficulties quickly, with a minimum of fuss and discomfort. Again, steady and patient parental direction is necessary to lead teens into learning adult standards.

Finally, teenagers lie to protect their privacy. Your teenager's new-found sense of privacy is very precious to her and she will do irrational things, including telling silly lies, to protect it. While you need to monitor your teens, they do have legitimate needs to have a (limited) part of their lives they can call all their own --where Mom and Dad are not barging in. This is a normal part of them growing up into someone like you, a mature person who also treasures privacy.

*****

Now that you've learned a little bit about what motivates liars, it's time to tackle that vast thicket of lies you encounter every day. The following chapters are divided by setting and are designed to be read in order. I'm sure that some of you rebellious types are going to skip ahead to the topics that interest you anyway ;-). Interspersed with these are case study chapters that attempt to pull together these concepts as they relate to topics of current interest. The penultimate section will discuss truth in the context of mental health and counseling. A list of principles rounds out the book, followed by the endnotes. For now, we will look at finding truth in, and getting truth from, the Bible.

Chapter 4

Biblical Truth

"Most people are bothered by those passages of Scripture they do not understand, but the passages that bother me are those I do understand."

~Mark Twain

Truth is a vital concept in the Bible. In the New King James Version the word 'truth' appears 210 times, 100 of them in the New Testament. In the New International Version it appears 214 times, of which 174 are in the New Testament. In the Bible, truth is not presented the same way it would be in a textbook. For this reason, understanding some of the Bible's internal rules is important to understanding Biblical truth. This chapter will not be a full exposition on Biblical truth. That would require several other books. I hope to share some general principles on how best to uncover truth as well as some valuable perspectives from which to view the Bible.

The most important thing to keep in mind when approaching the Bible is *humility*. The best way to approach the Bible is with the attitude that the Bible will change you, not that you will correct the Bible. Nor does it work for you to use the Bible to prove what you have already decided to be true.

Speaking of humility, I feel a great deal of it writing about the Bible. There have been thousands of authors who have gone before me with both more character and knowledge than myself. I also understand that many of the people reading this book will not have the viewpoint that I presently have: that the Bible is true and was written by God. I didn't always have that point of view, myself. After being saved, I was confronted with the concept of divine authorship and realized I did not share that belief.

At another Christian's advice, I read all of the way though the Bible. Fairly often, I would read something and think, "Well, that doesn't make a bit of sense." Shortly thereafter, God would convincingly show me why it did. This happened repeatedly. After this had gone on for some time, I joined millions of my ancestors in accepting God's authorship. There is no lack of other evidence that supports God's ownership,[7] but it was God's persistent point by point proving of its wisdom that convinced me.

More evidence that the Bible is the Word of God is that the Bible states that it is. Admittedly, if this was the only evidence we had, we would not have a very strong case. It is a start, however, and a necessary one. Many Scriptures support the God-breathed nature of Scripture. The ones discussed in this chapter are simply the most direct. The following are a few of the most relevant.

The New Testament states: "But know this first of all, that no prophecy of Scripture is a matter of one's interpretation, for no prophecy was ever made by an act of human will, but men moved by the Holy Spirit spoke from God" (2 Peter 1:20-21 NASB). Further, Jesus said: "If he called them gods, to whom the word of God came *and the Scripture cannot be broken...*" (John 10:35 NIV, italics mine).

Jesus also stated: "Do not think that I came to abolish the Law and the Prophets;[*] I did not come to abolish, but to fulfill. For truly I say to you, until heaven and earth pass away, not the smallest letter or stroke shall pass from the Law until all is accomplished" (Matthew 5: 17-18).

You'll notice that the quotes in John and Matthew, as well as many other that could be listed, are from Jesus. If you have any faith on the basic truthfulness of the person of Jesus, you have a very stark choice. He is not arguing for the Bible being a nice book or that some of it is God-inspired. He is stating that even the smallest marks in the Bible are God-breathed.

Your choices at this point are:

1) I guess Jesus is a liar after all. Darn, he seemed like such a nice guy too.
2) Someone has grossly misquoted Him for some unknown reason.
3) The Bible is inspired by God in its entirety.

Here is another verse to consider while you ponder your choice. The gospel of Luke, referring to Jesus' short time on earth following the Resurrection, states in Luke 24:27 (NASB): "Then beginning with Moses and with all the prophets, He explained to them the things concerning Himself in all the Scriptures." Now, which of the above three options most logically fits Jesus' behavior?

When you approach the Bible, you can have one of three possible attitudes. It is very important to carefully evaluate the attitude you have and to understand its implications.

Attitude 1: "I am not morally qualified to judge the God of the Bible."
Attitude 2: "I am morally qualified to judge the God of the Bible."
Attitude 3: "I am not sure if I am morally qualified to judge the God of the Bible."

---

* The entire Bible extant at the time.

If you hold Attitude #2, every action or attitude of God's that does not readily agree with your personal sense of morality will be a stumbling block for you in your acceptance of God. If you hold Attitude #1 or #3, you will be better positioned for the Bible to speak to you.

The first important principle to understand when trying to learn from the Bible is *exegesis*. Exegesis is simply the attempt to understand what the basic texts of the Bible *mean at face value*. Exegesis starts with the assumption that the Biblical messages were intended to convey a particular message to the readers that lived in that specific historical time, geographical location, and cultural context. Exegesis then, attempts to discover what the original Hebrew, Aramaic, and Greek texts meant to the original audience.

Pondering this assumption highlights some of our limitations in understanding Scripture. First of all, we are not native speakers of the original languages as they are no longer in use. So, we either need to learn them from scratch or rely on someone else who has. Also, we do not wholly share the mindset of either the author or his audience. While these difficulties do not make the word of God totally opaque, they must be given serious consideration and are cause to exercise humility.

The second principle is *hermeneutics*. Hermeneutics is also concerned with interpretation but, while exegesis is more concerned with the correct understanding of the words of the text, hermeneutics deals more with the interpretation of the text's spiritual significance for today's reader and context. To pick a simple example, when Jesus says in John 10:7b (NIV), "I tell you the truth, I am the gate for the sheep," good hermeneutics would inform us that Jesus is the entrance to salvation and we must go His way. Bad hermeneutics would inform us that Jesus was made out of wood.

To make the difficulties of interpretation a little more clear, let's look at a modern-day example of an interpretive difficulty. Imagine that you are at work. In the next room, you hear the voice of one of your co-workers repeatedly screaming these words: "I'm going to kill you! I have had enough, I'm going to get a gun and blow you to bits!" What you do next depends on how you interpret what is being said.

Since you are in the next room, you might not be sure you heard all of the words correctly. If you heard as few as two letters incorrectly, this might change the entire meaning of this outburst. For example, if you had instead heard your co-worker say: "I'm going to bill you. I have had enough, I'm going to get a bun and blow you to bits," you might react quite differently.

For our purposes, we'll assume you have heard the words correctly. If you know that the speaker has a history of being very laid back and calm, you will be much less likely to be concerned. Having the knowledge that the speaker is often frustrated with his computer and yells at it frequently might also be a key factor in your reaction.

Further, if your co-worker has yelled this before with no ill results, you would be much less concerned. The tone of voice would also be a key indicator. Their tone of voice may indicate that they are filled with hate, or simply mildly frustrated. Hopefully this illustrates just some of the difficulties, and opportunities for clarity, in employing interpretation. Returning to biblical hermeneutics, let's look at the hermeneutical aspects of context, perspicuity, and genres.

Considering context is fundamental to understanding the Bible. The most famous example is in Psalms 14:1b (NASB) which clearly states, "There is no God." This would seem to totally contradict the meaning of the Bible, but there it is in black and white. If you wished to discredit all of religion, you could surely walk about quoting this scripture as evidence.

Fortunately, a little attention to context makes this particular false reading readily apparent. You simply need to read the statement in the context of the rest of the verse and we learn that: "The fool says in his heart, 'There is no God.'" (Psalms 14:1, NASB). The simple act of reading the entire sentence gives us a totally different meaning.

It is important to remember that when Biblical passages were written, they were intended to have some level of logical flow to them. For that reason, understanding a passage requires you to look at the preceding and following paragraphs to help understand the overall gist of the message. Further, reading the entire chapter as well as the entire book, will give a fuller meaning to any Biblical passage.

It is also important to read passages in the context of the entire Bible. Recently, a member of the Jehovah Witnesses gave me a pamphlet that listed a few Scriptures that implied that Jesus was not God. If these few Scriptures were the only comments that the Bible made about Christ's divinity, then I would have valid reason for concern. The Bible as a whole, however, contains hundreds of other verses that directly or indirectly announce and affirm Christ's deity.

Another important interpretive concept is that of *eisegesis*. Eisegesis is the practice of reading the Bible with the conscious or subconscious desire to find passages that support attitudes and positions that you already hold. This leads to emphasizing only those verses that appear to support your positions, while discounting and ignoring ones that do not. In the preceding example, the Jehovah Witnesses were practicing eisegesis in how they selected verses about Jesus' deity. The purpose of reading the Bible is to gain wisdom and knowledge that is beyond what you have now. When you practice eisegesis, you are no wiser than when you started.

Let us turn now to the concept of *perspicuity*. Perspicuity means clearness or the ability to be easily understood. In Christianity, the Bible is widely believed to have perspicuity. This may seem confusing, as most everyone would agree that there are some Biblical passages that seem anything but straightforward and understandable.

The principle of perspicuity certainly does not apply to every message contained in the Bible. The central themes of the Bible, however, are repeated over and over throughout the Bible in ways that are clear to the average reader. For instance, that God is both loving and just is discussed from one end of the Bible to the other. That God is concerned about sin and provides a remedy for it is a recurring theme throughout the Bible as well.

Finally, it must be understood that the Bible was written using many different genres, including poetry, narrative, epistles, prophecy, law, apocalyptic, etc. To gain the fullest understanding of these different Scriptural writings it is helpful to understand more about how these genres are constructed and are intended to be understood. An excellent source for further reading on this is, *How to Read the Bible for All its Worth* (Grand Rapids: Zondervan, 1993), by Douglas Stuart & Gordon Fee.

The last important principle to understanding the Scriptures is the role of the Holy Spirit speaking to you as you read the Bible. The Holy Spirit is a person, and is both capable of, and willing to, speak to you about the Scriptures. Here are some basic guidelines on how best to hear from Him.

If in your life, you have chosen to largely ignore God and His rules, then you will probably not hear much from the Holy Spirit. If, through you choices and actions, you have effectively said, "I don't want you around God," then He will respect your wishes. By the way, God does not often speak audibly, so when I say "speak" I mean more along the lines of having thoughts occur to you that don't seem to have come from your own intellect. Hearing God speak out loud is quite rare.

Secondly, a very important rule to keep in mind is that *God's voice will not contradict God's Word.* For example, Biblical directives against sex outside of marriage are fairly well spelled out. Nonetheless, multiple people have tried to convince me that God told them that fornication was *OK for them.* If what you are hearing blatantly contradicts God's word, then what you are hearing is a deception.

The Analogy of *The Book*

A popular question is, "How can God know that something is going to happen, if it hasn't happened yet?

How is that possible"? We will answer this with the analogy of *The Book.*

Imagine a massive book lying on a table that tells the story of everyone's lives. In *The Book*, you and I and everyone else are all characters. We only know what has happened so far in the story and won't know what happens on the next page until the reader turns to it (i.e. time passes). We are confined to the current page (the present). We can't influence the speed at which the book is being read (how fast time goes). We can't change the size of the page or the typeset (the world we live in or its physical laws). We can't go back and change the dialogue that happened in the previous chapters (the past) and we don't know what the other characters will say on the next page (the future). How then, in this analogy, could God know what's happening in the next chapter?

Here is the secret:

God is not **IN** *The Book.*
God is the **AUTHOR** of *The Book.*

We mortals are totally confined by time. God, in contrast, *invented* time. He lives in something called *eternity.* Eternity is the ability to sit down on an enormous stool, looking down on *The Book* totally unconstrained by the boundaries of time. It is like being the author of a regular book. Though the impact of the author can be seen inside of a book, an author is not physically contained within his book.

As the author of *The Book*, God can look at any page of the book that he wants. God can not only look at any page he wants; he can also affect the action on any page he wants. It’s actually even more complex than that, as the characters in *The Book* have free will. God is such an awesome author, He can influence and interact with the characters on page 8 and simultaneously know the effect it will have on every single page after that. He can do this while simultaneously interacting with the characters on page 255, 368, and 512. That, dear reader, is how God can know things "that haven't happened yet."

Some Assorted Thoughts

Some people complain that the Bible doesn't make logical sense to them. If you're one of these people, try thinking about if from the following perspective. The Bible is a book that purports to be written by a being with an infinite intelligence. This book is intended to communicate not only all of the major truths, but hundreds of minor truths as well. It is intended to communicate these truths to every person of sound mind in not just one culture, but in thousands of cultures, with all of their respective ways of thinking and understanding the world around them, all across the globe. It is intended to do this at not just one point in time, but to every person in every culture in every nation in every point in time for the last two thousand plus years.

Now suppose that when you read the Bible, every part of it made perfect sense to you.

Wouldn't you be a little bit suspicious?

Here is something else to consider. My mathematics professor once stated that all systems of belief that claimed to explain <u>everything</u> were either inaccurate or incomplete. I agree with this statement. I believe that Christianity and The Bible are both incomplete. Many people find this incompleteness frustrating. I believe though, that the Bible is using this incompleteness to steer us further into God's arms. After all, if the Bible answered every conceivable question in every conceivable category, there wouldn't be much need to seek God out, would there?

*****

There is an old beginner Bible study question that I still remember well. It went something like this:

Pick the correct answer:
A) All of the Bible is inspired by God.
B) None of the Bible is inspired by God.
C) Only the parts that speak to me personally are inspired by God.

If you picked C, then, whether you realize it or not, you have a me-centered view of reality. That is, you believe that God's truth can only be understood when seen through your eyes. This is not a belief that holds up under much scrutiny. What if the person next to you has totally different passages that speak to her? Does that mean that God both did and did not inspire those words? Now multiply this by the seven billion people currently living on this planet and you'll find this works out to be quite a mess.

What I Learned in Seminary

When I started at Ashland Theological Seminary, there were people there from all types of faith backgrounds. There were Pentecostals and Fundamentalists. There were Methodists and Catholics. There were Presbyterians and Calvinists. As Ashland is a Brethren Seminary, there were many people from the Brethren denomination as well.

As I sat in my first theology class, we were being taught about the Holy Spirit, and I was focused on one important question. Would they teach correct doctrine? Correct doctrine, in my mind of course, corresponded to my own views. I wanted to see if they would teach the truth or if they would give into fear and teach things that would be non-offensive to the various denominations there. They surprised me and did neither and did it in a way that I was able to learn some things.

The professor divided up the major points of view into Sacramental, (Catholic and Eastern Orthodox), Regenerational (Mainline Protestantism), and Subsequential

(The churches that believe Holy Spirit baptism is real and for today). He then looked at the history and reasoning behind each group's position.

I had assumed that the other positions on these topics came about due to a fundamentally flawed reasoning process or through some other sort of foolishness. It turned out that each position actually had some well-thought out *reasons* behind them. Not just good reasons, but lines of reasoning that were produced in good faith. I had thought that the "others" in the class were there to learn about good theology and it turned out I was there to learn about my judgmentalism.

The other big thing I learned in Seminary was how to approach controversial issues. I had previously learned that there were "right" answers to all of these controversies and that if you simply looked at the verses correctly, then all of the verses on a topic would properly line up to support the correct answer. In Seminary, I learned to the contrary that if you're having a good, honest discussion of controversial issues, then you will need to admit that not every verse will clearly support your position. For instance, while I believe the Bible indicates that women should not be head pastors, I must admit that the Biblical example of the leader and judge, Deborah, does not support this position. The Bible, of course, is clear and consistent on the main themes, but God does not give a definitive answer on every conceivable topic. Again, I believe that this is God's way of encouraging our reliance on Him.

*****

So in conclusion, remember humility, context, more context, and more humility. This ends the more foundational chapters on truth. We now turn to more specific contexts for truth as well as some principles and case studies. Turning from deeper things to more commonplace things, our next chapter involves something we see every day: the interplay of truth and falsity in advertising.

Chapter 5

Truth in Advertising

"If you look for truth, you may find comfort in the end; if you look for comfort you will not get either comfort or truth, only soft soap and wishful thinking to begin, and in the end, despair."
~C.S. Lewis

Advertising. It's everywhere. Attacking your eyes. Assaulting your ears. Besmirching your clothing. Fetching premium prices on E-Bay. It clutters up unused parts of your brain and keeps you up late into the night as one noisome jingle after another paralyzes the executive functions of your brain. Advertising.

Before I start in on the evils of Big Business, especially its advertising arms, let me try to clear up a few myths. One of my degrees is a Master's in Business Administration, so I had a chance to learn about some of the limitations of Big Business. The degree of vulnerability that Big Business feels is largely unknown. Believe it or not, Big Business is incredibly vulnerable to us, the little guy. Big Business makes most of its money from the grand sum of all us little fish. Individually we don't count for much, but when you count up the cumulative effect of 300 million consumers, we can be a tidal wave that can swamp (or starve) these so-called big businesses.

Consider the following example. In the seventies, beta tape manufacturers made some sizable profits until the majority of consumers decided they liked VHS tapes better. VHS tape manufacturers, in turn, were forced out of business when customers at large decided they would rather watch movies on DVD. Fortunes large and small were made by video stores who happily rented out all three formats to customers. Their turn to shutter the windows came when customers decided they would rather rent their movies through Netflix and other avenues. Thousands of these stores all closed because the mighty little guy had spoken.

Big businesses are also vulnerable to bad publicity and bad luck. In 1982, Johnson & Johnson, through no fault of its own, had its market share of the pain reliever market drop from 35 percent to eight percent in the course of a few weeks.[8] The cause? One lone nut managed to bring this mighty company to its knees by injecting cyanide into Tylenol capsules and replacing them on store shelves. In addition to the seven tragic deaths, Johnson & Johnson was forced to recall $125 million dollars of product. A swift and honest response brought their reputation back, but at significant further cost. Despite their huge size, Johnson & Johnson had been shaken to its core by a single malcontent with a chip on his shoulder.[9]

Big Business is also very vulnerable to government action. Government can direct Big Business to follow whatever crazy dictate pops into its collective head. It is true that Big Business can afford to hire lobbyists and we can't. But, having lobbyists does not guarantee that you get whatever you want. After all, the opposing side in a legislative fight has lobbyists too. There is no lack of governmental creativity in crafting legislation and the effects of this legislation are cumulative. The total cost for federal government regulations has been estimated at $1.75 trillion annually[10]

That's a very big number to digest. To show you a more manageable example, let me tell you the riveting story of minimum wage increases from 2007 to 2009. The Fair Minimum Wage Act of 2007 increased the minimum wage in stages from $5.15 an hour in 2007 to $7.25 an hour in 2009. Whether or not the benefit to current job seekers from this legislation is worth the cost to future job seekers who remain unemployed is beyond the scope of this discussion. With the passage of FMWA, the main cost for some industries, labor costs, increased by 41% in the course of two years by the stroke of a pen. This happened to hard working and honest businesses as well as lazy and evil ones.

Well, you might ask, can't Big Business just use tricky advertising to make people (other than you and me, of course) buy stuff they don't need? Consider new product launches. Big Business loves to put out brand new products as these generate a whole new revenue stream. But, despite the large expense involved, only about 1% of new product launches succeed. These are products being introduced by businesses that have already been successful at launching other products and already have a lot of advertising know-how. If we were so easily tricked, the percentage of successful new product launches would be a lot higher than 1%.

So what am I saying? That advertising is all legit and all of that anger toward Big Business is misplaced? Sadly, no. While advertising is not a foolproof "weapon" that business uses against us, some of the most successful businesses wield it ruthlessly, with little or no regard for morality or ethics. Big Business often tramples the Golden Rule underfoot in their advertisements. So, with no further ado, let us see how advertisers attempt to confuse, deceive, steer, trick, and swindle us.

Lying in Advertising

In theory, it is illegal to lie in advertising. Actually it is a bit more than just theory, as people have been fined and sent to jail for lying in ads. Nevertheless, the lies continue, though they are more often lies of omission and implication. TV ads never state outright that drinking light beer will fill your house with bikini models, but they imply it very heavily by showing that very thing happening to actors. They also never state, "The food we are showing you is actually made by us and is edible." It very often is neither.

Advertisers are only convicted for explicit lies. You would think that sensible people would work hard to avoid such crimes, but these people continue to plague us, and often. It takes time and energy to sue or arrest these people during which time these liars can make a fair-sized bundle. Caution is also needed because businesses that have not been around long could be *fly-by- night* operations that take your money today and are nowhere to be found tomorrow.

In the fall of 1982 we were in the middle of a very bad recession. I gave $50 to an employment agency in Cleveland on the premise that they would work very hard to find me gainful employment. I was far from alone. The line of eager applicants went out the door. A week or two later I discovered that none of the agency phone numbers, including the special back-line number, worked. I must have called dozens of times and got only a busy signal each time. I didn't know enough to notice that the "employment office" had no office decorations, no personal photos, no potted plants or anything else that goes with an established business.

That experience paid off later in the 90s, when I went to what I thought was a job interview, but turned out to be another employment agency. During the thirty minutes of pointless questioning, I noticed through an open door that the back room equipment didn't sit on a table but was simply propped up on various boxes. Noticing those details, combined with the oily feeling I got from talking to the interviewer, saved me $3000 that day.

Why does being dishonest work? There is a saying among professional con men: "You can't con an honest man." In large part, con jobs work because of our own internal dishonesty. We should admit it; we don't want to face up to how difficult worthwhile things are, like building character or losing weight. The people who lie to us for fun and profit are counting on these shortcomings. They don't lie to you about things you don't have deep feelings about. They lie to you about things you desperately want to believe.

Advertising Techniques

Why should we care about advertising techniques? Well, first of all it's your money and you are the one responsible for it. Only you get to decide whether your money goes toward things that are life-affirming, useless, or somewhere in between.

Secondly, Madison Avenue has hired the best psychologists, graphic artists, motivational specialists, and supermodels that money can buy to get you to spend your money the way they want you to. Shouldn't you put some time and effort into fighting this onslaught? Madison Avenue has been studying you for a long time. You need to study them to help even the odds. The following are the most commonly used approaches to convince us to buy things irrespective of our actual need for them.

Sex Appeal

If their stuff is so good, why do advertisers need to use highly attractive semi-dressed people to demonstrate them to us? I'll tell you why. They know that we are attracted to attractive people and want to be around them and be like them. They are hoping that when we see their stuff with sexy people, we will transfer our attraction for the people to attraction to their product. They keep doing this because they are right.

Emotional Appeals

We are emotional creatures. Our emotional needs are complex and at times, overwhelming. For every emotional need you have, there are ten advertisers trying to appeal to them. They have studied us to see just how our emotions drive us. Then they break us all down according to demographics (male, female, young, middle-aged, suburban, ethnicity, etc.) and attempt to play to that demographic's most important need in a venue where that demographic is watching.

One of the biggest of these emotional needs is the need to be socially accepted. Social acceptance can be a complex need to fulfill, and advertisers can make it more complex still. They will tell us that in order to enhance our social desirability we need to look, smell, and sound not just good, but perfect. As if this weren't complicated enough, advertisers attempt to invent *created needs* as well. Would we have ever known that static cling was a threat to our social standing if we hadn't been told? Did you know that faded clothing was such a calamity before TV let you know?

The desire for safety is an important need as well. Who hasn't seen dozens of commercials where a helpless infant is rescued from a horrible accident thanks to the protective arms of the car or car part being advertised? There is also a huge appeal to your fear as well in their commercials. You are being invited to picture that infant as being your own helpless baby or child.

The wish to be loved and desired is yet another crucial need. People have risked kingdoms trying to satisfy these feelings. Look at the mockery that Prince Charles received as a result of his desperately trying to meet these needs with Camilla Parker-Bowles. It is this sort of desperation that advertisers are trying to tap into. If you, the consumer, can be convinced that the latest product has even the slightest chance of helping you accomplish this goal, isn't it worth five, twenty or five hundred dollars to try?

Make Outrageous Claims

This was famously practiced in the Old West by snake oil salesmen whose magic elixir was reported to cure an impossibly wide variety of ailments. These people are still with us, using weasel words such as "according to experts," "almost" and "has been demonstrated" to keep themselves on the outskirts of the law.

One of the best warnings ever given is, "If it sounds too good to be true, it probably is." This advice has saved millions of people from grief. It would be awesome to lose 30 pounds a week, but our instincts are an excellent guide on who not to trust. When our heart pulls us one way and our instincts and conscience in another, our conscience should be eagerly embraced.

Visual Appeal

Advertisers have learned to make things that look good. They may have briefly tried to sell things that looked horrid, but that really doesn't work. Instead, businesses work very hard to manufacture products that look appealing. Then, advertising agencies work twice as hard to make them look good on your TV screen or in other ads. Products are usually photographed next to attractive people or backgrounds to help with this.

The most painful (or tasteless) violation against truth is the visual presentation of food in advertisements. A friend of mine, William,* has a wife who is an exceptional chef. One day he came home to find a nice juicy hamburger on the table. He naturally assumed that his wife had thoughtfully prepared it for him. He warmed it up in the microwave and took a big happy bite. And then he promptly spit it back onto the plate. He had bitten into and half swallowed a chunk of raw hamburger.

The rest of the story is that his wife worked with a food advertising firm. She prepared foods for various "food photo shoots." In this case, she had made a hamburger patty out of raw meat. She then painted on a caramel color to make it look done. After this, she "cooked" the outside briefly using a blowtorch and added grill marks with a heating iron. The people that study these things have determined that food prepared in this way looks better than normal food that has shriveled up in the cooking process.

As it turns out, most food doesn't look its best when it is prepared naturally. Most food that you see, whether on TV or on the cover of a box, have been retouched or

---

* Most names used in this book are fictitious, and the identities of some persons have been altered to protect their privacy.

photographed in a way that has no association with reality. For example, a photo shoot of a cheeseburger may involve spreading Pine-Sol on the cheese to give it a freshly melted look. Turkey might be painted with soap for similar reasons. While none of this is illegal, it is an enormous lie.

Bandwagon

This technique overlaps with appealing to the emotional need to belong. The bandwagon approach attempts to send the message that "everybody is doing it." Think of every dance scene you've ever seen in a commercial. Whether it's Dr. Pepper, Pringles, or a score of beer commercials, everyone is totally thrilled to be dancing with each other in an atmosphere of total acceptance and happiness. Everybody is friendly, highly attractive, and having a great time. Who wouldn't want to belong to a fun group like that?

Testimonial

This is a fairly straightforward technique. The advertisers pay a notable or famous person to tell you that a product is wonderful. They are hoping you will transfer your admiration or star-struck feelings for the famous person to their product. It seems like it would pretty easy to see through this sort of thing. The vast majority of the time the celebrity is not an expert on the product's value and there is no obvious connection between the product and the celebrity. The practice must work. Advertisers, who are not in the business of losing money pay these celebrities millions of dollars a year.

It could be argued that when sports celebrities endorse sporting equipment, then they are the experts. I do believe them when they say they use these products. Often, part of the endorsement contract stipulates that they have to be seen in public using the sports product. I doubt that professional athletes would agree to use a product in their sporting career that they didn't trust to function well.

I strongly suspect when these contracts are put together it rarely happens that the athlete asks for the privilege of endorsing the product. For example, is it unlikely that Tiger

Woods approached Nike and said, "You know, I really love your sportswear. Nothing says comfort to me like Nike. I was wondering if I could have the privilege of being paid to wear it."

Advertisers approach celebrities, not the other way around, and they do it with check in hand. I'm sure that occasionally a sports start will reject sponsoring a piece of sports equipment that he doesn't like. On the other hand, I suspect their love for the equipment usually has more to do with the number of zeros on the endorsement check than their genuine affection for the gear.

Another type of testimonial is the endorsement from an average user such as Sally Rhodes from Grand Rapids, Michigan who wrote in to say that, "My family was lost at breakfast time until Corn Krunchies came along. They taste just like the Promised Land." Personally, I could see someone thinking something like that, but I am rather dubious that someone would spontaneously sit down, put their thoughts on paper, look up the correct address, and then spend money on postage to send their message to the company. Then again, I'm lazy and cheap, so that just might be me.

Having been involved in a testimonial, I might be able to shed a little light on the process. In one of my former careers, I was a buyer for an industrial parts distributor. One of my vendors was a local adhesives company who I thought did a really great job. Even though I didn't buy that much product from them, the owner would drive out personally to fix any problems. I suspect that a few of the problems weren't even caused by him or his products, but Steven happily fixed them anyway.

On a few occasions I told Steven that I appreciated what a great vendor he was, for which he was grateful. A couple of months later Steven called up and asked if I would write a testimonial for him so he could put it on the wall of his reception area. I happily agreed and mailed it over. So, was this from a real person and not just written by the company? Yes. Was the content heartfelt and not produced by the company? Yes. Was it totally spontaneous? In this case, no.

Bait and Switch

This tactic comes in three varieties, hard, medium, and soft (Yes, this is my own classification). In the "hard" bait and switch, advertisers offer goods for sale that simply do not exist. This is to get you into their store searching for that great deal at which point they attempt to sell you a more profitable product. The hard bait and switch is illegal in the United States, though it still happens.

This tactic is much easier to pull off with unique items. I remember in college looking at the Auto Classifieds in that day's paper. One of the used car lots listed about 15 different cars, all at very attractive pricing to a poor college student like me. Suspicious person that I am, I called the dealer before driving over and asked a little more about the deals. I was told, "Oh, we sold all of those." That was a different dealer than the one with the car where the engine still had radiator fluid pooled on top of it, but that's another story.

In the medium bait and switch, the advertised product may or may not be at the store. Sometimes stores will advertise inexpensive items but then purposely not order very many of them. If you get there much past the store's opening, they will be sold out, although you will have the option to get a rain check to purchase it a later date. The store's hope is that since you need the product and drove all this way out to get it, you will go ahead and buy the more profitable brand that they do have in stock.

With the in-stock variation, the product will be there, and in abundance. It will be such an obvious piece of junk, however, that most rational people will either leave or accept the sales pitch to buy the "upgraded" alternative.

Mild bait and switch is arguably not the same as your classic bait and switch. It does share some of the same aspects of your classic bait and switch, which is why I include it here. In mild bait and switch, the comparisons between products happen not at the time of advertising, but at the time you are already in the store, virtual or physical.

I have noticed in appliance stores lately, that they will often have one brand of appliance that is markedly cheaper than the rest of them. When I've looked at them, they were so horribly flimsy that even a person as legendarily cheap as myself* would not consider buying them. While I suppose the stores make some sales on the three people in the United States cheaper than I am, I suspect these appliances serve another purpose. My suspicion is that they serve the psychological purpose of making customers who buy lower end appliances more satisfied with their purchases. After all, "I didn't buy the cheapest one," so they have good reason to expect that their appliance is giving them good service and that the funny noise it makes is just a part of normal operation.

In virtual stores, mild bait and switch is also psychological in nature. Consider the following check-out options for a software purchase. First we have the old school check-out option:

_____ $50 for a two-year usage agreement
or
_____ $70 for a three-year usage agreement.

Compare this to the mild bait and switch version:

______ $100 for a two-year usage agreement
or today's special:
______ $70 for a three-year usage agreement.

In both deals the least expensive option is for the 3 year agreement and they are exactly the same price. The $70 bait and switch version, however, makes you feel like you have gotten the deal of the century and makes you feel quite happy about your purchase.

---

* It was once said of me that I had "gone through four years of college on the same two dollars."

Act, don't React

One of the best ways to deal with advertising's effect on you is to have a budget and stick to it. Decide at the beginning of the year where you want your money to go. Write it down, check it often and stick to it. If your budget for clothing is $50 a month and you stick with it, you won't find yourself with 6 pairs of $100 shoes that looked fabulous at the time, but don't go with anything.

If you've budgeted $100 a month for eating out, you have a built-in boundary to not be tempted by food ads past a certain point. For big ticket items, don't just budget well, but pray when it comes time to buy. It is much harder to be swayed by acquisitive emotions when you are in prayer. Some things to watch out for are the items on the shelves by the checkout counter. These are called "impulse items" because sellers know that most people don't come into the store with the intention to buy them. They think that if they present these items to you, you will have a sudden urge to buy them. Having a purchasing plan in mind beforehand helps to fight this as well. Know what you are in the store to purchase and only buy those items so you don't grab two tubes of lip balm, a Snickers bar, and a zip drive shaped like a lemon on the way out.

*****

Hopefully, I have helped to make you a little more prepared for the onslaught of ads attempting to convince you to spend money on things you didn't intend to buy. Always remember that God gave you free will and you are ultimately the person who decides what you do with your time, talent, and treasure. Proceeding from personal to national treasure, our next chapter tackles economics and the shenanigans of those who work in and around that field.

Chapter 6

Truth in Economics

"Figures don't lie, but liars figure."
~Mark Twain

Economics. Few things in life are as central to our daily lives and yet so poorly understood. Daily decisions such as when and where to buy gas, groceries, and bird houses are based on our understanding of economics. Our economic savvy also influences long-term decisions such as where to live, what kind of house to buy, which politicians to vote for, and what sort of job or career to follow. The better we understand our economic system, the better decisions we can make. If I were king for a day, I would decree that every citizen would complete one course in economics before they could graduate high school. A basic understanding of economics is key to not being fooled on some very important issues. There are a lot of people ready and willing to exploit this ignorance.

The following will not be an exhaustive treatise on all of economics, nor will I be telling you which economic theory is best or best explains how things work in the real world. This chapter will be a loose collection of observations on applied economics as well as some thoughts on how to understand the financial news. As with other areas of life, there are repeated patterns to both truth and lies.

One thing that smart people really, really, really like is to be thought of as *especially* smart. And nothing makes smart people think they are *extra special* than inventing a brand spanking new, nobody else has thought of it before theory, that explains everything. This is a very serious temptation to intellectuals. There is no greater intellectual high than to think that you now understand *everything.*

Economics, in many ways reminds me of the field of psychology as it progressed. Both fields of study had schools of thought which were initially thought to be THE EXPLANATION of how everything works. In psychology, Freud initially thought that all human behavior could be understood through studying sexual motivations (sex being defined somewhat broadly). When this quickly failed to hold up, Freud amended his theory so that sex *and aggression* explained all of human behavior. This didn't work out much better.

After Freud, we had Ivan Pavlov and B.F. Skinner, who were pretty convinced that *behaviorism,* the belief that human behavior can be reduced to animal impulses, explained pretty much everything. A number of other famous therapists followed them, all with their own clever theories. These new theorists were convinced that their theories were much superior to the ones that preceded them.

When you study the early psychological theories, something else interesting pops out. My very first psychology theory textbook[11] dedicated a lot of pages to discussing the personal background of the early theorists. A lot of these folks were, how shall we say, at least mildly disturbed.*

A close examination of the literature will show that the personal history of the psychological theorists greatly influences the theories they create. Harry Stack Sullivan for

---

* If you've guessed that some of your friends in the social sciences chose that career in order to figure themselves out, congratulations. **You're right!**

example, found his life greatly helped by a very good friendship he formed at age ten. In his theory of personality, there is a preadolescence stage which occurs from ages nine to twelve. An important hurdle in Sullivan's pre-adolescent stage? You guessed it, whether or not the child finds a good friend.

Of course, despite years and years of trying, these attempts to summarize everything that humans do into one single construct always failed. Human behavior was just too complex to fit into one simple theory, no matter how clever. This led, in fits and starts, to a system of eclecticism. Instead of rigidly trying to manage and predict all human behavior with one theory, social scientists and practitioners began to see the various theories not as competing "best" solutions, but as a collection of tools to explain human behavior.

Wait a minute! Weren't we talking about economics? Actually we were talking about its similarities with psychology. Let's get to that. At first glance, economics is just a study of a bunch of numbers. The laws of mathematics are logical and don't change, right? Generally this is true, but economics attempts to measure a very fickle thing, the behavior of human beings, which is what psychology does as well.

Economics also had an early period of theory development. The early theorists all hoped to develop the best theory to explain all of economic behavior. Most modern economists, however, are of the belief that theories useful for one situation may not be as helpful for the next. For example, a theory that works for a rapidly expanding agrarian economy might not work as well for an advanced economy in the middle of a depression.

These theories, just like psychological theories, appeal to their respective postulants and followers based on factors other than objective research. The economist's personality and values play a major role in how the data is collected, how it is interpreted, and how the resultant theory is applied.

Similar to psychological behavior, economic behavior is multi-factorial and highly complex. For this reason, theories that might have been highly predictive last week might be totally useless this week. In traditional science, experiments can be run on a static situation over and over. If you're studying gravity, for example, the gravity of the earth is a fairly constant thing to experiment with and past results are very predictive of future ones. This sort of constant background state is not available in either psychology or economics.

To take one example among millions, how readily can we predict that raising taxes will increase revenue? If raising taxes raised revenue by $100 billion in 1980, can we say that the same tax increase would bring in another $100 billion today? Probably not, as today's economic situation is very different from 1980.

Today the unemployment rate, the rate of consumer confidence, the labor participation rate, and the level of technological development are all very different from 30 years ago. So are state tax rates, home values, personal debt levels, stock market valuations, and prevailing interest rates. That's just from a domestic point of view. The level of international competition is also different from 1980. The export rate as well as the rate of currency exchange may be higher or lower. Foreign economies may be doing comparatively better or worse in regards to ours in 1980. All of this is just the stuff that can be measured.

People may have different attitudes toward charitable giving or the desirability of debt or the importance of a big car than they had 30 years ago. They certainly have different tastes in the things they desire to have in or around their homes. This is true for big-ticket items like stainless steel refrigerators as well as small purchases like disco balls, which no one besides my daughter want anymore.

So, each and every point of time in the timeline of the American Economy is like working with a unique person, one arguably more complex than an actual person. This doesn't mean that economists have no ability to predict economic events. They do and they're getting better at it. It does, however, mean that every citizen should have a great deal of skepticism toward the people giving them economic solutions. How often have you heard something like this:

"Stocks were up 100 points due to better than expected earnings reports"? Seriously? There are millions of people buying stocks out there! Do they really <u>know</u> this is the reason?

One of the central conflicts in economics is whether an economy should be more centrally planned or more laissez faire (unregulated). In practice, most people prefer a mixed economy where the government provides at least some minimal functions such as enforcing laws and regulating natural monopolies. Many people believe that the size and reach of government should be larger and provide a great deal more services than they do now. A growing number of people, however, believe that the US economy has become too centralized to the detriment of almost everyone. I would like to present my own thoughts on the matter in the allegorical story of Centralia which follows.

The Story of Centralia

In the country of Centralia are three kinds of people, the Controliken, the Makers, and the Little People. The Controliken make and enforce the rules. The Makers grow all the apples which made up the sole diet of the populace. The Little People do everything else.

About 70 years ago, a Controliken, whose name is lost in legend, witnessed a Little People child crying because she had no apples. To be sure, there were charities that provided apples for such occasions, but the heroic Controliken believed that this child had "fallen through the cracks" and drastic measures were needed to prevent such things from happening again. It is of note that a few historians suggest the child's family had stopped receiving charity only because the father kept using the apples to make hard cider.

In any case, the well-meaning Controliken vowed that they would increase their influence on apple distribution until---well no end goal was ever actually articulated. It was clear, however, that the Controliken felt that leaving things the way they were was a recipe for unhappiness. One of the first acts of the Controliken was to take away a percentage of the apples from the makers and give them directly to the Little People, or at least the Little People whom they thought deserved them. Most of the charities shut down as a result, but that was OK because apple distribution was now "fair."

The most nervous Controliken sat about imagining ways in which apples and apple production might harm people and then came up with rules to protect everyone from these dangers. Granted, some of these dangers had never actually harmed an actual person, but they could happen. Such a possibility was intolerable. The Controliken hired many helpers to assist them in creating and enforcing these rules. Their first important set of rules involved forcing the Makers to construct nets for all of their trees. This was their first societal safety net.* It was feared that without a net to catch the falling apples, one of them might hit someone in the head causing a serious concussion. One of the head Controlikens had a cousin who suffered from early dementia following a concussion. Granted, the concussion had been from a motorcycle accident, but you couldn't be too careful where the people's health was concerned.

The nets were strung, at Maker expense of course, and the Controliken and their staff congratulated themselves on a job well done. The next week, however, the Controliken staff found themselves without much to do. They enjoyed just goofing off for a while, but they began to grow leery lest someone notice their inactivity. They thought deep and hard about this problem and decided...that the people probably weren't safe enough yet.

Nets, after all, are just made of heavy string and can decay over time. As the Makers had whined and moaned like wounded wildebeest about putting the nets up in the first place, they obviously couldn't be trusted to maintain them. It was entirely possible that an unsuspecting Little Person could innocently walk under an apple tree just as an overly large apple was ripped off its skinny twig by gravity. That

---

* Rim Shot!

apple could then pass right though a soft spot in the net, and POW!, early dementia.

Predictably, the Makers complained bitterly about having to install the new, much safer, steel nets. Some of them even closed down their businesses just to spite the well-meaning Controliken, claiming they "couldn't afford" the new measures. To make up for the lost production, the Controliken formed advisory panels to help the remaining Makers increase their crop yields.

Many of the new panel members had taught highly acclaimed courses on growing apples for years. Other panel members had very strong feelings about how apples should be grown and had written emotionally stirring articles on the topic. None of them had actually grown any apples. Time passed and the new apple growing suggestions didn't seem to be working, so the Controliken went to the next logical step---making the suggestions mandatory.

Due to their ongoing dedication, the Controliken sought ever more creative ways to help with apple production. In a particularly famous program, they gave chosen Little People two apples for every apple that they threw into the river. As these two apples had to be confiscated from Makers in the first place, this spurred apple production all the more.*

The Controliken eventually came to realize that there was more involved in apple production than just trees. Accordingly, the Controliken took over fertilizer distribution as well. This was the only way to ensure that the Makers each got their fair share of the fertilizer. True, the Makers that were friends with the Controliken did get their fertilizer faster and cheaper. But, they were friends, so what could be fairer than that?

Of course there were small problems along the way; minor setbacks are to be expected. One time, a Controliken regulator was caught stealing apples and hiding them in his closet. The response of the ruling Controliken was swift. First, they denounced the guilty Controliken, publicly and

---

* Lest you think this is ridiculous, what I've described is merely a smaller version of the 2009 Cash for Clunkers program which spent three billion dollars paying people to destroy functional automobiles.

loudly. Secondly, they immediately moved their own piles of stolen apples out of their closets and into their basements. So, Centralia's apple economy plugged along, with its small upticks appropriately credited to wise Controliken interventions and its larger downturns just as appropriately credited to outside forces.

All of which brings us to the present era. Despite seventy years of interventions, the economy seems to be doing worse than ever. As a result, the Controliken have gathered together, discussed the situation logically, and concluded that they will greatly decrease the Controliken's interference in the economy since it clearly isn't helping.

I'm just kidding---they immediately unleashed an education campaign to inform the Little People that the economy was bad *because Makers are selfish.* Since I'm sure that strategy should work just fine, we'll leave this story of Centralia's pretend economy, and return to the discussion of our real one.

Unintended Consequences

Unintended consequences are the unexpected and usually highly negative results of well-intentioned tinkering. As we mentioned before, economics involves lots of numbers. This can give the illusion that those people using the numbers, our political leaders and their economic advisors, can just apply the best theory and everyone will be happier.

However, the numbers that are being worked with in economics are not really measuring something absolute, like the length of a stick. They are often measuring aggregate measures of human behavior, like total money spent or average consumer confidence. These things are very subject to human whims. One of the trickiest of human behaviors to account for is *self-interest.* What works really well on paper may not work so great in reality as human self-interest is very adaptive.

Why don't we look at an actual incident from Canadian history? In 1975, political leaders in the province of Ontario believed there was a problem with affordable rental housing. They felt that rents were too high and that the poor were being priced out of the market. With the very best of intentions, they passed the *Residential Premises Rent Review Act* that capped the price that landlords could charge to renters. The government mandated rate was significantly lower than the prevailing one. On paper then, the problem was solved and affordable housing was achieved for all.

This is what actually happened in the real world.[12] Landlords saw that the productivity of their rental units was greatly decreased and they were losing money on many of their units. So, when the opportunity came to buy or build more rental units, they put their money into other endeavors. When renters moved out, as they often do, the landlords did not advertise for new renters and used the rental property for other purposes.

What happened to the renters? Some people who had lived with their parents decided that renting was now an affordable option for them. Also, some people who would have bought houses, decided to continue renting instead.

The overall effect? The number of rental units (supply) decreased just as the number of people wanting rental housing (demand) increased. As there was no place to rent, many of the poor people the policy was intended to help ended up homeless instead. With no incentive to improve their properties, the existing rentals also declined in quality. All of these things were unintended consequences of government intrusion. This is an example of what happens when people, *with perfectly good intentions,* make autocratic economic decisions.

What gets even messier are the unintended consequences when people use economic arguments to deceive you. Some knowledge and a thirst for truth are necessary to counter the people who wish to feed us sweet tasting economic lies. First, we'll talk about one of the more popular theories, Keynesianism. One of the more important axioms of the theory involves its advice on how government should help to flatten out business cycles. In a typical business cycle you have an up period, a boom, followed by a down period, a recession, as shown below.

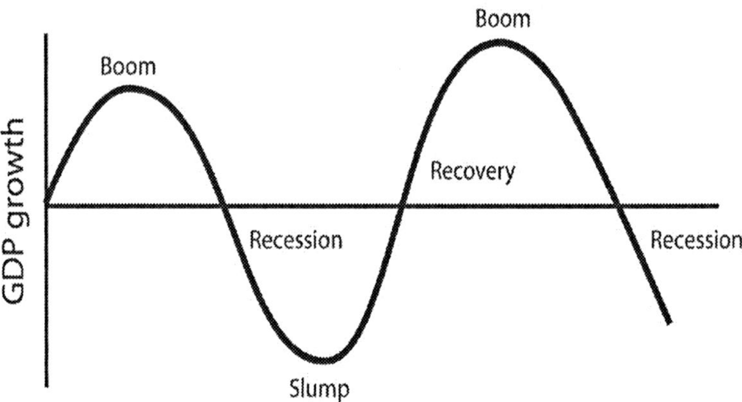

In Keynesian theory, both are problematic as too large of an expansion typically brings inflation and recessions typically bring unemployment. Keynesians prefer a much flatter cycle and believe that government is the best vehicle for bringing that about.[13]

In the recessive part of the cycle, Keynesian theory would advocate increased government spending to increase demand and decrease unemployment. This could take the form of increased payments to individuals through welfare payments, increased food stamps, unemployment insurance payouts etc. In theory, this additional money increases demand which in turn decreases unemployment and makes the recession shallower overall.

In the expansion part of the cycle, Keynesian theory advocates making the curve flatter through removing demand. Collecting taxes is one way this is done. Since expansions typically have higher employment, raising taxes takes more money out of the economy. To follow Keynesian theory, the government should also help put the brakes on demand by spending less money itself. Finally, any money the government borrowed during the recessive phase should be paid back at this time.

On paper, it works elegantly. In real life, not so much. The timing and size of the interventions are actually very difficult to determine and often make the situation worse instead of better. This, however, is not my primary interest. My interest is in what happens when a really nice theory which might or might not work at any given time if done perfectly, runs afoul of human self-interest. Not just ordinary human self-interest, but the extreme form of human self-interest, sometimes bordering on evil, known as:

*POLITICIANS!!!**

Politicians *love* Keynesian theory, or at least their own corrupted interpretation of it. Maynard Keynes receives a lot of grief for his theories and the perceived outcomes of their usage, but he is not responsible for the twisted, horrid creation that politicians have made of his work.

Democratic politicians are more likely to espouse Keynes, but many Republicans have as well. Here is what happens when politicians get a hold of a reasonable economic theory. During the recession phase, politicians loudly point to the wisdom of Keynes and vote for increases of payments to individuals as well as other types of government spending. Politicians love having a theory that justifies sending more money to voters. Political self-interest being what it is, there is also a strong temptation to use this additional spending in ways which benefit people who have been helpful to the politician in the past. After all, politicians want their friends to be helpful in the future, too. The people receiving more pork are happy. The people who are receiving checks in the mail like getting checks, so they are happy as well. These favors give the politicians an increased chance of getting elected, so they are the happiest of all.

---

* I couldn't make the politicians stay in their own chapter, sorry.

Now back to the business cycle. Eventually, recovery will replace recession, and who is to say that it didn't get started earlier thanks to the wise decisions of our politicians and their clever use of economic policy? But next comes the really sinister part of the plan.

When the economy recovers, something strange always happens. The politicians, who earlier could not stop talking about how wonderful Keynes was, now don't seem to remember his name. The recovery phase, remember, is where we pay back the money we borrowed to spend in the recession phase.

I have no memory of any politician citing Keynesian theory and demanding the government pay back the monies borrowed during a recession. During a recovery, Keynes no longer exists to politicians. To be sure, there are increased tax revenues during a recovery, but politicians focus their energy on finding some real or contrived crisis to spend this new money on rather than paying off our debts.

The last couple pages look more like opinion so I should pause for a minute to support what I'm saying. If what I'm saying is true, there should be one clear cut result. If the government is really manipulating an economic theory as an excuse to spend money even when it is unreasonable, there should be one inescapable result. We should be horribly in debt.

As of the date of my writing this, 9/22/12, our debts total over 16 trillion dollars.[14]

How big is a trillion? A trillion dollar bills stacked on top of each other with no air space in between would make a pile 67,000 miles high. Three trillion dollar bills would stack all the way to the moon. If you picked up a dollar bill every second round the clock without eating or sleeping, it would take you 31,000 years to pick up a trillion of them. Sixteen trillion dollars is ten times what the Federal Government earns in a year.[15] So to get a sense of how in debt the government is, imagine being in debt to the tune of ten times your annual salary. If you make $40,000 a year you would be $400,000 in debt. Remember, it's not ten times disposable income or even ten times net income; the federal government owes ten times its annual gross salary.

*****

I would now like to turn your attention to another reasonable theory which is sometimes corrupted by political tomfoolery. We are going to talk about Supply Side economics, specifically, the Laffer curve. As with Keynes, I think Laffer has some perfectly reasonable constructs which might or might not work very nicely in real life. The real problem comes in when politicians selectively omit parts of the theory in their implementation.

Here is a graphic of a typical Laffer curve:

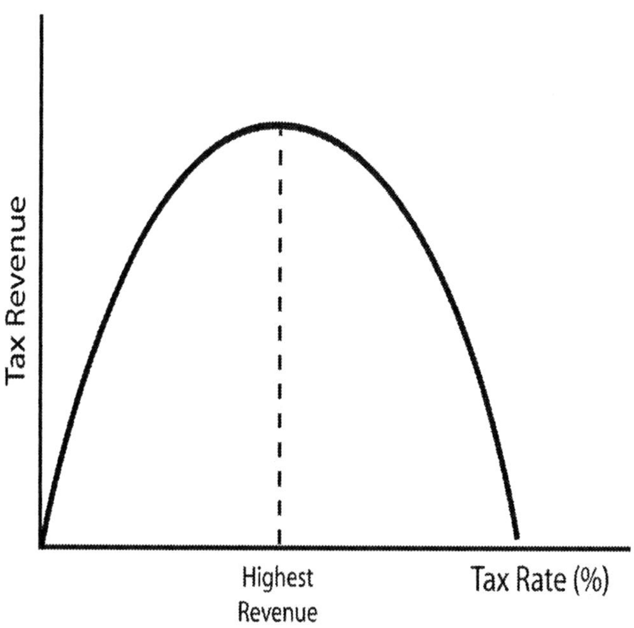

The Laffer curve is a representation of the relationship between different rates of taxation and the resulting levels of government revenue.[16] Look first at the left hand side of the curve. When the tax rate is 0%, 0 times any number is still zero, so no taxes are collected. When the tax rate is 1%, whatever number you collect will be higher than 0, so the curve goes up. At 2%, your collections are higher than they are at 1%, so the line goes up even more.

Now let's look at the other end of the curve. At a 100% tax rate, the revenue collected approaches 0. Given the choice of staying home and doing what you want and earning nothing, versus going to work and being told what to do and earning nothing, staying home would be an awfully popular option. Some people say collections would be 0. I'm hedging my bets and guessing that in a population of 300 million somebody would want to work, even if just for the fun of it. The total tax revenue would not be much though. At a tax rate of 99%, some more people would work, and the overall revenue would increase when compared to 100%.

So, assuming a unimodal curve, working backwards from the both ends we can draw a curve that meets in the middle somewhere. The highest point on the graph is the point where government revenue reaches its maximum.

This leads to an interesting yet counterintuitive conclusion. Namely, that it is possible at some points of the Laffer curve to actually increase revenue by *cutting* tax rates. It sounds magical, but on paper it works just fine. The appealing political pitch that can be made is that sometimes you can cut tax rates, while simultaneously raising more money to spend on important government programs. This approach is primarily advocated by Republican politicians, but has been put forth by Democrats as well, most famously President Kennedy.[17]

"Well," you're probably thinking, "I can see a problem with this already. How do you know where that point of maximum revenue is?" That's a great question. As we've discussed before, by the time you finish your exhaustive research into every single factor that goes into an economy, that economy has changed. In truth, there *are* multiple historical incidences of revenue rising following tax rate cuts.[18] But this does not *necessarily* mean that it will work for present or future economies.

The main problem in implementing this theory is, once again, politicians. When the Laffer curve is discussed among the economically savvy, it is much simpler to say by way of shorthand, that: “tax cuts lead to increased revenue” when what is meant is “tax cuts on points to the right of the maximum revenue point lead to increased revenue.” If everyone involved in the discussion is familiar with supply-side economics, no harm is done by this verbal shorthand.

The problem comes when politicians use this shorthand with the general public and announce: "I'll cut your taxes and you'll get to keep more of your money and tax revenue will go up too." It is simply dishonest to state that because tax cutting worked when tax rates were over 70%, that you *know* that tax cutting will work the same way when tax rates are at 40%.

What's the connection between these maladaptations of Keynesian and Supply Side economics? Promising something for nothing and using economic theory to justify it. Oh yeah, and politicians.

So, what approach should we take toward economics? Total and utter skepticism, I say. Economics is the study of fickle human behavior as understood by frail humans and further distorted by self-serving politicians. Do yourself a favor and educate yourself on how economics works. You would be surprised how easily authority figures' arguments fall apart when confronted with some basic knowledge and healthy incredulity. Your truth muscles will be strengthened and your wallet will thank you too.

*****

Authority figures play a huge role as well in our next chapter on science. Many people you encounter will expect you to be quiet because they speak for SCIENCE. Next we'll delve into how to tell when science is truthful, when it's full of hot gas, and how we can tell the difference.

Chapter 7

Truth in Science

"Christianity has nothing to fear from science; only from small scientists and small followers of science."
~C.S. Lewis

In our society, science is relied upon as one of the few final arbiters of truth. It behooves us then, to examine how science works and doesn't work in sorting out truth from fiction. There are two main components to science. The first is the scientific method, which I will argue is good. The second are the scientists, which I will argue are questionable. If you remember nothing else from this chapter, remember this: Trust the scientific method, but question the scientists.

The Scientific Method

In my view, the scientific method is a gift from God. It has allowed us to organize our knowledge in such a way that we can discover wonderful things like the smallpox vaccine, the automobile, the ink pen, and one of my personal favorites, the IJOY, a combination easy chair and back massager. Many of the things that are true about our physical and psychological world are not obvious to the naked eye and cannot be discovered or divined through intuition. Prior to the scientific method, human civilization advanced very slowly for thousands of years. After the scientific method came into common usage in the nineteenth century, human progress (on a material level at least) grew exponentially. Standards of living increased and the human lifespan increased not just a little bit, but by decades.

As we have seen, the assumptions we start with often determine our outcomes. The scientific method is built on three central assumptions: Order, Determinism, and Discoverability.[19] The presumption of order assumes that things do not occur in a random fashion and if something worked a certain way yesterday, it should continue to work that way tomorrow. Yes, this applies to computers as well. They do stop working for a reason, just don't ask me why.[20]

The presumption of Determinism assumes that preceding events determine the nature of the events that happen next. For example, your teenager will try to convince you that his having the car last night had *nothing to do* with the six inch hole in the driver's side door. But you know better. Lastly, the presumption of Discoverability assumes that each step in the chain of events can be traced and measured even if those means have not yet been invented.

In addition, there are three important rules that regulate whether scientific observations are "permissible in court." The rules on scientific observations are that they must be Empirical, Public, and Repeatable.[21] An empirical observation is one that is real and objective, as opposed to one based on feelings, hunches, or intuition. It is an observation that a reasonable person standing next to you would be able to see as clearly as you do.

A public observation is one that can be seen by others, by either looking where you looked or by being able to run a similar experiment themselves. Real science isn't interested in "Secrets known only to the Ancients." Finally, an observation must be repeatable. Other scientists must be able to get the same results when they run the experiment in their own labs. If these rules are followed honestly, then real progress can be made in human civilization.

At first glance, some of these principles might seem to preclude a discussion of a belief in a divine person that works supernaturally. Introducing an untamable God into the mix would seem to muddle the usual path of scientific discovery. The term "supernatural," by definition, means "above or superseding the natural." If, however, there really is a God that is both capable of and willing to disrupt nature, then we will never fully understand reality until we make room for Him in our inquiries.

This is something that scientists disagree on. Many scientists apply the assumptions in the scientific method to *everything* and find it difficult to flexibly address issues outside of science. Many other scientists recognize that the scientific method is a great tool for understanding natural laws, but it is not so useful in understanding spirituality and the non-material world.

Returning to the scientific method, there are three goals scientists are trying to attain. These are the more self-explanatory concepts of Understanding, Prediction, and Building on an Organized Body of Knowledge. These principles do have a concrete impact on how science is performed. In the early 80s, when I was working on my bachelors in Psychology, the textbooks of that time stated that while Evolutionary Psychology had previously been an active field of inquiry, it had since been dropped as a useful tool. This was because evolutionary theory had proved to have no practical value in predicting psychological behavior.

If we want to gain a better understanding of how the scientific method works, we will have to first learn a few of the basic terms. The first term is "hypothesis." A hypothesis is a suggested explanation for an event. It's an educated guess. A hypothesis must have three attributes. It must 1) potentially answer a specific question, 2) be stated clearly and simply, and 3) be provable or falsifiable.[22] Falsifiability is the capability of being proved wrong, a term we will look at more closely in the chapter discussing Evolution.

The other important term to understand is "theory." A theory is a collection of hypotheses that have been tested and are commonly believed to be true. This collection can be used to explain and predict a group of observed results. The general theory of relativity is a good example. It seems to explain a number of things quite well such as gravitational time dilation and gravitational red-shifting, but it is still possible that it could be proved wrong in the future as new data is collected.

The scientific method gives us a set of rules to let us know if our ideas work. If they do work, they are considered trustworthy and can be passed on to others. If they don't work, they are reworked or discarded. Repeat this thousands of times and the result is scientific progress. When used correctly, it leads us to many truths.

The Scientists

Let us turn now to the discussion of the other important element in science, scientists. I used to think of scientists as smart, dispassionate pursuers of objective knowledge who sat about all day thinking up new theories and testing them. They would occasionally disagree about ideas, but by and large would agree on the principles of science and how to go about doing things. Their main desire was to learn new things, and based on that new knowledge they would try and learn other new things. Then I grew up.

It turns out that scientists are actually... people.

I'm not attempting to impugn them. I'm not saying that they are worse than average people or stuck in the clouds, or lost in their ivory towers, or any of the usual complaints. The problem I have found with scientists is that they are people and hence, *sinners*. Sinners like you and me. They have the same barriers to knowing truth that you and I have. This prevents them from pursuing truth in a purely objective fashion. The scientific method both relies on and rewards objectivity. Scientists are subjective beings, however, and this interferes with their ability to do objective science when left to their own devices. Add in the effect of outside influences like the media and government, and the waters get muddied still further.

There is no better way I know to illustrate this point than with an experience I had in college. In order to graduate from the Honors Tutorial College at Ohio University, I had to complete an undergraduate thesis. I had to synthesize a theory, read through and report on research done in the area of that theory, use experimentation to test that theory, use statistics to analyze the results of the experiment, and then write up the results of the whole process.

The theory and experiment were very interesting and exciting to me. The experiment tested elements of color perception, culture, language, and physiology. My thesis panel consisted of two full professors who seemed interested in my topic and were supportive of my efforts. The process was designed to take a year, but I managed to extend it out to nearly two.

What were the results of all of my work? Well, I got to graduate. That was certainly good. But, in terms of experimental results, I had discovered absolutely nothing. I found no support for my theory. There were lots of results and lots of numbers and the ANOVA (ANalysis Of VAriance) statistical package computed, sorted, analyzed and then produced an impressive sized stack of green and white computer paper. I had hoped there would at least be gender differences, as I thought that women would be superior in discerning subtle color differences. After reading through my impressive green and white pile, however, I had found no significant differences between the test group and the control group; not even a trivial one.

About mid-way through the experiment, I had noticed that the Psych 101 students I was experimenting on were memorizing the test control colors in pairs rather than separately. As my theory was that the test color would be more memorable, this behavior threatened to corrupt the whole experiment. In my discussion section I duly reported on this, and what could be done in future experiments to remedy the issue. I theorized that once the testing process was improved, my theory might still be proved to be correct.

I then added about a half a page of material discussing the fact that I might have had no useful results because my theory was *simply wrong*. I wrote that particular page without giving it much in the way of thought. This simple discussion, however, absolutely amazed the two professors on my thesis board. One of them, Dr. Schumacher, said something to the effect of, "Wow, NO ONE ever says that in their conclusion. They ALWAYS say that if they did the experiment differently or did more experiments that they would be able to show that their theory is right." Dr. Bellezza chimed in and said much the same. It was a telling moment for me and I still remember it vividly 27 years later. It was then that I really began to understand how science works in the real world.

I am tempted to claim that my behavior differed from my fellow scientists due to my superior virtue. I certainly thought so at the time. The truth is more likely that my behavior was different due to circumstance. You see, at that time I had no long-term goals to be a scientist-practitioner in the social sciences. Frankly I had no long term goals at all. My only goal was to graduate, at which point I would then think of something else to do. No need to hurry things. It didn't really matter to the world of Ron if my theory turned out to be true or not. It would have been fun and personally gratifying if it had, but I was graduating whether my theory panned out or not. Real scientists do not have it this easy.

As a matter of routine, Honors Tutorial theses were placed on file at the OU library.* In the same meeting with my thesis panel I described above, I asked if there was any chance of my thesis being published to a wider audience. Their answer was, well....definitely not. In order to get published you have to show results. Your theory has to be supported. You have to actually find something. The one exception to this is if you find convincing evidence that

---

* Mine was subsequently lost and only restored due to the labors of my younger brother.

disproves a popular and well-known theory. I was disappointed my thesis wouldn't see wider circulation, but I was far from crushed.

Nothing could be further from the truth for full-time scientists. Their livelihoods, fame, and reputations depend on such things. They are not rewarded for diligently applying scientific principles in the purity of their integrity and then discovering nothing. Fame, tenure, and yes often financial gain, depend on finding something new and publishable.

Perhaps you begin to see the problems that even an honest scientist faces. Do you study an interesting and important area of science that may well not yield much of publishable papers in the short term? Or, do you study something bland as oatmeal but likely to yield several publishable works? There is a saying in the field, "Publish or Perish." By and large, you're not going to get tenure unless you publish and publish often.

Worse yet, let's say you are a scientist that is not 100% honest or who is not an entirely free agent. What if you lived in a country where the government only approves of certain results? Under Stalin's regime in Soviet Russia, Lamarckian genetics were approved of because Lamarck believed that developed strengths were passed on to the children, a notion which Stalin regarded as in keeping with communist principles. Mendelian geneticists were criticized or crushed.

This effect is not limited to dictatorships. Imagine the plight of a scientist who lives under a government which has a definite opinion on global warming. The U.S. Federal Government spent 2.12 billion dollars on global warming research in 2010 alone.[23] As the vast majority of climate research is federally funded and that government currently favors research that supports man-made global warming, what effect does that have on scientists who have other opinions or even other interests in the field?

While we're supposing, what if you're the head of a multi-million dollar drug company whose future rests upon showing a certain set of experimental results? My brother-in-law found his lucrative job come to an end when the pharmaceutical company he worked for falsified test data in an attempt to gain FDA approval. They were caught and the company fell into ruin.

Role of the Media in Scientific Confusion

Experimental scientists generally know how scientific research works and how to interpret it. As it turns out, a large number of things can go wrong in experiments. My own field of psychology used to be notorious for badly designed experiments that produced results that were useless. It is out of the wreckage of some of these experiences that such things as single-blind and double-blind experiments were invented. In single-blind studies, the experimental subjects are not told what is really being tested, so that they can not try to "please" the experimenters by changing their responses.

In practice, even single-blind experiments were often found to be insufficient. Test subjects were uncannily good at picking up non-verbal cues from the experimenter. This led to the invention of double-blind studies. In double-blind studies, even the person running the experiment is deceived or kept ignorant as to the real purpose of the study. This aids greatly in removing experimenter-induced error.

A host of other factors can ruin experiments as well. These include such things as having subjects not really randomly placed into groups or having test subjects that do not resemble the population being studied. If you're trying to learn something about the geriatric population, a study based on college students may not help you much. Other confounding variables include measuring devices that don't properly measure what they're supposed to. IQ tests from the 1950s, which tended to heavily penalize non-whites, come to mind.

Another important concept in understanding scientific experiments is the *alpha level*. The most common alpha level is .05, although more ambitious studies have an alpha level of .01. What an alpha level of .05 means, is that there is a 5% chance that any positive results may be entirely due to chance. This assumes that *everything else* in the experiment goes *exactly as planned*. As we can see from the above, it often does not.

Wait. Doesn't this prove that experiments are unreliable? Doesn't this show that scientists are running a total scam? After all, they know up front that their experiments may be wrong simply due to random chance, don't they?

Well, any <u>one</u> experiment is not much to get excited about. The general public doesn't usually know this, but scientists do. Scientists understand that before a lot of enthusiasm should be shown about experimental findings, there needs to be a <u>pattern</u> of consistent results from multiple iterations of an experiment. Ideally, a number of different experimenters should find the same results. This is because any <u>one</u> experiment, as we've seen, has the potential to be profoundly flawed. A cogent example of why excitement should always be tempered is the story of cold fusion.

In 1989, Stanley Pons and Martin Fleischmann at the University of Utah conducted an experiment that they believed demonstrated the attainment of "cold fusion." Hot fusion, also known as nuclear fusion, is the creation of large amounts of energy by combining or fusing elements together at an atomic level. This typically happens in the core of stars or in small inefficient amounts at very large, very expensive labs. Cold fusion is the same process, only at room temperature and without the huge expense. If cold fusion could be developed, it would create an almost limitless source of cheap energy.

After their "successful" experiment appeared to produce cold fusion, Pons and Fleischmann spurned the usual scientific process and proceeded instead to hold a news conference. Most journalists lack scientific training and run the results of experiments through their own filter. If the story serves the journalist's interests, it's carried. If not, it's ignored (further discussion can be found in the Truth in Journalism chapter).

In this case, cheap energy spelled VIEWERS and all of the news agencies rushed to scoop each other. There was wild excitement as speculations of revolutionary developments filled the airwaves. It was only *after* the press conference that other labs had the opportunity to attempt to replicate the experiment.

All repetitions of the cold fusion experiment failed miserably. The scientific community quickly agreed that Pons and Fleischman's claims of cold fusion were mistaken and the excitement soon faded. While there was some belief that they had found something interesting, their claims of achieving cold fusion at 70 degrees Fahrenheit could not be repeated. Here in a nutshell is a telling story of how science works and how it does not.[24] As the theory was a readily testable one, it was fairly easily resolved. This arrival at the truth happened due to the diligence of good scientists winning out over the desire for fame of a few.

In the cold fusion experiment, as in many "breakthroughs," there was breathless excitement on the part of the media after the very first experiment. Thankfully, the nature of the experiment allowed the scientific community to respond swiftly, allowing the error to be quickly discovered and put to rest. Things did not go nearly so smoothly in an earlier incident: the saccharin scare. In this case outside interference caused a great deal of harm.

In some preliminary saccharin experiments, rats were fed the equivalent of 1200-1800 cans of diet soda a day.[25] This was not done out of carelessness on the part of the experimenters, but out of economy. It is much cheaper to feed 100 rats the equivalent of 1500 cans a day of saccharin, than it is to feed 10,000 rats the equivalent of 15 cans a day. These studies were intended to be exploratory. If the results turned out to be positive, as they were in this case, (male rats developed elevated rates of bladder cancer) then the scientific community would know that this would be an interesting area for future study. This was done with the full understanding that any positive results might be simply due to high dosage effects.

The media, however, heard the word cancer and the news spread far and wide that saccharin was a major health risk. To make matters worse, the government also became involved with the science. Not the real science, of course, but the hyped-up reporting on the science. In response to the media attention, the FDA was prepared to ban saccharin in 1977. In a partial victory for the checks and balances system, Congress canceled the ban in favor of warning labels. These warning labels were finally removed in the year 2000 after further experiments were completed showing no human risk. The rats, I presume, are still in danger.

As the disproving of the significance of earlier results was more difficult in this case, the official change at governmental levels required 23 years. In the meantime, significant mischief was done. Warning labels had to be added at significant expense. Sales were lost as consumers avoided non-existent cancer dangers. The scientific establishment had proceeded with the proper care and methods, but the addition of journalists and politicians to the process proved to be a disastrous mix.

*****

In conclusion, I urge you to trust the scientific method, but question the scientists. Corrupt or sloppy scientists take away from, rather than add to our informational store. In addition, most of our knowledge of science is filtered through the media. The media can and does pick and choose which science stories are important based on their own subjective criteria. When journalists and politicians come along to "help" science, you should question the results three times as much.

With that in mind, we tackle our first case study, this one concerning evolution and creationism. Hopefully we can separate the wheat from the chaff in these two oft-criticized sciences.

Chapter 8

Case Study 1: Evolution and Creationism

"No wonder paleontologists shied away from evolution for so long. It seems never to happen."
~Niles Eldredge

"What is man, that thou art mindful of him?"
~Psalm 8:4, KJV

There are few places where the search for truth can be more instructional and challenging than in the Evolution versus Creation debate. In this case study, we will evaluate the arguments for the Theory of Evolution as well as for Creationism. I won't be trying to pick a winner. I'll be suggesting some ways to examine the arguments that will give us a better understanding of the issues.

It is vital to apply the principle of clarity when discussing evolution and creation. The term "evolution" can mean either of two very different things. The first thing evolution can refer to is microevolution. Microevolution is the change over time *within* a species. This can refer to such things as the forced evolution of dogs through breeding or to changes within species in the wild. In microevolution, a species retains its essential characteristics. Over time a bird's beak may become shorter, longer, or more curved, but it will still *have* a beak.

Most creationists do not have any complaints with microevolution. Their disagreement is with macroevolution. Macroevolution refers to species evolving into a totally different species over time. Often people will not distinguish between the two terms, which leads to much confusion. Much mischief and contention is generated through this lack of clarity.

When creationists say that evolution is false, the creationist is typically referring to macroevolution. When the evolutionist says, "The evolution debate is settled"[26], he can plausibly make this case for microevolution, but not for macroevolution. For our purposes, further discussion of the term "evolution" will refer to macroevolution. So, as radio talk show host Dennis Praeger has often pointed out, the simple act of clarifying terms can resolve a great deal of debate. We'll first look at some methods of discerning truth in the arguments for evolution. Following that will be a similar section on Creationism, and finally a discussion of the challenges found in both camps.

Evolution Examined

Questioning and examining assumptions is a powerful tool for discerning truth. Evolutionists, in common with most other scientists, assume that only mechanistic causes can be examined. As a result, they demand that no one introduce supernatural forces into scientific inquiry. I *am* sympathetic towards this attitude in most scientific pursuits. Trying to convince everyone that a disease is *not* caused by invisible demons can take up a lot of time.

It is inappropriate, however, to exclude the possibility of a prime Creator when you are talking about---how things were created. There is obviously a high level of commonality between all species. This suggests either one common source or one common Creator. It strikes me as cheating for scientists to declare at the start that the only other possible theory for creation is not allowed.

Let's look at another assumption. Many evolutionists, though they don't state this out loud, assume evolution itself. Evolution is an intellectually appealing theory. Having a simple tool that appears to explain everything about an extremely complex topic can be an intoxicating experience for intellectuals. It's not only exhilarating, but highly comforting to believe you have the answer to all questions. Once you assume evolution, evolution always works.

There are many honest questions about evolution. For example, if you ask why we have a sense of humor, the evolutionist will answer that it must have helped us survive in a way we don't fully understand yet. This is a roundabout way of saying, "Well, evolution made it that way." This is circular reasoning.

Another example of circular reasoning is the radical evolutionist's "proof" that there is no God. There are a lot of words involved, but when you strip away the extraneous ones, it boils down to this argument:

Assumption: There is no God.
Premise 1: Evolution provides many explanations for where things come from.
Premise 2: Other stuff about evolution being great.
Premise 3: Something disparaging about religion.
Conclusion: Evolution proves there is no God.

This is called assuming your conclusion or circular reasoning.

How can we use our guidelines for discerning truth to help us evaluate the evolutionist position? Look again at the issue of reputation from Chapter Two. The first element of reputation is expertise. For evolutionary biologists, studying evolution is their job. Before they even began their careers, they spent extensive periods of time working on the subject in college. Since their graduation, they have spent a large amount of time and energy studying the issue. This doesn't mean they're always right, but it does mean that they know *something*. A casual dismissal would be inappropriate.

Now let's consider the second element of reputation, character. Unfortunately, evolutionists have a history of discredited, fallacious and questionable claims. The number of fossils put forth as proof of the "missing link" between man and apes is fairly small. None of these finds have been very complete. "Lucy" was hailed as a major, major, find because her skeleton was a whopping 40% complete[27].

Considering the relatively small number of fossils involved, the number of problems with missing link claims through the years is surprising. They include:

1) Piltdown Man. An "early human" which was a total and complete fraud consisting of a human skull that someone paired with an orangutan jaw and then "discovered" at a dig site. It took 40 years for the scientific community to uncover the hoax.

2) Nebraska Man. A "missing link" based on a single tooth. This later proved to be the tooth of a peccary, a type of pig (this particular species of peccary had been extinct for some time).

3) Peking Man. Numerous partial fossils found in China. Some copies were made, but the vast majority of the original fossils disappeared in 1941.

4) Orce Man. A "missing link" based upon a single skull fragment. A symposium dedicated to it was canceled when it became clear that the specimen could not be clearly distinguished from that of a donkey skull fragment. To this day, evolutionists have not reached a consensus on whether it is of hominid or equine origin.

From a character perspective, what is troubling about these discoveries is their ready affirmation when they were first announced. This ready gullibility of evolutionists is troubling. I'd think that after these numerous setbacks they would be a little more tentative in their excited announcements.

Finally, consider the third component of reputation, objectivity. Evolutionists face severe challenges in being objective. To question evolution would be to question the basis of their entire careers. Since their livelihood relies on evolution being true, it would be very difficult psychologically for them to accept different conclusions. Also, it is more difficult to be objective in a field that faces repeated questioning. A sense of "us" vs. "them" can easily form in these circumstances.

When dealing with a difficult task, a common response is to toughen up and press on while simultaneously understanding that the limitations of the situation might lead to something short of clear-cut success. Proponents of evolution need to work hard, but also need a strong sense of humility to appreciate the complexity of the problems they face. Instead, when questioned they often exude the cockiness of Central American gang members.

How is it that the branch of science that has the least proof is the one that is the most dogmatic about its accuracy? In traditional scientific experimentation, scientists take repeated measurements. As we saw, they can rerun, for example, cold fusion experiments to see if they work the same for different people and adjust the theory accordingly. The development of life on earth, to the contrary, only happened once and can't be replicated.

Evolutionary science has to satisfy itself with examining the fragments of evidence left behind rather than being able to test and retest the process in real life. Evolutionary science is inferential rather than observational. This doesn't mean they can't do real science, but it does mean it is a weaker science. Evidence of this continuing weakness is the fact that the number of transitional species, even by the evolutionist's count, has grown scarcely at all in over a hundred years of searching.

*****

In 1972, Stephen Jay Gould and Niles Eldredge presented a paper which greatly changed evolutionary theory.[28] In contrast to the theory of gradualism, where evolution occurs at a more or less steady pace, Gould and Eldredge observed that species seemed to have long periods of no change, or stasis, interspersed with short periods of very rapid change. Their term for this pattern of change was "punctuated equilibrium."

This theory has been characterized by creationists as a frank admission of the failure of gradualism: "...how can you believe in evolution, or change, when the fossils testify to stasis, or lack of change?"[29] It has been characterized by evolutionists as simply an addition to the existing theory.[30]

What interests me is this: Just like my experience in Chapter 7, the people pushing the theory never paused to consider that maybe, just possibly maybe, their main theory could be wrong. Instead we have a situation where: "... even more than before, whatever the fossils show, 'evolution' can account for it! If lineages can be found, that is evidence for gradualistic evolution; if lineages cannot be found, then that is evidence for punctuational evolution."[31] When I listen to discussions of evolution they often sound more like religious conversations than scientific ones. A science that can't consider its own fallibility is a badly damaged one.

One indicator of scientific validity is the issue of falsifiability, or the ability for a theory to be definitively proved wrong. Many people, I among them, have argued that evolution is a poor theory due to its lack of falsifiability. Falsifiability is hard to come by in evolution. Since much of the hard evidence is "missing," we can't prove that the missing evidence is not there. Some evolutionists have argued that evolution is indeed falsifiable stating that it could be falsified by the discovery of, for example, "fossil rabbits in the Pre-Cambrian era."[32]

This is patent nonsense. If rabbits were found in the pre-Cambrian layers, I confidently predict that exactly zero evolutionists would give up on evolutionary theory. Instead, I predict that most of them would immediately, without examining a scrap of evidence, declare that the fossil rabbits were obvious fakes. If the fossils were thoroughly verified, other evolutionists would come up with multiple possible explanations that "obviously" settled the matter. They would claim the rabbit fossils were the product of an inversion layer or that softer rock had been eroded away and the fossil rabbits had collapsed into a lower layer. They would claim that Ken Ham put them there. There would be some internal debate, the most favored explanation would become the official version, and the science would remain "settled."

If I may, I would like to offer up some constructive criticism to evolutionary biologists. This is what I think your issue is in convincing others. You're like a group of nomadic teenagers that wandered onto someone else's basketball court and noisily demanded that everyone else stop counting free throws and dribbling with one hand and play by your rules instead. This bossiness has guaranteed that the original players won't listen to you *even when your ideas are good ones.*

In evolution, science has wandered onto religion's home court as it attempts to answer such questions as "Where does man come from?" and "How did life come from non-life?" When evolutionists dictatorially insist that we only play by their rules, (i.e. discussions of God are too distracting so they are not allowed) we're not inclined to listen to you. If scientists want us to listen, it would work a whole lot better for them to show some respect for our rules. After all, we've been playing on this court for 6000 years.

Creationism

Creationists have assumptions as well. First of all, they assume that God is behind everything that exists. So, they're not going to give credence to any theory that removes God from the picture. I'm not disagreeing with them; I'm just illustrating how assumptions work. Also, some creationists assume that the days in Genesis refer to 24 hour days. This makes it difficult for them to account for much of the scientific findings in regards to the age of the earth.

Now we'll apply the same reputation tests to creationists that we did to evolutionists. In the area of expertise, most creationists spend the majority of their career pastoring and/or being authors, rather than studying evolution. We should keep this in mind when evaluating competing claims. In all fields of endeavor, people make the noob mistake of concluding that they, after ten minutes of thought, have discovered a fatal flaw that the people in that field have never thought of. This doesn't work. People are sometimes wrong about concepts in their own field. But, identifying these errors takes a great deal of thought and research. If a newcomer notes an error, chances are the practitioners in that field have also noticed it and have already discussed it at length.

When examining objectivity for the creationist, we find a similar situation to that of the evolutionists. To some extent, creationist "job security" also rests upon their assumptions being correct. In a situation similar to that of the evolutionist, a creationist's belief in macroevolution would probably cause a deep questioning of his core beliefs. To be sure, some creationists have beliefs like theistic evolution, but it is not a topic on which the creationist can easily be objective.

Evolutionists have had a history of scams and disappointments and some pretty bad science. Creationists have had a history of even worse science. One of the most painful creationist arguments is that the Second Law of Thermodynamics proves that evolution can't be true.[33]

The Second Law of Thermodynamics states: "In any closed system, the entropy of the system will either remain constant or increase."[34] In more commonplace, but less exact language, it states that the complexity of a system never increases. Some creationists reason that since the complexity of a system always decreases, evolution must be impossible. A planet bursting with life is obviously more complex than one filled with protein soup.

This argument was obviously flawed even when I first heard it and discussed it with my fellow teenagers in the eighties. If you followed this line of reasoning, then it would be impossible for plants to grow from seeds. Actually, the Second Law of Thermodynamics, in and of itself, leaves room for one part of a system, the earth, to become more complex at the expense of other parts of the system. The sun is also a part of our solar system and is becoming much less complex as it burns out.

I think the medieval struggle over geocentrism helps to illustrate some of the shortcomings of creationist thought. Let's face it, church. We got our nose badly bloodied during the whole Galileo thing. As in today's evolution debate, the church tried to take descriptive Biblical language and apply it as though it were science textbook language. In the Galileo controversy, church leaders censured Galileo for noisily insisting that the Sun was the center of the Solar System. Church leaders stated that, in fact, the Earth was the center of the Solar System. If you read some of the verses from the Bible as you would a science textbook, this makes perfect sense. Consider the following verses:
1 Chronicles 16:30 (NIV): "Tremble before him, all the earth! The world is firmly established; it cannot be moved."
Psalm 93:1 (NIV): "The LORD reigns, he is robed in majesty; the LORD is robed in majesty and is armed with strength. The world is firmly established; it cannot be moved."
Psalm 104:5 (NIV): "He set the earth on its foundations; it can never be moved."
Ecclesiastes 1:5 (NIV): "The sun rises and the sun sets, and hurries back to where it rises."

The natural conclusion when reading these verses, when combined with ordinary observation, is that the sun moves around us. It was a reasonable enough deduction at the time, but further evidence demonstrated that this was phenomenological rather than scientific language.

Why then do we turn around and read parts of Genesis in the exact same way, expecting that this conflict is going to turn out any different? Yes, that God used 24 hour days is the most apparent meaning of the text. But, creationists embrace the obvious simplicity of the repeated "and there was morning and there was night on the nth day" without struggling with the puzzlement of how there were 24 hour days before the sun was made. Many have argued that the *Biblical* conclusion should be that Genesis days are actually unspecified long period of time *irrespective* of any outside evidence.[35]

Speaking of extra-biblical evidence, the outside evidence that the earth is older than 8000 years old is both extensively cross-checked and voluminous. To review all the research would take a book of its own. But, to name just seven, some of the dating methods are: 1) Tree Rings (11,800 years),[36] 2) Ice Core Layers (160,000 years),[37] 3) Coral Reefs (400 million years),[38] 4) Deep Lake Varve layers (35,00 years),[39] 5) Lake Suigetsu Algae Layers (45,000 years),[40] 6) Radiometric Dating using at least seven different elements (Four billion years),[41] and 7) The ability to see stars that are millions of light years away.[42]

Many Creationists put forth their arguments out of a fear that if one part of Scripture is shown to be "wrong" (e.g. Genesis) then believers and non-believers alike will feel that all of Scripture is subject to dismissal. For this reason, they believe that Genesis, or at least their understanding of it, needs to be fiercely defended.

I don't think Holy Scripture needs our help. It has survived burnings, bannings, poor interpretations, reinterpretations, deliberate misinterpretations, false gospels, and intense hatred from the gates of Hell. Through it all, it has survived, thrived, and is the best-selling book in the history of the human race. I believe what we really need is a deeper trust in Scripture. It doesn't need our help.

Remember how in *Raiders of the Lost Ark*, Harrison Ford suffered something like 87 separate injuries trying to rescue the Ark of the Covenant from the Nazis? In the end he failed, only to have the Ark of the Covenant rescue him.[*] We need to trust that the Bible is strong enough on its own to withstand the silly assaults of atheists et al.

I would further contend that some of this fear comes from a lack of understanding of the Bible's nature and its total awesomeness. Many Christians believe that if the Bible addresses a topic then other books on that topic are not necessary. As a therapist, I sometimes encounter this attitude toward the practice of counseling. This appears to be the belief of some creationists as well.

---

[*] Yes, I know that *Raiders of the Lost Ark* is not theologically correct. Work with me here.

As for me, if I had to choose between two auto mechanics, one of whom used only the Bible as an instructional guide and a second one who only used shop manuals, I would pick the guy with the shop manuals every time. True, the one with the shop manuals is more likely to overcharge me, but at least I'd know my car would work.

So, if the Bible is not our sole resource for every topic it addresses, what is its role? I think it does a much bigger job than just being the best advice and information that God could cram into 1500 odd pages. While for its size, it does a miraculous job of that, it actually does something much more incredible.

I can take my Bible, and using it metaphorically as a viewing lens, I can evaluate the truth and falsity of every one of the *millions* of books that have been written throughout human history. I can take The Bible and view evolutionary textbooks that claim there is no God and know those texts are filled with nonsense on a spiritual level and quite possibly a technical level as well. I can do this without knowing a single thing about science. I can pick up a book about Intelligent Design, see that it honors both scientific truth and God as Creator and know it probably has something useful to say. Without knowing any sociology, I can deduce that any book which concludes that some men are better than others isn't worth my time.

I could go on and on. My point is this: The Bible is The Book through which all other books are judged.

*****

A common question young earth creationists hear is: "If the earth is only 6000 years old, how can we see stars that are millions of light years away?" A common response is that perhaps God made the universe "with age" much as he created Adam as an adult rather than a baby. This theory does provide a possible explanation for the multiple observations of the earth's great age. As God is omnipotent, this explanation is both logical and entirely possible.

To address this issue, I use the technique of Occam's razor. The use of Occam's razor assumes that the simplest answer is most often the correct one, especially when compared to a convoluted one. To frame this issue I ask myself the following question: "Is it more likely that: a) God created the Earth with age or b) our interpretative skills involving a few pages in Genesis are not as good as we thought?" Offhand, I can think of no reason for God to create the universe w/ photons in mid-flight. On the other hand, I can think of lots of times when Christians interpreted Bible verses incorrectly. For that reason, I have chosen "b" as the more likely answer.

Difficulties that Evolutionists and Creationists Share

What difficulties do they share? There are a number of them, but most of them come down to issues of humility and insecurity.

Humility on the part of new-earth creationists is often lacking. Very regrettably, some new-earth creationists have asserted that if you don't believe in new-earth creationism then you can't be a Christian.[43] The message is clear, if you're not with them, you're a terrible person somehow. This is how insecure people talk. People that are confident in their positions don't need to put others down to feel better about themselves.

What about evolutionists and humility? Refusing to look at other people's ideas doesn't convince me that you're very confident about your own. That God made everything is not some random idea that popped up a couple of years ago. It has been the main belief of pretty much all of humanity for all of human history. Now we're not even allowed to think about it? On whose authority?

Evolutionists use science as a club to stop the debate before it starts. They begin by demanding we don't talk about God because he's "not scientific." So there. When this doesn't work, evolutionists will often use lawsuits to keep schools from teaching alternatives to evolution. What other science uses lawsuits to shut down people's discussion of it? How insecure can you get? Most evolutionary biologists do not have the commensurate humility to match the difficulty of their task.

Both creationists and evolutionists are very fond of their respective solutions. Creationists are enamored with the simplicity of the most apparent meaning of the Genesis account. Evolutionists are similarly captivated by the simplicity of survival of the fittest. Simple solutions can be both elegant and accurate, but they should be open to questions and alterations if reality doesn't line up with them.

An approach that creationists and evolutionists share is something I call "eisegetical science" or "fudge-factor science." As you may recall from the "Truth in the Bible" chapter, eisegesis is the process of reading the Bible, not with the intent of finding its meaning (as you would with exegesis), but intending to prove a position you already hold. Most Christians I know are aware of this tendency and work quite hard, usually successfully, in avoiding eisegesis when they study the Bible. Many of these same Christians, however, will readily cherry-pick scientific facts or factoids based on how it helps their position and consider those facts definitive while ignoring the rest.

I've heard on many occasions the story of the guy who carbon-dated a live leaf and the instrument showed the leaf to be millions of years old. It wasn't until I researched it that I learned about the tens of thousands of internally consistent measurements done by carbon dating and other methods. Focusing only on the live leaf guy is eisegesis.

"Fudge-factor" is another way of explaining this tendency. When I was in high school, we would jokingly discuss the fudge factor in math class. The fudge factor was the number that you had to multiply by to get the correct answer. The fudge factor, of course, was never really used as it was totally arbitrary and didn't help you learn anything.

In creation science, the fudge factor rears its ugly head quite often. See if you can spot the fudge factor in the following quote:

> A global flood like the one described in the Bible would invalidate this assumption. Creation scientists have estimated (based upon the amounts of organic matter thought to be contained within the sedimentary layers) that the carbon in the pre-Flood biosphere may have been 300 to 700 times greater than what is present in today's world.[44]

This "300-700 times greater" number is then used to multiply the age of the earth out to be in the thousands of years. An examination of the geographical evidence from point zero does not lead us to the conclusion that the earth is young, quite the opposite. When I read creationist discussions, I don't hear an evenhanded analysis of the strengths and weaknesses of a proposed solution. Instead, I hear, "Oh, wait, this can explain it, so that must be what happened." Perhaps creation scientists are making valuable discoveries every day. But, when they stop the discussion after they've found a possible solution that supports their assumed dating, they lose credibility. If creation science hopes to convince a larger audience, it will have to take a more exegetical approach to science rather than the present ad hoc one of plugging gaps.

This is a reachable goal. It has been done by Biblical archaeologists who have successfully moved the scientific field as a whole. For instance, the existence of the Hittites has changed from a reason to mock the Bible to standard fare in secular history books.[45] This is because Biblical archaeologists proved, via patiently collecting evidence and adhering to the standards of proof of that scientific field, that the Bible was indeed factually correct.

Evolutionists, similarly, do eisegetical science when they ignore the millions of fossils showing no inter-species changes and herald the (three?) fossils that appear to illustrate it as "the real evidence." This is because these few fossils illustrate what they want to be true, clear evidence of macro-evolutionary processes. This is cherry-picking. Similarly, when I viewed the Lucy skeleton at the Cleveland Museum of Natural History, I saw the bones arranged in their presumed locations with the missing bones filled in with drawings. What I did not see was a drawing of the *size of the area* that they retrieved the bones from. This is an important piece of the context of the discovery.

*****

What do I believe about evolution/creation? I am encouraged by the field of intelligent design. While it is a young science, it seeks to establish evidence of God's handiwork within the boundaries of the scientific method. I go back and forth between identifying with Intelligent Design and calling myself a "None of the Aboveist." I believe it's a huge jigsaw puzzle where evolutionists and creationists both have some legitimate pieces. But, even between them they don't have enough pieces to get even a partial picture of what happened. We humans like to understand how things work. It gives us a feeling of accomplishment and control. It may well be, however, that the detailed sort of final answers we're looking for may not be available. This may be true no matter how much we sift through the fossil record or Genesis.

It's not a breach of either scientific rigor or your relationship with Christ to question accepted answers about our mutual origin. Both God and science are big enough to withstand our skepticism. I believe that both of them require us to embrace some level of uncomfortable uncertainty.

Speaking of uncertainty, we turn now from the discussions of the somewhat private domain of cloistered scientists to the much more visible and public world of journalism. I hope to offer some tools for clinging to the uncertain and slippery surface that is American journalism.

Chapter 9

Truth in Journalism

"There can be no liberty for a community which lacks the means by which to detect lies."
~Walter Lippmann

I remember listening to a radio interview of a famous rock band in the early 70s. The interviewer asked the band members what the most important things in life were. The band members immediately replied that young people needed to ask their ministers and other responsible adults for the answers to those questions. They knew they were not qualified.

That is the childhood I remember. Make no mistake, there *were* people spreading naughty messages back then, but they did it in a furtive, nervously self-conscious fashion. This was because almost all of the responsible adults knew right from wrong. Even irresponsible rock stars realized they were bad examples.

Sadly, we now live in a culture where the majority of society's voices affirm that what has been evil for the last 20 centuries is now good. We don't only hear these things from the usual suspects either. Finding truth in today's culture is particularly difficult because even the majority of "responsible adults" now constantly repeat or invent gross falsehoods.

Many of these contemporary voices come to us as either "news," or commentary on the news. Sadly, much of the media has joined the rest of their broadcast brethren in either overt or covert support of an agenda that is contrary and counter to the Judeo-Christian roots of this country. Thankfully, alternative media has sprung up to counter this monopoly of the airwaves. This new media comes with its own problems, however, and a keen desire for truth requires we view these newcomers with a jaundiced eye as well. To demonstrate that there is "nothing new under the sun" let's examine an ancient group of folks from Jerusalem.

The Pharisees

The elite of Jesus' time were the Pharisees. They weren't just the religious elite. They were the social, political, cultural, and educational elite of their day. They were in charge of telling other people what to say and think. They started out well-intentioned, but their self-righteousness ultimately devoured their souls. We have a modern day equivalent to Pharisees.

Journalists.

Too harsh? To support this statement, we can look at a snapshot of how Pharisees behaved and see if there are any correlations to our modern day journalists. In Luke 20: 20-26 (NASB) we find the following exchange:

> So, they (the Pharisees) watched Him (Jesus), and sent spies who pretended to be righteous, in order that they might catch Him in some statement, so that they could deliver Him to the rule and the authority of the governor. They questioned Him, saying, 'Teacher, we know that you speak and teach correctly, and You are not partial to any, but teach the way of God in truth. Is it lawful for us to pay taxes to Caesar, or

> not?' But He detected their trickery and said to them, 'Show Me a denarius. Whose likeness and inscription does it have?' They said, 'Caesar's.' And He said to them, 'Then render to Caesar the things that are Caesar's, and to God the things that are God's.' And they were unable to catch Him in a saying in the presence of the people; and being amazed at His answer, they became silent.

The Pharisees had brainstormed a question they thought would trap Jesus any way He answered it. This was the first, "Have you stopped beating your wife yet?" question. If Jesus said that people should pay the tax, He would lose political power with the masses (this was the Pharisee's real concern). If He said to not pay the tax, then He would be in trouble with the Roman government. The Pharisees figured their cleverness had Jesus trapped. Being God Incarnate, Jesus left them in frightened silence instead.

What does an analysis of the Pharisee's behavior show? 1) They pretended to admire and respect Jesus when they actually felt fear and loathing. 2) They feigned agreement with Jesus' value system, but had no interest in following it themselves. 3) They asked questions with the pretense of nobly seeking knowledge for the benefit of the public. 4) They asked questions that were solely intended to embarrass and destroy Jesus.

So, to summarize:

- They didn't want new information.
- They didn't want to clarify some confusing points.
- They weren't seeking Jesus' insights.
- They didn't care about anything he thought.
- Their sole purpose was to discredit him.

Has anything like this happened lately? Well actually, it happens all the time. For an infamous example, let's look at:

The 2008 Katie Couric and Sarah Palin Interviews

In 2008, Sarah Palin was running for vice-president on the Republican ticket headed up by John McCain. In the last week of September, 2008 she had several interviews with Katie Couric. Many point to these interviews as a turning point in how Americans perceived Governor Palin. I won't be addressing here whether Sarah Palin was a good or bad candidate or whether she did a good or bad job in the interviews. I'll be looking at Katie Couric's question selection as it relates to journalistic Pharisaism and other journalistic misdeeds. For the record, there were many appropriate questions during the course of these interviews. My focus is on the obnoxious ones.

We'll start with the question: "You've said, quote, 'John McCain will reform the way Wall Street does business.' Other than supporting stricter regulations of Fannie Mae and Freddie Mac two years ago, can you give us any more examples of his leading the charge for more oversight?[46]

On the surface, this is a fairly innocuous question, but I believe it was designed so that Katie could "win" no matter what the answer was. Sarah Palin had been pulled from her job as governor and launched into the vice-presidential business rather quickly. It could be expected that her knowledge of Congressional minutiae would be limited. Throughout the campaign, she was asked a variety of questions designed to make her look dumb for not knowing the answers that the interviewers themselves probably didn't know until they had looked them up beforehand. This looks like one of those questions. Plan A for Katie was for Sarah Palin to admit she doesn't know about Senator McCain's financial legislation and look dumb. If that didn't work, Plan B was to dismiss whatever legislation she did identify as being insufficient.

More evidence of Couric's duplicity comes in her very next question: "But he's been in Congress for 26 years. He's been chairman of the powerful Commerce Committee. And he has almost always sided with less regulation, not more."[47]

Katie was not interested in what Sarah Palin actually thought; she was interested in making the point that McCain was soft on regulation and probably a bad person somehow. This shows that Ms. Couric was not seeking new information, but was editorializing.

The next question of interest is taken from the interview in front of the UN: "In preparing for this conversation, a lot of our viewers ... and Internet users wanted to know why you did not get a passport until last year. And they wondered if that indicated a lack of interest and curiosity in the world."[48]

Maybe it's a personal thing, but it really burns me when journalists don't have the courage to take responsibility for their own questions. They already have the microphone, the platform, and the power to edit at will. Why can't journalists put on their big boy pants and admit it's their own question they're asking? Here Katie is blaming the viewers for her question. She goes on to blame Internet users as well, in case the TV audience did not provide enough cover.

Among other things, this is a leading question, as evidenced by the phrase "they wondered if that indicated a lack of interest and curiosity in the world." It's also an editorial comment rather than a question. And yes, it's Pharisaical as well. Katie doesn't care about whatever Sarah's answer might be. She knows there is no real good answer to the question. She is trying to make her own point while disingenuously blaming the question on somebody else.

Another question from Couric: "Let me get your take, if I could Governor Palin, on a number of social issues. Because that's, they've gotten some attention, your position. If a 15-year-old is raped by her father, you believe it should be illegal for her to get an abortion. Why?"[49]

Here Katie Couric shows her own extreme views by focusing on one extreme end of an issue in lockstep with partisan supporters of abortion (See the Arguing for Abortion chapter). She's obviously already taken a side of the argument and trying to win it. She's not trying to find out new information.

And finally, there was the infamous: "And when it comes to establishing your worldview, I was curious, what newspapers and magazines did you regularly read before you were tapped for this to stay informed and to understand the world?"[50] It's true that Governor Palin didn't help herself by not naming a single source in her reply. But, look closer at the deviousness of the question by playing through some scenarios:

Scenario A: Sarah Palin doesn't answer.
Response A: She can be mocked for dodging the question and it can be openly opined that she doesn't read anything.

Scenario B: Sarah Palin says she mostly reads McCall's and Family Circle.
Response B: The governor can be ridiculed for being ignorant and stupid.

Scenario C: Sarah Palin says she reads mostly Alaskan newspapers and magazines because her job is, duh, governing Alaska.
Response C: Sarah Palin can be made fun of as a lightweight who knows nothing about foreign affairs. Obviously then, we'll all die from a nuclear holocaust after the aged John McCain dies in office and President Palin mistakenly invades NATO.

Scenario D: Sarah Palin sensing the trap in the question, attempts to lie about what she reads claiming she reads things she does not.
Response D: Follow up questions and spies discover the claimed periodicals are not in her living room or trash can and she can be exposed as a liar.

Scenario E: Sarah Palin states she reads Time, Newsweek, and the New York Times.
Response E: It can be impugned that she is lying because duh, everyone knows she's a moron and can't read.

Alternately, they can claim that Sarah is lying about being a conservative because all she reads is liberal periodicals.

And here you thought journalists didn't put any thought into their questions. I have many more examples, but I think you get the idea. We turn now to some of the root causes of distortions in both the old and new media.

Media Distortions

Today we have a journalistic environment where the majority of the media outlets can be classified as either "left-wing" or "right-wing." Increasingly, the population of the United States is split along these lines. All news sources have their weaknesses, deficiencies, and temptations. If you want to understand which parts of the news are true, false, or a little of both, being informed on how the media operates is paramount. We will next discuss left-wing distortions, right-wing distortions, and difficulties common to all news sources.

Left-Wing Distortions

When I refer to the left-wing media or to the old media I am including such far left sources as MSNBC, PBS, and the New York Times as well as more center-left organizations such as ABC, CBS, NBC, and CNN. These will serve as rough classifications as I am sure arguments could be made to place these organizations elsewhere on the continuum.

First of all, left-wing media organizations obscure the truth by insisting that they are nonpartisan, neutral, and impartial. A large body of evidence shows that this is nonsense.[51] They vote in overwhelmingly lopsided proportions for Democrats, and believe predominantly in liberal positions.[52] These attitudes do not remain hermetically sealed within the journalists either, as reporting by left-wing media almost always leads to left-leaning news. This is understandable. What is infuriating is the old media's stubborn insistence on their neutrality.

One oft-repeated defense to their demonstrated lack of neutrality is that they get complaints from both the right <u>and</u>

the left.[53] I have noticed, however, that they never tell you how many complaints they receive from each side. Is the ratio one to one? Ten to one? Fifty to one? I strongly suspect they get a lot more conservative complaints than liberal ones. If they were receiving more liberal complaints, I'm pretty sure they would mention it.

Another left-wing journalistic distortion is their predilection to frame the news in black and white terms. There's always a victim and there's always a villain. Watch the news for a while if you doubt this. The "villain" will be portrayed as acting out of sheer malice and innate evil. The media will not explore the possibility that the villain is merely mistaken or operating under extenuating circumstances. The "victim" will always be portrayed as 100% helpless and 100% innocent. Generally, there will not be any discussion of the victim's contribution to the conflict.

While this is compelling story-telling for children, it greatly distorts reality. Most people and issues are more complex than this. Unfortunately, three dimensional people do not condense well into a two minute segment. Rather than examine the nuances, left-wing journalists prefer instead to instruct their audience via suggestion on how they should think and feel about stories and issues.

Another common distortion is the liberal media's heavy emphasis on emotion. To pick one example among millions, I recently saw a news report on some local police officers who were caught on tape having a snowball fight. Rather than leaving it to the viewer how to feel about this, the news anchors made it clear through the content of their statements and the emotion in their voices, that this was shocking, absolutely SHOCKING behavior. It was apparent from their analysis (i.e. the officers couldn't be identified, so they couldn't immediately be punished) that they felt this was irredeemable conduct and obviously everyone else should feel that way too. There was no discussion of why this behavior was terrible. The snowball fight was terrible simply because the journalist said so.

Left-wing journalists also often use misleading language. For example, while you will commonly hear about arch-conservatives, you will never hear the term arch-liberal uttered. Further, if a Democrat is in trouble, he will more often be referred to by name rather than by their party affiliation, whereas a Republican in trouble will usually be identified openly as such.[54]

Finally, left-wing media will distort the news by the selectivity of their coverage. I was present at the Promise Keepers gathering at the Washington D.C. mall on October 4th, 1997. It was the largest gathering of men ever in Washington, D.C., even bigger than the Million Man March.[55] What I'm trying to say is; there were a *lot* of men there.

I heard second hand reports of there being a few National Organization of Women (N.O.W) protestors at the rally as well. I didn't see any protestors first-hand, but I heard that the press (who I didn't see any of either) were all busily clustered around the N.O.W. protestors and ignoring the thousands and thousands and thousands of Promise Keepers. While the press accurately stated that there were both Promise Keepers and protestors attending, their selectivity distorted the actual event greatly.

More informative ground-level coverage came to me from my friend Ralph. He was part of our group that came to DC via bus from Northeast Ohio. He told me about his own encounter with one of the N.O.W. protestors. It was a very bright, hot day in Washington and shade was very hard to come by. Ralph had somehow wrangled himself one of the six trees available. As he stood under it, he noticed a young lady nearby wearing a great big button which announced, "I want my abortion N.O.W." No, I'm not making this up.

Ralph, being who he is, invited the young lady to share in his shade. They stood there for a while under the tree and the young lady asked Ralph, "So, what are you guys doing here anyway?" Ralph politely answered that we were all there to have God help us to be better fathers and husbands. "Oh," she said, "Well, at least one of us knows why we're here."

I wish that had made it onto TV.

Right-Wing Distortions

When I refer to right-wing media, I include such right-wing talk show hosts as Rush Limbaugh, Michael Medved, and Bill Bennett on the far right as well as center-right organizations such as Fox News and the Wall Street Journal. Again, my love to those who would place them elsewhere.

Right-wing talk show hosts readily identify themselves as such which I both appreciate and applaud. As a long-time listener to these programs, I have become increasingly aware that they have distortions as well. Most talk show hosts would probably object to me lumping them in with journalists and would prefer to be thought of as commentators.[56] For practical purposes, however, many people look to them as their primary news source and I want to point out the weaknesses of that approach.

First of all, talk show hosts are hampered by their lack of any significant reporting staff. This means they are reliant upon the old media to provide them with the basic facts of most news events. Their commentary is based on second-hand information. If there are additional relevant facts to be gathered, talk show hosts are reliant upon either speculation or second party sources (i.e. blogs, callers etc.) to provide them.

Secondly, the approach of many of these programs is to find the most outrageous liberal behavior and report on the most shocking facets of it. If your main goal as a listener is to stay informed on ridiculous liberal behavior, all is well. If, however, you listen to these programs because you enjoy the feeling of being outraged, this can become a destructive trap. There is a certain warm, but dangerous, self-satisfaction that comes from knowing that your "opponents" are really and truly horrible people.

But, speaking to the Christian readers here, we always need to remember that our real opponent is Satan, not other human beings, however deluded they may be. This feeling of self-satisfaction can grow into a destructive self-righteousness. This approach does sell. So, please keep in mind while listening that talk show hosts are constantly tempted to shape their stories to encourage maximum outrage.

There is one example of this that haunts my memory due to the flagrant nature of its spin. It involves the talk show universe's reporting on the 2005 arrest of two border patrol agents. Jose Compean and Ignacio Ramos had been placed in custody for their role in the shooting and wounding of a Mexican drug smuggler. The outrage factor was high and talk show hosts loudly opined on the ludicrousness of arresting these honest border patrol agents for simply doing their jobs. The lie in this case was one of omission. This story was repeated over and over but with one important fact left out. Namely, that the two Border Patrol agents had failed to report to their bosses that they had fired upon someone. Omitting this fact from the broadcast helped keep the focus on making people feel outraged.

When talk radio was younger, there was less temptation to choose extreme stories. Now that there are multiple talk show hosts and commentators, there is an incredible temptation to report on increasingly outrageous stories so as to increase market share.

Temptations Faced by all Media

There are many barriers to accurate and balanced reporting that bedevil all media outlets. First among these is the necessity of gathering and then keeping an audience. After all, more viewers means higher advertising rates and more profits. For example, Americans highly prefer news about other Americans. So a story about Lindsay Lohan's legal troubles might get a lot more coverage than an arguably more important story about massacres in Darfur. Also, if your audience likes to see stories that vindicate and celebrate their worldview, a news agency might be tempted to highlight those stories as opposed to more neutral ones.

Another difficulty encountered by both sides is the "bubble effect." Both right and left-wing media tend to hire people that agree with their worldview. As mentioned earlier, media tends to create content for people that share their way of thinking. This means that the people they to talk to as well as the people they "work for" think very similar to them. The result is an artificial world where everyone around the journalist or commentator "knows" certain things are true. Since everyone believes pretty much the same thing, these views often go unchallenged. Unfortunately, this tends to turn any discussion between the two sides into shouting matches. There is a tendency for left-wingers to assume that right-wingers are evil (there's always a villain, remember) and for right-wingers to assume that left-wingers are ignorant and driven by emotion.

With all media, topic selection is a prime area where bias shines through. In the right-wing media, stories tend to be chosen that vindicate right-wing positions. Stories that illustrate liberal failures (Detroit, Obamacare, etc.) are much more likely to be chosen for discussion than generic stories on current events. Conversely, stories with some sort of victim are heavy favorites with the left-wing media. Reporting on plight of various victims shows that there are still villains out there and highlights the need for left-wing style compassion.

The Nervous Aunt Approach

I don't know if anyone else has noticed, but a great deal of the news sounds like it is being reported by someone's nervous aunt. I can picture in my mind the news anchor giving the news in a high-pitched nervous voice and jumping out of their chair with a scream when someone accidentally drops a book.

"And the other thing we need to be worried about, I mean it is soooo frightening, is... (Thud)-- YAAAAAH!" There <u>are</u> nervous aunts out there and occasionally they have a point, but I'm mystified as to why so much of our national dialogue is driven by their soul mates. There are thousands of examples of this type of reporting, but a particularly poignant tale is the story of:

The Time my Family Caused a Bomb Scare

In, I believe it was 1996, the three Leonard boys (I being the middle child) were gathered at our stepmother's house. Our father had passed away the previous year and we had gathered to sort through some of his possessions. "While you're here," my stepmother said, "Can you look in the crawl space under the house? Your father seems to have shoved something under there." (Cue foreboding music).

A little background is necessary here. Before my father went into Special Forces, he had spent some time in the Army Engineers. Engineers work with dynamite a lot and, much as you might accidentally bring an office pen home from work, my father would absentmindedly bring home explosives. As it happened, our hobby farm had a number of inconveniently placed trees. Cutting them down was difficult enough, but removing the stumps from the ground was a royal pain. A little bit of dynamite provided both labor savings and cheap entertainment.

Our father and we three boys would sit on the back porch and wait for the timed munitions to go off much as other people would wait for a parade. The resulting explosion would blow the tree, roots and all, right out of the ground and across the driveway as debris rained down on the porch roof overhead. Ahh, the innocence of youth. We sat there with no awareness whatsoever that this might be even remotely dangerous.

So, with this glorious childhood, we were not terribly surprised at the contents of the garbage bag stuffed under our stepmother's house. We began neatly piling the contents on the side lawn as we took them out of the bag.

First, there was a glass jar filled with black powder which dad probably used with some of his primitive firearms. Next was a small spool of detcord, a high speed fuse that looks like a thick plastic wire. Then we pulled out a smaller bag containing blasting caps. You can blow off several fingers if you handle those wrong, so we quickly set them down. Lastly, we pulled out a decaying white box which contained some very decomposed looking cylinders roughly a foot and a half long by a half-inch wide. I pulled those out for a better look, poked around in the box a bit, and placed that on the ground as well.

We stood there pondering our next move for a few minutes. Suddenly my older brother blurted out, "You know, that white thing looks like Dad's old dynamite box!" I was five years younger and had never seen the box, so this was a surprise to me. I gave Leonard Leonard* some harsh words for allowing me to play with what could well have been unstable dynamite.

Do you remember the episode of "Lost" where the science teacher yells at the main characters for carelessly handling the century old dynamite sticks? And how his whole body just disappeared when the stick he was waving around to emphasize his point exploded? Fortunately, I saw that episode many years after this incident.

Anyway, we brothers figured that identifying the threat level of the decayed cylinders was important, so we called the police to come have a look see. A particularly bored looking representative of the constabulary arrived shortly thereafter and ambled up the driveway towards us. His mood instantly changed when he saw what we had and he struck a pose that looked, I swear it, exactly like Barney Fife from the Andy Griffith show. After a moment of shocked silence, he yelled out, "Oh my god! That's detcord!!"

Now, if you were to wrap detcord around your arm and attach a blasting cap to it (the detcord, not your arm), that <u>could</u> be a pretty dangerous situation. This detcord, however, was simply sitting on the ground attached to its little detcord spool minding its own business. Before we had a chance to say, "Yes, we know that's detcord, but could you take a look in the little white box?" Barney ran out of the driveway and began flinging open the doors of other houses in the neighborhood.

We were a little too far away to hear what he was saying. It might have been a calm explanation of what was

---

* Not a typo!

happening nearby, but for all we know he was simply yanking doors open at random yelling, "Oh my god! That's detcord!!" His concern for the safety of the neighbors notwithstanding, he apparently felt we were perfectly fine standing three feet away from the dreaded detcord. He never talked to us again.

Barney apparently knew how to work the police radio, as we were eventually joined by a fire truck (maybe it was two fire trucks, it's been a while), an ambulance, and several more police cars. The firemen were a bit more social and actually asked some questions about what we had found. They finally suggested: "Well, let's move you away from here. Because, you know--- paperwork." This latter approach was more the sort of thing we expected from Southeast Ohio emergency personnel.

It turned out that the closest bomb expert was an hour and a half away in Columbus, so we mostly just hung out for a while, with a few members of the media taking pictures from the fringes. The bomb expert finally arrived, poked at the materials briefly, and declared that the decayed cylinders were actually ammo for a flare gun. He then directed his teenage assistant to toss all the stuff in his trunk and they drove off. This was a bit of a letdown. Not only were the materials not exciting enough for him to open his eyes all the way, they weren't even dangerous enough for him to go the trouble of bending over.

Perhaps wanting to salvage some dignity from this debacle, the powers that be then decided it was time to search the house. The problem with this plan was "The Beast." My father and stepmother had somehow acquired a bizarre looking mixed breed pit bull. In some freak of genetic recombination, The Beast had a normal large dog's body, but the head of a pit bull. It looked like the alien creature from "The Thing" had taken over a retriever's body and had popped off the original head, replacing it with the new pit bull head. If someone had painted stitches all over the base of the dog's neck it could not have looked more abnormal.

The Beast would not have mixed well with a bunch of strangers searching through the house. Fortunately, it was very fond of my aged and perpetually soft-spoken stepmother and meekly followed her out of the house. This comically mismatched pair went for a walk as the police and firemen conducted their fruitless search for hidden contraband.

Getting home shortly before six, we turned on the news wondering if we would get a brief mention. The opening credits rolled and the camera zoomed in on the anchor's face, her brow furrowed in concentration. There was a dramatic pause. Then, a little more dramatic pausing. Then suddenly:

"BOMB SCARE!!!---IN MARIETTA!!!"

There were some long shots of the emergency vehicles and of us walking about. There was a brief outline on the facts of the case. Then it got weird. They cut to a shot of the side of my stepmother's house. A reporter breathlessly intoned, "This is the *actual crawl space* from which *the explosives were removed*." Then they cut to another shot of some bedraggled elderly woman inside of her house dragging an oxygen tank behind her. Another reporter, partly in the shot, dramatically declared in her best nervous aunt voice, "Because of her oxygen, this woman *could not be evacuated from the danger zone."*

I sat there in the living room with a number of confused impressions. My first thought was, "Wow, that was a lot more exciting than actually being there." It had been an interesting day, but not nearly as breathtaking as the news report. The other impression I had was that while the story they were reporting was certainly dramatic, <u>it wasn't the story that actually happened</u>. They didn't show my brother saying, "You know, that white thing looks like Dad's old dynamite box!" They didn't have a shot of "The Beast." They hadn't filmed the anticlimactic ending of all the Scary Things being offhandedly dumped into a trunk.

Obviously they couldn't be everywhere to film all of this, but there wasn't even a mention of the fact that the devices had turned out to be relatively harmless. Instead, they somehow found some sweet elderly lady attached to an oxygen tank to exploit. How did they find this woman anyway?

They told their story, but it didn't seem to have much to do with the one I had been in.[57]

*****

You probably have your own preference on the kind of media you like and I won't try and talk you out of it. Please remember that whatever you watch or listen to has both economic and political factors which impact its veracity. I'd advise you to gather your news from a variety of sources. As the Scriptures say: "But in abundance of counselors there is victory" (Proverbs15:22b, NASB). We turn now from victory to despair, as we contemplate the role of truth in the lives of politicians.

Chapter 10

Truth in Politics

<This page intentionally left blank>

Chapter 10

Truth in Politics

"The inquiry knowledge and belief of truth is the sovereign good of human nature."
~From a plaque on the Reading Room in the Library of Congress, Washington DC

I talked to a lot of people about this book while I was writing it. I would mention the title and about a third of them would immediately blurt out, "You've got to talk about politicians." Unfortunately, I've only got one chapter to address what probably deserves a trilogy. Rather than addressing the most shocking political behavior as some writers have, I will try to highlight some perspectives I haven't heard discussed elsewhere, because I like that sort of thing. Much of the focus will be on seeing the temptations from the politician's perspective. Yes, sometimes they have reasons for their behavior.

The Constant Need for Reelection

First, stare closely if you can stomach it, at the nature of a politician's job. Most of us have some level of job security. If you are self-employed, for instance, you're never going to fire yourself (although your customers might). If you're in a regular job and the boss likes you, your employment can be fairly consistent. Of course, this is less true than in the past and varies from job to job.

Contrast this with politicians. Politician's jobs always come to an end. Typically this happens every two, four, or six years. If they want to continue to work in the same job, they have to earn the right to that job all over again. Certainly politicians in "safe" districts do not need to worry nearly so much, but these politicians are the exception rather than the rule.

This need to be continually rehired is a prime motivator for the way politicians act and think. Every term they have to convince a large number of people they don't know and have never met, to both leave the comfort of their own homes *and* choose them over the other guy. Not only are they reapplying for their job, but there are usually several other people applying for the same job. A great deal of a politician's energy goes into being reelected rather than doing the job they were hired for: governing.

Consider the example of a politician who we'll call Lucky Pierre. Lucky Pierre sees his opponent, Albert, (who is also trying to get or hold a job) promising more results with lower taxes. Albert is also promising that his voters will at last experience true love. Lucky is probably not going to counter this with a promise that he is a good guy and will do his best. Lucky will probably feel the urge to either make even larger promises, or try to convince voters that Albert is ridiculous. Lucky Pierre may decide to do both.

Our hero Lucky wins the election, and once he is in office, he becomes keenly aware that in a few short years, he has to audition for his job all over again. While Lucky Pierre truly has a desire to do what's right and effective, he has this often conflicting desire to improve his chances of reelection. If he is basically honest, he may make all sorts of minor compromises to ensure the "greater good" of his reelection. If he is dishonest, Lucky's only boundaries on his behavior are the credulity of the media and the voters.

The Need to Give and Receive Favors

Pretend that you have decided to run for local office. Now imagine that there are roughly 50,000 people that you have to reach out to and convince to vote for you. Where do you start? Do you have the resources to reach them all? Nope, me neither. Suppose that through your own personality and networking you know that 300 of these people will probably vote for you already. That leaves you 49,700 people short.

You are probably beginning to see the need for a *lot* of help. Lacking a private fortune, you are going to need to convince other people to give you their own money so you can afford the resources you need to reach the voters. A lot of money. Since you can't talk to all of the voters personally, you are going to have to convince other people to help you get your ideas across. Yes, some of this help may be given altruistically as people are spontaneously motivated to support your ideals and goals. Much of the help you get, however, will have strings attached. Many people will want something in return for their help.

It is generally understood that donations to politicians do not necessarily buy votes, but do buy some access.[58] That sounds less sinister than buying votes outright, but note that in the mind of the giver, *something is being bought.*

Also, many volunteers work with the hope that there will be some reward later on. There's usually not an official agreement, but if none of your volunteers get jobs as a result, you will discover that you have a lot fewer volunteers in the next campaign.

Ed Koch has written a very good book about his political career, *Politics*. In the very first chapter, he discusses the role of patronage, the giving of jobs to people who have been helpful to you.[59] Koch talks at length about his efforts to keep patronage at as low a level as possible.[60]

Almost immediately, Koch proceeds to discuss several instances of how he engaged in patronage. I mention this not to criticize the mayor, but to illustrate the pervasiveness of the conflicts of interest involved in getting elected and reelected. In a telling section, Mayor Koch recounts the following conversation at a political dinner:

> I once attended a dinner for the Borough President of the Bronx, Stanley Simon, and there were one thousand people at that dinner. I said to Stanley Friedman, the county leader who had arranged the dinner, "I don't know how you did it. I couldn't get a thousand people to attend one of my fund-raising dinners." He said, "If you give me a thousand jobs, I'll get them there for you." While that was an overstatement, he in fact could point out how each of those who attended, whether they were working in government or were in the private sector, owed something to him or Stanley Simon--not in a corrupt way, but just in terms of the regular glue of politics.[61]

Look at the tail end of this quote: "...not in a corrupt way, but just in terms of the regular glue of politics." That's ridiculous. What Mayor Koch describes as the "regular glue of politics," is corruption, plain and simple. It appears that career politicians, even well-intentioned ones, can no longer tell the difference between what's "corrupt" and what is "regular." What Koch has described isn't illegal. That might have something to do with the fact that the politicians who benefit from this corruption are the same people who write the laws in the first place.

The constant need to give and receive favors in politics is pervasive. In Koch's concluding section of chapter one, he blames his loss in the governor's race partly on his reluctance to support patronage. The subsequent lack of support from party officials crippled his chances.

The Desire for Power and Money

Another concept necessary to understand politicians is their desire for power. Politicians desire power for many different reasons. Some of them want to change things for the better and see politics as a way to bring about that change. Some desire power for emotional reasons. The power and control that comes with political office makes them feel better about themselves. A central feature of both narcissistic and borderline personality disorders is the need for external power and control to compensate for the chaos they feel inside. Politics can be a natural career path for people with these disorders.

Power is also a common reason that wealthy people will seek political office. They could retire comfortably at any time and relax however they liked, but they still put a huge amount of effort into getting elected. Since they are already wealthy, it is usually not for material gain. The kind of personal power that political office can give them is more than they can get in any boardroom.

*****

Many politicians do indeed seek office for personal gain. It is fascinating to look at the before and after financial standing of members of Congress. Even though they only have a salary in the low six figures, many members of Congress become very wealthy.[62] This financial gain can come about through legal as well as illegal means. There are some controls on profiting directly from legislation that congressmen vote on, but with a little ingenuity, a politician's insider knowledge can open up multiple rivers of income. The kind of insider trading that would put Wall Street executives in jail is perfectly legal for most politicians. The gravy train doesn't stop when the politician is out of office either. Speech-making pays top dollar as does being paid to lobby your former co-workers.

The Snare of Type A'ism

As I explained in Chapter 1, I have a Type B personality. While I was writing this book I often yearned to have what Type As have, the ability to stay on task and get things finished. I wish I had a switch that I could flip to "Type A" when it was time to write, and then flip back to "Type B" when it was time to relax.

I haven't seen any polls on the topic, but I am reasonably sure that the majority, and possibly the vast majority of elected politicians are Type A. Let's face it, Type Bs are usually not going to be self-motivated enough to add a political campaign to their regular lives and jobs.

While there are many organizations that would delight in having mostly Type As on staff, I do not think this is the best arrangement for a government. Other types of organizations have natural limits to their growth which governments lack. While growth is most always a good thing for business, the excessive growth of government is usually harmful.

Let me share a few personal examples that will help illustrate this point. Some years ago, I worked with a local lawyer on some estate matters following the death of my mother-in-law. If there is any truth to the stereotypes about lawyers, none of them applied to this fine man. He was supportive, entirely honest in his dealings with me, and both emotionally and personally real. He was a fine Christian man, with drawings from his children decorating the walls of his office. Furthermore, unlike most other lawyers I've known, ***HE RETURNED MY CALLS***!

It just so happened that this wonderful lawyer was involved in politics as a member of the local school board. I honestly don't know which political persuasion he was. On one occasion, he told me with a voice filled with pride, that he had helped bring about the building of a science lab in the high school that was the equal of any college in the area.

This particular high school only has a couple hundred students in all four grades. Colleges, of course, have considerably more students. The question of whether this was a responsible use of a sizeable chunk of somebody else's tax dollars did not seem to occur to him. Nor did it occur to him that the folks in that town might have preferred to keep their money instead.

No, what motivated him was that he had helped build something **REALLY COOL!** This is what Type A's like to do; build more and better programs and things. If the program is cool, clever, and impressive sounding, then they like it three times as much.

That is an example of what happens at the local level. Now consider an example of what happens at the Federal level. A few years ago, I attended a Social Security Administration presentation for behavioral health organizations and practitioners. There were several presenters and between them they described a growing problem they had been noticing in payments to persons with disabilities. They were finding that there were many SSI recipients who could hold down a job and get off of disability if they were just given a little help. In one example, they spoke of a gentleman with mental health issues who simply needed a small refrigerator at work to keep his medications in.

They spoke very articulately of the increase in self-esteem and life satisfaction that happened in the lives of disabled people when they moved into the world of work. They spoke convincingly of the large amounts of money that could be saved by no longer paying out disability claims.

I found it very heartening to hear from government officials who had a clear desire for, and understanding of, the need to cut government spending when it was unnecessary and counterproductive. The goal of their presentation was to convince the organizations and practitioners present to work with the disabled to assist them in moving into employment.

To motivate us to do so, they announced the formation of a new program that would give cash payments to private organizations that succeeded at placing and keeping the disabled in gainful employment. These cash payments would grow larger the longer the person was kept off of disability; but always at a smaller amount than the actual disability check had been.

This seemed like a reasonable plan. As I mulled it over, though, I had some second thoughts. Historically the Social Security Administration (SSA) was formed to help seniors with retirement by sending them checks when they reached retirement age. Later, Social Security Disability (SSI) was formed to help disabled people by sending them checks when they were adjudged to be too disabled to hold regular employment.

These folks really seemed to understand and care about the problem. They also seemed to recognize the very real shortcomings of a program that addresses problems by handing out checks. Their solution, however, was to create a brand new program that handed out checks. To my knowledge, just doing less of what they were already doing wasn't considered. Again, the default is not to do fewer, less expensive things, but to create something new that does things better and cooler; even if that new thing is saving money.

In the preceding examples, I have illustrated the behavior of some of what I consider the better people in government. Now imagine what happens when dishonest people work in political office. Rather than just building up government in a naive attempt to help, evil politicians with hungry egos can quickly consume everything in their path to feed their need for self-aggrandizement. This is why we citizens can not just trust that the government is going to work in our best interest. We should assume that politicians will energetically, and often with the best of intentions, find ways to grow and expand the government's reach and spending unless we actively work to stop them. Government needs our constant and very active oversight.

Propaganda Techniques

Speaking of politicians, now is a good time to peruse some very good work done in the 1930s by an organization known as The Institute for Propaganda Analysis. Their goal, which fits in very well with the goals of this book, was: "To teach people how to think rather than what to think." To this end, one of the Institute's major contributions was the identification of seven common propaganda techniques. I will list them below along with some associated commentary. While some of the information is dated, it still serves as a good starting point for analyzing political speech today.

Technique 1: Name Calling

It's not just for unruly children. Name calling is an attempt to discredit your opponent by attaching negative, two dimensional labels to your opponent or his ideas. If someone is using name-calling, you should ask yourself if their arguments are not strong enough to hold up on their own.

Technique 2: Glittering Generalities

Using glittering generalities is an attempt to identify your own ideas with ideas or concepts that are universally liked or admired. For example, a politician may state that his cause supports or protects, "the family," "children," or "the environment." Their hope is that your feelings for this universal good will attach to whatever bill they are promoting or to the prospects of their own reelection.

Technique 3: Transfer

When the transfer technique is used, the propagandist is moving or transferring the argument to another area where they have better arguments. This is similar to changing the subject, except that you are trying to convince people that your discussion of Topic B is actually relevant to Topic A. For example, a politician might discuss the virtues of upholding the Constitution when the topic being discussed is not a constitutional one. Or, a politician might discuss the virtues of protecting children when children have nothing to do with the legislation being discussed.

Technique 4: Testimonial

In the testimonial technique, the opinion of a famous or popular person is sought to buttress the claims of the politician even if the person giving their opinion has no real expertise in the matter at hand. For instance, a popular actress who appeared in a movie about farms might testify about farm legislation.[63] After all, nothing gives you an understanding of agriculture like pretending to be a farm hand in front of a camera. A modern twist on this approach is the use of mothers of slain family members to argue for a political cause.

Technique 5: Plain Folks

In this technique, the politician attempts to convince people that he understands and identifies with "the common man." They may dress like "regular folk" or relate childhood stories of poverty to convince their audience that they empathically relate with rural, poor, or blue-collar voters. Other plain folk's activities include being photographed with their family, wearing jeans, going duck hunting, or temporarily adopting an accent.

Technique 6: Card Stacking

Card Stacking involves the selective use of facts, half-truths, and plausibly deniable falsehoods to present the best or worst case presentation of a person or program. A current favorite is the selective use of scientific studies that support your position without regard for the strength of the study being used or the strength of studies with an opposite conclusion.

A variation of this is known as the straw man argument. In the straw man argument, an opposing politician's actual views are replaced with one that is superficially similar (and usually despicable). This replacement straw man argument is then cleverly and readily dispatched. The hope is that the observer will conclude that the actual argument has been destroyed as well. For example, a politician might ignore an opponent's complex views on immigration and express disgust because his opponent "hates foreigners."

Technique 7: Bandwagon

In the Bandwagon Technique, the hearer is assured that everybody else is doing or thinking the same thing so they should get out of their intellectual pigsty and join all the reasonable people. This can be a positive appeal to join what is being portrayed as a very wonderful idea or program. Alternately, this can be a shame based appeal, in an attempt to convince others that they are bad people if they don't support the idea or program.

Another device that is used to help create a bandwagon effect is the introduction of polls designed to solicit responses favorable to your position. The then favorable results of the poll are released in an attempt to get others to join the bandwagon that is evidenced by the poll.

*****

I wanted to find some illustrations of this technique that were non-partisan. To this end, I will be identifying propaganda techniques in Andrew Jackson's 1830 speech on removing the native American Indians from the then western frontier of the United States. It is considered by many to be one of the lower points of his career.

Portions of Andrew Jackson's Speech to Congress on Indian Removal

> It gives me pleasure to announce to Congress that the benevolent [Glittering Generality] policy of the Government, steadily pursued for nearly thirty years,

in relation to the removal of the Indians beyond the white settlements is approaching to a happy consummation [Glittering Generality]. Two important tribes have accepted the provision made for their removal at the last session of Congress [Testimonial], and it is believed that their example will induce the remaining tribes to seek the same obvious advantages [Bandwagon].

The consequences of a speedy removal will be important to the United States, the individual states, and to the Indians themselves. The pecuniary advantages which it promises to the Government are the least of its recommendations. It puts an end to all possible danger of collision between the authorities of the General and State Governments on account of the Indians [Card Stacking]. It will place a dense and civilized population in large tracts of country now occupied by a few savage [Name-calling] hunters...

It will separate the Indians from immediate contact with settlements of whites; free them from the power of the States; enable them to pursue happiness in their own way and under their own rude institutions; will retard the progress of decay [Glittering Generality, Card Stacking], which is lessening their numbers, and perhaps cause them gradually, under the protection of the Government [Transfer] and through the influence of good counsels [Glittering Generality], to cast off their savage [Name Calling] habits and become an interesting, civilized, and Christian nation [Transfer, Transfer, and Transfer].

What good man [Plain Folks] would prefer a country covered with forests and ranged by a few thousand savages [Name Calling] to our extensive Republic, studded with cities, towns, and prosperous farms embellished with all the improvements which art can devise or industry execute, occupied by more than 12,000,000 happy people, and filled with all the blessing of liberty, civilization, and religion?"

[Transfer, Glittering Generalities, Card Stacking, Straw Man Technique, and Bandwagon].

The DC Bubble

Living in Washington DC has often been compared to living in a bubble.[64] More so than ever before, the attitudes, beliefs, and lifestyles in DC are radically different from those in the rest of the country. This is an extension of an old trend. In 1984, for example, when Ronald Reagan won a 49 state landslide, Washington DC voted 85% for Walter Mondale.

Our federal representatives and senators begin their lives in their respective states and hold attitudes that are similar to their constituents. Since *everyone* they know holds the same beliefs, people inside the Beltway often have no comprehension of how the rest of the country thinks. The attitudes in DC are so pervasive and so homogenous, however, that the peer pressure is often overwhelming. The freshman congressman soon discovers that political advancement and prized committee membership is tied to this conformity.

Elsewhere in this book I discuss some of the effects of groupthink. Washington is an exercise in groupthink done large. As you know, “bad company ruins character” and our elected representatives often end up looking much like the people that they were sent out to influence.

*****

The politician's temptations to mislead, confuse, confound, and tell enormous whoppers are multitudinous. When a politician tells you something, your question should be, "How does it benefit the politician to say this?" The next question after that should be, "Has he told the truth in the past?" The next question after that next question should be, "If this politician actually does this, will it really have the benefits they promise in the long run?" When you have figured these questions out, for goodness sake go vote and get involved.

We turn now from the seemly world of politics to some more general rule of thumb guidelines to discernment. They're not terribly precise, but when you're lost in a fog of deceit, they're better than a lighthouse.

Chapter 11

Practical Discernment: Tools and Tips

All falsehood is a mask; and however well made the mask may be, with a little attention we may always succeed in distinguishing it from the true face..."
~Alexandre Dumas, *The Three Musketeers*

In this chapter, we will focus on practical guidelines for discerning truth. Rule of thumb methods such as these don't always lead us directly to the truth, but they can get us a whole lot closer. We'll also be using some metaphors, allegories, and miscellaneous exercises to give us some different perspectives on where truth lives. First, we'll begin with some guidelines.

Follow the Money

Though he was not the first to say it, one of Rush Limbaugh's favorite maxims is "Follow the Money!" If someone is very eager for you to do something, check first to see if they will profit from you somehow. Often this is fairly straightforward. Deke Zing appears on a TV ad begging you to buy his anti-gravity mop. Deke invented it, so when you buy one, he gets a cut. His opinion of how much cat hair the mop will pick up is not going to be very objective. That's why customer reviews are great. If they're not secretly written by Deke, they give us some unbiased views on whether the anti-gravity mop can hold 12 pounds of cat hair or if it breaks on contact with oxygen.

People who stand to gain from us monetarily will attempt to hide their financial interests. Take the case of a coworker inviting you to a jewelry party they are hosting. If they tell you they are hosting it to help out a friend, they might be telling you the unbiased truth. Then again, they may be motivated by the free jewelry they receive for hosting the party.

In 1996, Steve Forbes ran for president on the Republican ticket. One of his political positions was the support of a flat tax. Critics suggested that Forbes, being very wealthy, strongly supported a flat tax because it would benefit him financially.[65] I have no personal insight on Mr. Forbes' intentions, but it was a legitimate question from a "Follow the Money" standpoint.

A good place to apply this principle is in interactions with doctors. Often, you will find that a doctor orders more tests than you may think necessary. Ideally, a doctor is making suggestions that have your best interests in mind. Perhaps these tests have provided early detection of horrible diseases in previous patients. I know a lot of doctors and suspect the latter is usually the case. Unfortunately, this is not always true. Some doctors have a financial relationship with the laboratories doing the testing. Studies have shown that doctors who have these ownership interests do indeed order more tests.[66] Knowing your doctor's relationship with the lab can help you "follow the money" and give you a better idea of your doctor's objectivity.

Following the money will help you evaluate advertising as well. Some advertisements make it sound like businesses are purposely losing money on their latest sale just to help you out. Businesses are not in business to lose money. It is worth your while to try and figure out how the store or business is making money on their latest promotion. This will forewarn you against some unpleasant surprises such as hidden charges or over-inflated starting prices.

Overall, you should be more trusting of situations where the financial interests of the other person is clearly known and straightforwardly presented. If costs are difficult to determine or the person is hiding their potential profit from you, chances are they are hiding other things as well.

Look for Secondary Gain

"Secondary Gain" is a closely related concept to "Follow the Money," although it usually refers to non-monetary rewards. This term is commonly used in the psychological field to refer to the manipulative behavior of some patients. Most people requesting help for mental health or drug issues just want help for their issues. On the other hand, some of them are seeking something else entirely.

Some of my more honest clients have told me after an hour-long evaluation that they are happy to be getting help with say, their anger issues. Then they'll offhandedly mention that their lawyer told them it would look good in court for them to be in counseling. This courtroom bonus is the secondary gain to coming to counseling. They might have some desire to deal with their issues, but the courtroom benefits are the real driving force.* In this context, "secondary" means secondary to the stated goal, not secondary in importance

That is an example of mixed motives. At my hospital job, some patients do not have psychiatric help as a real goal at all. Some homeless people know that saying the right words will get them a stay in a warm safe environment where they bring you three meals a day. Similarly, some prisoners know that faking a suicide attempt can get them to a place

---

* These people tend not to make much progress in counseling.

that's more comfortable than jail and may give them an opportunity to escape.

Be suspicious when teenagers volunteer for things. There *are* those joyful moments when they overcome their dominant egocentrism to do something truly altruistic. More commonly, if they volunteer for something unpleasant it is to place them closer to desired food, desired others, or the freedom from some unpleasant future task. Volunteering to do an errand may have more to do with a desire to use the car for their own purposes than out of any sense of family obligation.

My final example of people looking for secondary gain is an unpleasant one. Feel free to skip down to the next section if you are easily upset. Some men are very, very, eager to help single women with childcare. Of these men, some of them are very giving and really love children. Some of them are trying to impress a potential new girlfriend, another form of secondary gain. And some of these men, are child molesters.

Child molesters are often very helpful with children, spending a long period of time establishing themselves as indispensable to the young mother who lacks other family supports. This free childcare gives the molester the opportunity to spend uninterrupted time with the children during which he can slowly groom them for future molestation. The lesson here is yes, background checks are sometimes appropriate. Also, when someone seems <u>too</u> willing to do something, always ask yourself why.

If it Seems too Good to be True, it Probably is

This is a fairly basic principle, but one that will save you a lot of money and trouble. Just today I heard on the radio someone promising to give people who signed up for their financial services a 15% bonus on their money up-front and a 50% bonus on their money later on. Since a 2% return is currently considered really good, this seems too good to be true.

Experience has taught me that this remarkable "bonus" will never be mentioned again, or turn out to be some sort of barely legal fraud. It will consist of bonus "points" or require a $50,000 minimum deposit or only apply to the first $10. I know for a fact this advertiser isn't paying for radio ads so he can give away money. I also know I shouldn't trust anyone who tries to convince me otherwise. This ad was designed to appeal to my greed, in the hopes I will be enticed into visiting or giving them a call.

And yes, you haven't just won ten million dollars, you can't lose weight by eating ice cream injected with butter, and those friendly folks in Nigeria are not going to share their money with you. When you receive junk mail and e-mails promising you all of this, ask yourself why these people are spending good money to reach you in this way.

Change Your Point of View

A useful truth-finding tool in many contexts is changing your point of view to help reveal your own biases. Think about something your significant other or family member does that is particularly annoying. Perhaps they interrupt you a lot. Next consider why they might be behaving this way.

Now imagine that you are the one with the frustrating behavior. What do you think your motivation would be to do this heinous thing? Do you imagine that your motives would be purely evil? Or would your motives be fairly understandable? If you think your motivations would be about the same as theirs, do you react with as much rage towards yourself? Nah, probably not.

Late-night talk show host Jimmy Kimmel has done a number of "man on the street" interviews asking people their position on political events that were totally made up. In one video, Kimmel's camera lackey reversed the political positions of two candidates and asked people if they thought it was the right stance on those issues. Sure enough, people fiercely supported their candidate's political position even though they were the opposite of the real ones.

If the interviewees were to watch these episodes, they would have the opportunity to learn something about themselves. Namely, that their political positions were based on their fondness for the candidates and/or political parties, not on their core principles.

Proverbial Ways of Finding Truth

The Biblical book of Proverbs contains timeless wisdom on what works and what doesn't work in real life. Proverbs are not meant to be ironclad rules with guaranteed outcomes. Rather, they are very significant hints on how to make our lives run more smoothly. We will focus here on those proverbs that deal with separating fact from fiction. A helpful passage from Matthew is included as well.

Proverbs 9:8a (NAS): "Do not reprove a scoffer or he will hate you."

This doesn't mean that some mockers don't need corrected. It points out the natural consequences of doing so. There is a similar modern expression: "Don't pick fights with people who buy ink by the barrel."

Proverbs 9:10 (NIV): "The fear of the Lord is the beginning of all wisdom, and knowledge of the Holy One is understanding."

This is a foundational principle of discernment. The things others tell you to believe either line up with God's Word or they don't. Some very smart people end up in some very foolish places because they don't recognize that God is much smarter than they are.

Proverbs 11:2 (NIV): "When pride comes, then comes disgrace, but with humility comes wisdom."

I can't add anything to that.

Proverbs 14:12 (NIV): "There is a way that seems right to a man, but in the end it leads to death."

This is what happens when a man or woman makes up their own rules on how to live life. The "death" spoken of here is spiritual death, or separation from God.

Proverbs 14:15 (NIV): "A simple man believes anything, but a prudent man gives thought to his steps."

It is not safe to leave our decisions to the talking heads. Beware of people that are very eager to convince you of something new. What are the odds your welfare is their highest priority? Before you commit to something new, talk to people that are for and against it, not just people you know will agree with you.

Proverbs 15:22 (NIV): "Plans fail for lack of counsel, but with many advisers they succeed."

Don't put all your trust into any one person, even if they happen to be an expert. Try and get all sides of the story and then decide.

All of Proverbs 18.

More truth on humility and a dozen other pieces of awesome advice in just 24 verses!

Proverbs 19:9b (NAS): "and he who tells lies will perish."

You might not be seeing it, but the liar is definitely dying on the inside.

Proverbs 26:4 (NAS): "Do not answer a fool according to his folly, or you will be like him."

I can't help it. These proverbs keep making me think about journalists.

Proverbs 26:17 (NAS): "Like one who takes a dog by the ears is he who passes by and meddles with strife not belonging to him."

This is a very vivid picture of what happens when you try and "help" when you're not a part of the problem or the solution. This truly is what happens in real life. I can attest to that.

Proverbs 28:26 (NAS): "He who trusts in his own heart is a fool, but he who walks wisely will be delivered."

The foolish deer hunter shoots at something he thinks is a deer. The wise hunter only shoots when he is 100% sure. The first is following his heart, and the second is submitting his will to an outside rule.

Matthew 7:16-20 (NAS): "'You will know them by their fruits. Grapes are not gathered from thorn bushes nor figs from thistles are they? So every good tree bears good fruit, but the bad tree bears bad fruit. A good tree cannot produce bad fruit, nor can a bad tree produce good fruit. Every tree that does not bear good fruit is cut down and thrown into the fire. So then, you will know them by their fruits.'"

Here is a shortcut to doing in-depth research on every nuance of a situation. What kind of fruit does it bear? Take a look at gambling. Many people argue that it is a fun activity that generates money for our children's schools. But, if you examine the lives of people who gamble, you very often find a very different result, or "fruit" to their behavior.

I learned firsthand in college that gambling is a bad idea. I didn't come to that belief because someone convinced me intellectually. Instead, I observed the fights, animosity, and breakdowns in friendships it caused in my fellow gamblers. I thought beforehand that gambling was OK if done "properly," but my experience of its fruit showed me otherwise.

A Thought Exercise

For something a little different, follow with me on a mind-stretching mental exercise. Just pretend I am that exercise instructor you secretly hate. Let's see if we can recruit the right side of your brain in helping us find truth. Ready?

Imagine a one-dimensional point. It doesn't take up much room and isn't very interesting. Do you understand it? Now imagine another point. Connect the two points and we have a line. That's a little more interesting. We now have something with two dimensions and a large number of one dimensional points (an infinity of them perhaps). Add two more lines and this forms a triangle. This form is still two dimensional, but more complex than just a simple line. It contains three lines, three corners and three angles all which measure some number of degrees. We know there are complex mathematical formulas which can describe the relationship of the angles to the lines and to each other.

We're getting somewhere now. But, do we understand what we are looking at yet? No, not yet. This two dimensional construct is only the description of one face of a three-dimensional object. How many faces does this three dimensional object have? It has six. Does that mean we understand 1/6 of the whole object yet? Probably not.

Stick with this, your brain hasn't worked up a sweat yet.

Let me describe the object further. The faces of the object we are after consist of two triangles and four rectangles. Being three dimensional, there is something in between these triangles and rectangles called *volume*. I will tell you something else, as well. There is not just *volume* in between these triangles and rectangles there is actually *something* in between them. What does this tell us? This strongly suggests that I am not talking about some imaginary construct, but an actual *thing*.

Let's go further and see if you understand it. Two of the rectangles are oblong and measure roughly six inches by two inches. They are on opposite sides of the object. One of the rectangles, the "top" of the object, is two inches square. The rectangle on the opposite side of this rectangle is two inches long and 1/64" wide. In other words, the object comes to a point. Since it comes to a point, (part of your brain is no doubt thinking, what is the *point* of all this?) we can say that the object is tapered. The two facing triangles are two inches high at top, tapering down to a 1/64" wide point at the bottom.

Well, now we know more about the six faces of this object, but do we understand it? We understand some things about it. We know about points, we know about lines, triangles and rectangles. We've gone from one dimension to three dimensions. How deep is our understanding now?

Those of you following closely may have figured out that the object is wedge shaped. What sort of a wedge is it? Is it a wedge of cheese? As we attempt to understand the truth about this object, we will need to know more about its various *aspects*. What is its color? What is its hardness? What is its conductivity (i.e., is it cool to the touch)? What is its weight? What is its ability to reflect light? What is its sharpness? If then, we learn that it is black, very hard, cool to the touch, "heavy," doesn't reflect light, and is slightly sharp, we can deduce this object's name. It is a *splitting wedge*.

For those not familiar with splitting wedges, they are placed into logs pointy end first. They are then struck with heavy objects, like sledgehammers. This transfers the power of the accumulated force of the swing into the point of the wedge. When done properly, this makes the log split in half.

So, we understand three of the dimensions and at least six of its aspects. We also have a name, a working description, and probably a mental image of the object at rest and in action. Do we understand it?

Well, I doubt that unless you have used one, you would understand the feeling of mastery involved with using a splitting wedge. You might not understand the inherent coolness of being able to start out with a sledgehammer *behind your back* and somehow *just know* how to swing it up over *the top of your head* and hit the little 2" x 2" area on top of the splitting wedge. And then do it again.

Or, the feeling of accomplishment and power when, on the third blow, the left and right hand halves of the now split log fly in opposite directions. Or, the enthrallment of small boys watching who are convinced that you must be *awesome.*

Finally, we will add a fourth dimension; time. What happens if next week my neighbor steals the splitting wedge and melts it down into an irregular circular blob? How much of what we knew of the splitting wedge is still true?

So, what is my point? My point is *not* that truth is relative. My call is not to squishiness, but to *humility*. Some people will understand fewer dimensions and aspects of a situation than you. This does not make them bad. Some will focus on different aspects and dimensions than you. This does not make them wrong. Some people, will actually see *more* dimensions and aspects than you do. You will often find yourself mocking people who actually have a fuller understanding of the situation than you. Our first inclination is to dismiss ideas that don't match ours. If they don't match our understanding, we assume they must be wrong. This will happen most often with God.

God's Word and His rules often seem obscure if not downright bizarre. Deciding to argue with Him, however, is foolish. You can tell Him the line is crooked and it should be straight all you want. He knows that this crookedness in your life is the key piece in a much larger picture that you have no clue about.

You can reason and think harder and catch up with some people, but you can't make yourself as smart as God. He will always have a fuller view than you do, and your life will go much more joyfully if you embrace this.

Groupthink

Groupthink is an example of a problematic approach to reasoning. Groupthink is the tendency for all of the individuals in a group to end up thinking the same way. In contrast to *consensus*, which refers to the positive aspects of thinking as a group, groupthink refers to the negative consequences of doing so. In this section I want to discuss not just groupthink in small groups, but also in terms of much larger groups, up to and including the entire culture.

Using groupthink is convenient in many ways. For one, if you follow what everyone else already thinks, you can save all the energy of figuring out your own values from scratch. Researching, pondering, and working through every aspect of proper thinking and behavior can be a daunting task.

Allowing the group to provide all of this for you is a real timesaver.

Secondly, adopting group standards helps immensely with getting along with others in the group. Group dynamics being what they are, following the crowd also makes you feel good about yourself as well as giving you the added benefit of being able to look down on people outside the group.

Problems with groupthink are both legion and legendary. In the late 1930s, the Germans "knew" that Jews were responsible for Germany's problems and should be treated appropriately. In the 19th century, the Southern states "knew" that slavery was perfectly acceptable. You can list 20 more examples of your own. What is much tougher is identifying groupthink's influence on your <u>own</u> thinking and behavior.

An Exercise in Confronting Groupthink

Groupthink can operate in any group we happen to be in. For instance, if you're a teenager you probably have a group of friends that feel very strongly and surely about certain things. You may feel, for example, that you understand many things much better than your parents. That is certainly possible, but what is the basis of your belief? Is your group of friends inherently superior in intelligence, knowledge or experience? Do they have something that helps them to overcome the handicap of having brains that won't grow all of the way in until age 25?

Moving on to you adults, how about your ethnic group? Do you think it has the best understanding of the causes of racial tensions and interactions? You, too? That's great. Let's try something. Mentally list five attributes of your ethnic group that make it more insightful than the others. It's OK; you can put the book down. I'll wait.

How's it going? Harder than you thought, maybe? OK, can you list just two?

Do you have your list of very good reasons ready? Good. Now tell me this, why don't the other ethnic groups recognize the wisdom of your viewpoints?

Hmm.

OK, I see, go on.

And finally---Yes, I see.

One final question. Can you explain why other ethnic groups don't get it, but this time do it without denigrating them?

Yes, that is tougher isn't it?

Congratulations. If you worked through this exercise, you've now learned something about groupthink.

Reasoning that Will Please Those around You

Another problematic form of reasoning is rationalizing our decisions because of peer pressure. As you can imagine, truth is not the main feature of this kind of reasoning. It is also far too common.

In the 1950s, Solomon Asch conducted a series of studies on conformity. In the first round of experiments, a test subject was placed with three or more confederates who were secretly working with the experimenter. The experimenter announced he was doing "an experiment in visual judgment" and showed the group a series of white cards depicting four lines of various lengths. The test subjects were then asked which of the last three lines was equal in length to the first line.

The differences were quite obvious, and on the first few trials everyone agreed on the correct line. Beginning on the third trial, however, the confederates would all pick the same incorrect line. Sometimes the differences were absurd. In one trial, the test line was three inches long and the incorrectly chosen line was ten inches long. The test subject was always seated last or next to last. When he gave his answer, he had to decide if he agreed with the group or with his own senses. The results are either shocking, or all too predictable depending on how you view your fellow man.

Three out of four test subjects agreed with their peers and picked the wrong answer on at least some of their responses and some of them agreed with them on every single wrong response. Many of the trial subjects admitted in post-experiment interviews that they knew they were giving the wrong answers, but didn't want to look stupid by disagreeing with the group. The power of group coercion was so strong, that some test subjects actually *saw* the lines as being equal.[67]

This experiment illustrates the pressure we all feel to conform to our peers and our culture. Embracing truth requires having the courage to speak up when everyone around us is mouthing lies with the utmost confidence. The Asch experiments were done on college students sitting in a group they would never see again. I suspect that this desire to conform is even stronger in the groups that surround us all the time.

There was a very telling follow up study to the first conformity experiment. In one of Asch's experimental variants, two real subjects were used instead of one. The addition of just one other honest person greatly increased the incidence of both test subjects giving the correct answer. These subjects voted against the group in much greater numbers.[68] Of course, Jesus knew this nineteen centuries earlier when he sent the apostles out in pairs to do their ministry.[69]

*****

Hopefully, this chapter has given you some tools to use in unearthing truth from lies. I know it's unpleasant to hear that a lot of error comes from our own desire to take shortcuts or to be popular. Accepting this, however, will have a profound effect on your life.

Shifting our focus from self to others, our next chapter takes a break from studying truth and lies from our society to looking at lies from the person right next to us. Falsehood is not an abstract thing that only floating heads on the television engage in. It comes from your brother, spouse, boss, employee, and child. Fortunately, we are not at the mercy of their deceitfulness and can, with some careful study, learn much more about who's lying to us and when.

Chapter 12

Face to Face Truth

"For every good reason there is to lie, there is a better reason to tell the truth."
~Bo Bennett

In this chapter I will be discussing how to detect a liar right in front of you. We will be looking at the body language, affect, and behavior of the liar. In this chapter I am greatly indebted to Mark McClish, author of *I Know You are Lying*. Mr. McClish, a former Secret Service Officer and Deputy U.S. Marshal, has worked extensively with people known to lie the most; criminals. If this chapter is the one you were most interested in reading, Mr. McClish's book is the one you will want to pick up next. The long stories are mine, but the principles and ideas in this chapter are all Mark's.

The Principle of Excess Energy

When people lie, they have a rush of adrenaline.[70] This creates excess energy in the liar. It is hard to tell exactly where this energy will go, but it will come out <u>somewhere</u>. It might show up in the liar's words, their behavior, their eyes, or even their hands. It might show up in their mood. This extra energy does not go away on its own. Allow me to illustrate this with a story from my youth.

When I was in high school, we would have various "Spirit Days." I still don't know what the point of Spirit Days was. Maybe other teenagers get something out of it or maybe it's just something to keep the faculty entertained. I couldn't tell you. I was once told by our principal that he had bought a fancy floor mat in order to increase our school spirit. I am not making this up.

Anyway, when I was a freshman we had an entire week of spirited days. One of these ill-planned events was called "Dollar Day." It turned out slightly less disastrous than the Cleveland Indian's infamous "Ten Cent Beer Night,"* but only because there were fewer people involved. On "Dollar Day," five separate dollar bills were given to randomly chosen students. The rest of the students were to ask everyone they met, "You got a dollar?" If the person asked this question was in possession of one of the dollars, she was supposed to hand it over. If you still had the dollar at the end of the day, you got to keep it.

This may seem like a lot of hoopla for a dollar, but you need to keep in mind that: 1) it was 1980, 2) this was Appalachia, and 3) we were children. To give you a sense of how much a dollar was worth; Matt Wolfe had accidentally hit me in the jaw the year before. As he was only messing around, Matt was grief-stricken and by way of penance, gave me all the money in his pockets, a grand total of sixty-five cents. I was of the opinion that I had made a killing on this transaction.

A dollar being so valuable to us, and the passing on of the dollar based entirely on the honor system, dishonesty

---

* I am not making this up either. On the night of June 4th, 1974, the Cleveland Indians, as a marketing technique, sold each and every beer for just a dime. Even in 1974 this was a heck of a bargain and the fans took full advantage of it. The deeply inebriated fans rushed the field in the ninth inning and a widespread brawl ensued. Many fans and players were injured and the Indians had to forfeit the game.

was almost guaranteed. Steve Yeater attempted to beat the system by laundering his dollar into the school lunch program. The lunch lady, showing more foresight than the administration, had a list of the serial numbers on the bills and caught Steve red-handed.

During the course of this hoopla I thought I saw J.L. Rupinski receive one of the dollars.* I said the magic phrase to get my dollar and J.L. denied any and all knowledge. I pressed the point, explaining that I thought I saw the handoff. J.L. at this point became very animated, strongly denying that he had the dollar and loudly slapped me on the chest several times. It didn't hurt in the least and J.L. was a good 4 inches shorter than I was, so I didn't feel threatened, only annoyed. As I saw no way of proving my point, I went back to my day.

My friends, on the other hand, thought this was a serious situation that demanded **A RESPONSE**. They insisted that I now had to fight J.L. in order to preserve my honor. In Appalachia, honor is very important, and any young male knows that he must be ready to fight at any point if challenged. My best friend, Ted, who was usually much classier than this, aggressively used shame to provoke me into fighting.

Caving in to peer pressure, I challenged J.L. to a fight under the bleachers after that night's football game. J.L., loudly and quite publicly, suddenly became my instant best friend and grabbed me in a near-embrace declaring our wonderful friendship to everyone who would listen. I don't think we had touched that much in all of junior high.

Thanks for letting me reminisce. What does this tortured memory from my past tell us about the extra energy brought about by lying? Look at this story from J.L.'s point of view. J.L. has the coveted dollar bill in his possession and thinks that by running away quickly he has broken the chain and can simply hang on to the dollar until the end of the day. He almost makes a clean get-away but I call him out. He lies to me and this doesn't work. Since he's already committed,

---

* I never did find out what "J.L." stood for.

he has to lie even harder. This created a lot of extra energy. This energy quite visibly exploded onto my chest. It also came out with his raised voice and some serious attitude.*

As noted, J.L.'s response to my challenge to a fight was also over-exaggerated. A full understanding of this story requires a little knowledge of Appalachian culture. J.L. wasn't afraid to fight any more than I was. Fighting, when it wasn't absolutely necessary, carried with it a sense of social failure. Fighting to preserve your honor was O.K., but fighting to cover up a lie would be mildly criminal. Since he wasn't that bad of a guy, J.L. quickly decided that formulating a new, milder lie that we were tremendous buddies was the best solution. The stress of this new lie created the extra hugginess.

Sticking Close to the Truth

There are a number of reasons why liars stick close to the truth. For one, it is easier to keep track of your lies that way. Mark McClish notes: "In an open statement in which a person can say anything he wants to, most people will not tell a lie. They will tell you what they saw or what they did. They will not say anything incriminating."[71] Lying is also problematic because: "Another reason people choose not to lie is because they do not know what you, the interviewer, know. If they tell you a lie and you have information that directly contradicts the lie, then they are in big trouble."[72]

Liars know that lies cause stress, which can cause unwanted attention. Besides, your average non-sociopath prefers not to lie. Most everyone knows at some level that lying is wrong. Given the choice, people will pick the truth over lies. When they do lie, their lies will remain as close to the truth as possible, even if only technically.

So, when a guilty person is asked if they stole your $20 and half of the marble cheesecake, the liar, instead of saying, "I didn't take them," will more likely respond with, "I

* For the record, this was totally out of character for J.L. Dollar Day seemed to have had everyone out of sorts.

wouldn't do that." When she says "I wouldn't do that," what she is really saying is "I wouldn't ordinarily do that." As she doesn't go around stealing twenty dollar bills and foodstuffs on a regular basis, this is technically a true statement.

Corollaries to Sticking Close to the Truth

It might seem that this tendency for liars to stick close to the truth might make it very hard to detect them. Once you know the pattern, however, your knowledge of this behavior gives you a number of tools to catch them with. These concepts are detailed below.

Words that Indicate Deception

When a person is answering a direct question from you, pay careful attention to extra words, or words that aren't needed to answer the question. Short answers such as, "No, I didn't" are the most indicative of truthfulness. Some words that are especially suspicious are: "Honest to God," "I swear," "To tell the truth," "I swear to God," and "To be honest."[73] Use of these words indicates the person is going to some lengths to convince you of their truthfulness. When you hear these words, you should wonder if the other person thinks you have reason to doubt him.

It could be that they have been deceitful in the past and want to emphasize that this time they are telling the truth and it's important for you to believe them. It's also possible that they think you should distrust them because they are in fact, lying to you.

Finally, be suspicious of words like "really" and "kind of." These may be extra words or they may be the liar's attempt to verbally distance themselves from the truth.[74]

Not Answering the Question

Mr. McClish writes: "However, when people do not want to tell us certain things, they may avoid answering the question. Common sense tells us if people refuse to answer our questions, there must be something they do not want us to know."[75]

This is straightforward enough, but deceivers do not formally tell us, "I do not wish to answer that question. It may make me look bad." Instead they will try to artfully provide some answer that has the surface appearance of total truthfulness.

Consider the following exchange of a mother asking a child about a cookie theft. "When his mother asked him if he took a cookie he replied, 'I don't like those kinds of cookies.' That may be a truthful statement, but he did not answer the question."[76]

This previous example involves a rather short conversation. More commonly, people will want to explore related themes in their answer and discuss all of their related thoughts, feelings, and experiences related to the question. This is commonly known as "beating around the bush." That is fine, but at the end of their long story you still have to ask yourself if they ever answered the question. If they didn't, than all the other words are distractions, not helpful details.

Answering a Question with a Question

Another form of distraction is answering a question with a question. On this, Mr. McClish states:

> This is a delay tactic which gives a person time to think about his answer. Typically a person will do this by repeating the question. However, asking any question is a sign they are thinking about their answer. The question you should be asking yourself is, 'Why does this person need to think about his answer?' 'Why can't he give me an immediate straight answer?"[77]

Questions can also be designed to distract the questioner by putting them on the defensive. The liar might ask, "Why don't you trust me?" Or, "What do you care? Aren't you the one who got two speeding tickets last week?"

If successful, this technique will leave you defending your own behavior while leaving the original question long forgotten.

I've found the best counter to this technique to be something similar to the following statement: "Well, if you are concerned about my speeding tickets, I'll be happy to talk about that. First, I want to finish discussing why the car no longer has a back seat."

Pay Attention to Pronouns

Pronouns are very small words, but they can tell us a lot about a person's inner state. They reflect how someone feels about a person or object. If they refer to something as "my" or "mine" then they feel a sense of ownership (of objects) or closeness (to people). If they refer to something as "that car" or "the wife" they have, or want to have, a feeling of distance from that person or object. For instance, stating, "I left the car in the parking garage," may reveal the liar's knowledge that the car does not really belong to him. If he did own the car, he would more likely say "my car."[78]

Pronoun usage also reflects the speaker's feelings of ownership. You are looking for the word "I" to see if the person feels responsibility for poor behavior. If the person discusses what "we," "they," or "one" did or should have done, they are distancing themselves from responsibility.[79]

When a person is telling you a story about something they did recently, they can give you a clear account of what happened because they lived through it, recording it in their memory in real time. When they repeat to you what happened, they merely describe the events from memory. When liars make up a story from scratch, all of these details are missing and they sometimes lose track of what they said a few sentences ago. If the story changes from "he" or "she" to "someone" "that person" or "whoever" then the pronoun change may indicate that the person is inventing, rather than remembering the story. Sometimes even the gender will change and "he" will become "she" or "they" as the story progresses. This is often not a simple misstatement. This may be an indication that the liar is too busy focusing on inventing the larger details of the story to keep track of little things like pronouns.[80]

Verb Tenses

Changing the verb tense in an answer is a simple but tricky way of lying by telling the truth. In my line of work, I see a lot of drug users. Due to the shame that drug users and alcoholics have, they often lie about their drug habits. When they lie, it will usually be with a statement somewhat close to the truth. So if, for example, I ask "Have you ever used illegal drugs?" A common response is, "I don't use illegal drugs." When the user responds with "I don't" it sounds like a strong denial. But, it is not answering the question in the same verb tense. He may be referring to his usage in the last two hours. By answering this way, the drug user has avoided completely lying by answering a question of his choosing by changing the verb tense.[81]

A similar example can be found in President Clinton's response to a journalist's question about Monica Lewinsky. The exchange looked like this:

Matt Lehrer: "You had no sexual relationship with this young woman?"

Clinton: "There is not a sexual relationship -- That is accurate."[82]

This was technically true. Bill Clinton was not having sex in the middle of the interview. Even though Bill Clinton was well known to lie long and often,[83] his answers to questions in many of his scandals reflect this sort of hairsplitting response. This desire to tell the truth, even if a perverted form of it, is universal. Even politicians have a strong subconscious desire to produce an answer, however twisted, that they can consider the truth.

Body Language

Watching body language is an exercise in applied excess energy observation. You can quote me on that. What you are looking for in another person's body language is extra movements caused by the adrenaline added to their system by lying. They might, "...begin to squirm in their chair, rub the back of their neck, run their fingers through their hair, or look away when speaking."[84]

Please note that due to the widespread dissemination of the fact that liars look away when talking, liars have learned to look people in the eyes, sometimes fixedly so. This leads us to the topic of overcompensation. Liars may try to disguise their extra energy by overcompensating. They might hold their bodies very stiffly or stare fixedly. Their arms and legs might not move at all.

I remember watching *Survivor: Marquesas* where the Maine lobster boat captain, Zoe Zanidakis, was a contestant. A teammate asked her if she was in an alliance with Boston Rob and a few others. As Jeff Probst had revealed this to be the case earlier in the show, I already knew the answer was yes. So, I was watching closely to see how she would react. She lied to the other contestant in a calm voice, saying something to the effect of, "No, I'm not." Sure enough, excess energy kicked in and her arm flew up of its own volition to swat at an imaginary fly or something. Her voice and face seemed clam and honest, but her right arm announced the truth.

If you are intuitive, you will sometimes notice that something is off in a conversation. It may well be your subconscious telling you that your friend is talking a bit differently than normal. Your brain might be noticing subtle changes in their body language.

Intuition is good for clueing you into other subtle changes in behavioral patterns as well. I hate to think that my teenage son is doing naughty things, but there are times I suspect he is. When confronted, he always has an innocent explanation. I accepted this for a while, but I became increasingly suspicious. It was my intuition telling me that the pattern for other teenagers was for them to misbehave, even if only infrequently. My intuition was increasingly suspicious of this kid who never misbehaved. It knew the complete innocence he protested didn't fit the normal teenage pattern.

Observing How a Story is Told and Retold

One key to discerning whether a story is true or not is to keep track of the details. If a response to a question contains too many details, the person may be guilty of something. They may be inventing minutiae so the story sounds more plausible and natural. When you hear a multitude of details, you should ask yourself if this is how your friend or family member normally answers questions.

Related to this is the level of detail in repeated retellings. If a person is telling the truth, the level of detail usually increases when the story is repeated. This is because the speaker is recalling more details of the event from his memory. If the speaker is lying about an incident, the level of detail will usually remain the same, as there are no new details to add to a story that was made up to begin with.

Asking "How Would I Answer This?"

If you are even slightly suspicious, a good question to ask is how you would answer if you were asked the same question.[85] If you would give a simple answer to a question and their answer takes five minutes, investigate why that is. If you would answer a question matter-of-factly, and their response is hyper-emotional, check into that as well.

Lie Catching Practice

A study of daytime court cases is great practice in identifying liars and their lies. Usually one, if not both, of the litigants are lying so there is plenty of material to work with. The judges on these shows have seen thousands of these jokers and simple repetition has given them a keen sense of who the liars are. Sometimes the judges will explain how they know they are being lied to. This is a great service to you, the lie-catcher-in-training. Even if the judge only points out which litigant is the liar, this gives you an opportunity to try and figure out what gave that person away.

As noted, watching the TV series, *Survivor* is also a good opportunity to watch people lying. Taping the show and watching people lie in slow motion can give you practice at catching the sometimes subtle clues to people's deceptions. This will prepare you for the next step, practicing on the devious characters in your own circle of friends and family.

Truthorfiction.com is a website that I've found to be very good at researching and giving unbiased assessments on internet rumors, urban legends, religious claims, and questionable stories of all sorts from our culture. I highly recommend it for its accuracy and its approach to handling truth.

Summary

With all of these tips and techniques, keep in mind that no one word or behavior is definitive proof that your friend or significant other is lying to you. What you are looking for are indicators that a person's statements merit closer scrutiny. You can't double-check everyone all the time, so you need some indication of who deserves closer scrutiny. Once you start the investigation, look for a *pattern* of deceptive words and behaviors. Everybody uses extra words, confuses verb tenses, or misuses pronouns at some point. Liars, however, will show multiple indications that they're being deceitful.

*****

Most of the chapters in this book approach the issue of truth from a straightforward logical approach. The next chapter, in an indirect way, attempts to extract a general truth from a single instance in time. Thanks again dear reader, for allowing me to be autobiographical.

Chapter 13

A Refutation of Atheism; From Nicaragua

"And the king shall say unto them, Verily I say unto you, Inasmuch as ye have done it unto one of the least of these my brethren, ye have done it unto me."

~Matthew 25:40

In January of 2014, my family and I went on a mission trip to Nicaragua. Our first two days we ran medical clinics in Messiah Project's garage. My wife, the highly attractive and awesome doctor that she is, ran the medical side while the patients needing physical therapy were shuttled over to the main building. My job was to do some prescreening and information gathering for my wife.

My helper was Alondra, 16 year old language whiz and easily the prettiest translator in Central America. During the interviews I insisted on trying out my college Spanish on the locals. This worked better than I had feared, but was still bad enough to frustrate my translator terribly. The linguistic haze I was creating became so confusing that Alondra took to yelling at me in Spanish and the Nicaraguans in English.

We had assigned numbered index cards to everyone wanting to see a doctor. I remember #17 the most.

Even though she topped out at less than five feet, I was afraid of her at first. She wore a white cloth covering her lower face. I feared she had something communicable, or worse, tuberculosis which I am greatly afraid of.

As I asked her about her medical problems, she haltingly mentioned a few routine afflictions but didn't mention the cloth over her face. This was not terribly uncommon. Some of the people we were seeing were very sick; medical care in rural Nicaragua being what it is. Some of the villagers with horrific medical issues would casually report headaches and neck pain. After dutifully writing this down, I would prompt them for "otras problemas," and they would finally mention their diabetes or recent open heart surgery.

I prompted Alondra to delicately ask about the cloth and received the response, "She's shy." Perhaps taking courage from my calm response to this, #17 lowered her cloth to reveal-------- a slightly swollen lip.

*****

Later that day, I learned more about Maria (not her real name). For some unknown reason, at a very early age she had been rejected by her entire family and kicked out of the house. Only her grandfather cared for her and took her in to live with him. Two months before our arrival, Maria's grandfather had died. Not content to throw her out of their own home, her family had begun legal proceedings to throw Maria out of her grandfather's house as well. As we talked, Maria didn't know if she would continue to have a home or not.

I didn't know those details when I began praying for her in Messiah Project's garage. What I did know was that my soul was appalled to its core at the starkness of the lies about her worth that had been told this woman. Never before have I seen someone so filled with shame--simply for being. A woman who God Himself loved before time began. A woman who God would rather come to earth and die for than be separated from.

My limited Spanish flowed miraculously smoothly as I prayed for her, so I know she heard me. She heard me as I prayed for God to obliterate the lies in her life. She heard me as I prayed for her to see her true and awesome worth in God's eyes. I don't cry very often, but I was crying then.

She continued through the process and my teammates all loved on her. Our team leader, Carrie, said it best, "Nobody here wants her, but we'd all take her home." I don't know if she took my prayers for her to heart. I don't know if she was convinced that the love from my teammates was both real and deserved. What I do know, is that when she left that day, her face was uncovered.

I'd like to see atheism do that.

Chapter 14

Formal Logic

"Logic: The art of thinking and reasoning in strict accordance with the limitations and incapacities of the human misunderstanding."
~Ambrose Bierce

Throughout history, mankind has made the same mistakes over and over. There's been a lot of trial and error in our attempts to think clearly. The good news is that we can learn from history and from other people's mistakes. We have made progress in finding better ways to solve problems. Logic is one of the tools our ancestors developed to sift truth from falsehood. It's not foolproof, of course, because fools are so ingenious. But, a good knowledge of logic beats the heck out of guessing.

Useful Logical Concepts

In this chapter we will look at a number of logical dos and don'ts. First we'll examine several foundational concepts for understanding arguments. This will be far from an exhaustive list as we only have one chapter to work with.

I will also be illustrating principles and fallacies from some popular arguments.

Whose Hand is it?

First-hand information refers to information you saw or heard personally with no intermediaries. First-hand information is not considered perfect. You may have been drunk, distracted, or demented when you witnessed the event. Even so, it is considered much better evidence than second-hand information. *Second- hand* information comes from someone, a friend or a journalist perhaps, who has talked to someone who directly witnessed an event. The person who saw the event would be called the "first-hand source" of the person giving you the second-hand report.

If you went and told your mother what you thought you heard the journalist or friend say, your mother would be getting the information *third-hand*, as she would be the third person in the chain of communication. There isn't a fourth, fifth, or sixth hand. I don't know why. If there are four or more people in the line of communication, it is still referred to as third-hand.

Having more hands involved, very much like having too many cooks, makes the broth, or communication, much worse. Each new person in the chain adds a new level of bias, miscommunication, selective attention, and downright error. Also, as school-day games of telephone demonstrate, the more complex the communication the worse this distortion becomes.[86]

Correlation is Not Causality!

"Beetle larvae cured my cancer!" yelled Susan, a person I just made up. "I ate a pound of them a day for a month and when I went to my oncologist he said my cancer was in total remission!" Here we have a *correlation* between the practice of eating beetle larvae and the event of having cancer go into remission. They are correlated because they happened around the same time.

Susan additionally believes that the beetle larvae *caused* her cancer to get better. She does have some reason for this belief. The person who sold her the beetle larvae said they would. Why else pay $70 a pound for them? And oh yes, her cancer is now in remission. How much more proof do you need?

There are actually at least four possible relationships between the cancer and the beetle eating:

1) Beetle larvae ingestion did indeed cure the cancer.

2) The beetle larvae contributed to the cure, but were not a major factor.

3) Beetles have no effect on cancer and some third factor, such as prayer or chemotherapy actually brought about the cure.

4) The beetles actually made the cancer *worse*, but other third factors overcame their negative effect.

The classic example of correlation being different from causality is the link between reading ability and shoe size. Did you know that in children, the bigger the shoe size, the better the reading ability? It's a perfect correlation. Honestly. Do you suppose that having big feet somehow stimulates the reading center of the brain?

What's really happening is that both reading ability and shoe size are being influenced by a third factor: age. The older a child is, the bigger their feet are. The older a child is, the more developed their brain is and the more experience they have with reading. So, even though increases in shoe size and reading ability match perfectly, they have no causal relationship to each other. Shoe size doesn't increase reading ability. Reading ability doesn't make feet grow.

I remember when I was a young boy listening to the radio announcer report that a recent study had shown that married couples who shared a goodbye kiss in the morning were much more likely to stay together. The clear implication was that you should rev up the smooching so as to safeguard your marriage. This was most likely a case of *reverse causality*. Rather than morning kissing causing harmonious relationships, it is far more likely that morning kisses are caused by harmonious relationships.

The argument over correlation versus causality rages on in many current day topics. In the global warming debate, many people believe that global warming is caused by increased levels of carbon dioxide from burning fossil fuels. Many others believe that while there are correlations between warmer weather and more carbon dioxide, the two factors are unrelated or that perhaps warmer weather leads to increased levels of carbon dioxide instead.[87] I'm not going to weigh in on that one for the moment as I've probably collected enough enemies already.

Argumentation is not Quarreling

When you argue, it should be productive. There should be a point to it. As D.Q. McInerny points out, "The object of argument is to get at the truth. The object of quarreling is to get at other people."[88] The sort of name-calling that passes for arguing in much of our world leads to plenty of hurt feelings, but little in the way of increased knowledge. A discussion where neither party has any possibility of adjusting their opinion to fit the facts is not an argument, it's just conflict. If your flame-war isn't doing anything constructive, douse it and find something better to do.

Occam's Razor

An important concept in discerning truth, and one referenced elsewhere in this book, is Occam's Razor. This principle was developed by William of Occam, a philosopher and Franciscan monk who lived in Occam, England around 1300 A.D.[89]

Occam's Razor states: "among competing hypotheses, the one with the fewest assumptions should be selected. Other, more complicated solutions may ultimately prove correct, but—in the absence of certainty—the fewer assumptions that are made, the better."[90] Occam's Razor is a good way of excluding more comprehensive, but much worse explanations that rely upon layer after layer of ad hoc explanations. Consider Liam's conversation with a conspiracy theorist:

Conspiracy Theorist: "I know that President Reagan was not shot by John Hinckley Jr. He was shot by an alien from the star system Rigor Mortis!"

Liam: "But wouldn't they have found out he was an alien when they caught him and examined him?"

Conspiracy Theorist: "Oh, they found out alright, but the Republican Party covered the whole thing up. They don't want us to know aliens exist. Duh!"

Liam: "Wouldn't President Clinton have discovered the conspiracy when he took office and got access to all of the records?"

Conspiracy Theorist: "He did, but President Clinton didn't want to talk about it because he's an alien too!"

The use of Occam's razor would very strongly suggest that John Hinckley Jr., acting alone and, influenced by mental illness, shot President Reagan. That is the simplest explanation that fits all of the facts. While it does not prove it beyond all conceivable doubt, it does suggest that that this is the most likely and accurate explanation.

Hanlon's Razor

Hanlon's razor is a more modern saying loosely related to Occam's Razor. It is intended as a rule of thumb method to better understand other people's behavior. Hanlon's razor states: "Never attribute to malice that which is adequately explained by stupidity."[91] This does not mean, of course, that people are never malicious. Instead, it highlights the fact that we are very quick to attribute malice to others when we would attribute our own failures to mere incompetence. Also, when you think about it, there are a lot more failures from foolishness than mistakes due to malice.

Explaining versus Explaining Away

When someone answers a question, look to see if they are trying to explain all of the facts as best they can or just trying to discount them. Consider these two excerpts from a writer who is answering objections to the belief that global warming is real and manmade.

> In September 2013, the Daily Mail — a British newspaper that frequently publishes articles presenting climate change as a hoax — trumpeted its latest evidence, in the form of researchers' findings that the Arctic ice cap actually had increased 29 percent over the previous year. 'And now it's global COOLING!' the paper's headline gleefully proclaimed.
>
> On the face, increasing polar sea ice would seem to be a powerful refutation of the scary scenario presented by mainstream climate scientists, which is that the shrinking ice is causing sea levels to rise dangerously. But again, the flaw in the argument is that a single year doesn't make a trend. The amount of northern polar ice varies from year to year, but the long-term pattern is one of severe decline. From 1979 to 2014, the average ice cap in January shrank from 15.5 million square kilometers (6 million square miles) to 13.7 million square kilometers (5 million square miles). The only way that 2013 looked good was because it was a little better than 2012, which was one of the worst years on record.[92]

In this discussion, the author thankfully sticks to the facts and appears to apply them relevantly. He is explaining why he thinks the Daily Mail is wrong. I can't attest that the author is wrong or right about global warming. But, in this small section, the author argues in a way that leads me to some level of trust that he is addressing the topic in a non-distorted way. On the other hand, our next selection from the same article makes me suspect the opposite is true.

> To climate change deniers, this is the slam dunk argument. If the rise in global warming has stopped, even as human civilization has continued to pump increasing amounts of carbon dioxide emissions into the atmosphere, that should prove that the whole greenhouse effect thing is bunk, right? Radio commentator Rush Limbaugh certainly thinks so. 'There is no warming, and there hasn't been for 15 years,' he proclaimed in an August 2013 broadcast.
>
> That sounds convincing, except that it isn't correct. In fact, data from the Met Office, Britain's equivalent of the U.S. National Weather Service, and the University of East Anglia's Climate Research Unit shows that the global temperature did, in fact, increase between 1997 and 2012— roughly the period Limbaugh is talking about —by 0.09 degrees Fahrenheit (0.05 degrees Celsius).
>
> It is true that the increase was relatively flat, compared to other periods in the past century. But as climate scientist and National Academies of Science member Peter Gleick has pointed out in a Forbes article, global surface temperature has had similar plateaus in the past. But the overriding trend is still that the planet is getting hotter.[93]

How you feel about this response may well depend on how you feel about the debate in general. To my eye, this looks much more like <u>explaining away</u> the evidence. An increase of 0.09 degrees over fifteen years is not significant enough to be called warming. Would the author argue that a yearly decrease of 0.006 degrees[*] would constitute *cooling*? I wouldn't either. Other than claiming that it is still "getting hotter," he attempts no factual explanation. He makes references to science, scientists, and "similar plateaus," impressive sounding words all. Strip away the extra words and we can see that he is trying to argue that temperatures staying the same are as predictive of temperatures going up as---temperatures going up. When stated this way, of course, it's patent nonsense.

Also note he has not addressed the initial objection that temperatures would be expected to increase the most in recent years when carbon outputs have been the highest. These are the sorts of obfuscations you need to identify when people are explaining things away. It tells you they're not confident in their position.

Logical Errors and Poor Thinking

Following are a list of poor ways to argue and think. This is not an exhaustive list by any means. It's some of the more common problems you'll see in both national debate and everyday discussion.

Arguing from Selective Evidence

Unfortunately, this constitutes most of persuasive speech today. If you are arguing for a certain position, you *do* want to highlight the facts that support your case. Honest argumentation, however, takes account of the other side's facts and important points. It engages those points, shows why they are not applicable, and demonstrates that they are weak or misleading. Arguing from selective evidence, on the other hand, simply leaves out your opponent's best arguments altogether. This is done so that the audience will not be exposed to good counter-arguments and the deceptive speaker can win by default.

---

[*] 0.09/15 years = 0.006.

For instance, if your teenager wants to convince you that he is a reliable driver, he might point out that he's never gotten a ticket, never ran a red light, and has never gotten home late. This sounds very impressive, but your teenager has left out the most important fact about his driving ability. Namely, that he wrecked the car while it was still in the garage. It is true that he's never gotten into any of the other trouble he has pointed out; only because the car is now inoperable.

Ad Hominem Attacks

Ad hominem attacks are a very primitive form of argument. Although simple, they are still widely employed today. The smallest child will try to win an argument by yelling, "Oh yeah, well you're fat!" The adult form is not much more sophisticated.

Ad Hominem is Latin for "to the person," a fancy phrase which means "name calling." If you're losing an argument, simply call your opponent an idiot, a neocon, a liberal, a homophobe, or whatever you think will impress your audience.[94]

If you wish to see ad hominem in action, tune into any of the daytime court shows. These cases are often disputes over who owes who money. It is amazing how much we learn about the plaintiff's marital infidelities and drug use when the defendants plead their cases. Of course, these sins are totally irrelevant to whether the defendant owes money or not.

The internet is filled to the brim with ad hominem attacks as the comment sections on most any controversial topic consists mainly of personal jabs and insults, all in the name of "proving" a point. When you see such arguments, it is often a signal that the poster knows they are losing the debate.

But it's Not Peer Reviewed!!

This one is a logical fallacy category of my own naming albeit not my own construction. Peer review refers to: "the evaluation of work by one or more people of similar competence to the producers of the work (peers). It constitutes a form of self-regulation by qualified members of a profession within the relevant field."[95] Most typically, this peer review process is used to review articles before they appear in scientific or medical journals. These journals are referred to as *peer reviewed journals* which contain only *peer reviewed articles.*

A very common criticism of late is that an idea is without merit because research supporting it has never appeared in a peer reviewed journal. The inference is that if such a journal has never published it, then that idea must be baseless. After all, professionals in that field have not signed off on it. This is not a bad indicator of an idea's merit, but very problematic when used as an absolute criteria. It may actually indicate nothing more than that the idea reflects a minority opinion. The number of people involved in journal production are very small compared to the number of people in the field overall. For this reason, it is not hard for one mindset to take control of a journal or even a category of journals.

Consider say, *Christianity Today.* Odds are pretty good that the writers, publishers, and employees believe in God. Chances are even better that the few people with real authority to decide what gets published in that journal believe in God rather deeply. This is not a conspiracy; it's just that people with common ideas tend to concentrate around a project of mutual interest. Now imagine that someone argued that atheists were wrong because none of their articles ever got published in *Christianity Today.* In and of itself, this would be more evidence about the worldview of the publishers than anything else. It would have very little logical relevance to whether atheists were right or wrong.

People will often claim that because there are no peer-reviewed articles supporting a certain point of view, that point of view is wrong and the matter is settled. These points of view include such issues as reparative therapy (therapy to remove or reduce same-sex attraction), intelligent design, global warming, and many others. Such difficulties are not only encountered in right versus left arguments, they are endemic to all of science. Wikipedia notes that any ideas outside of the mainstream of the field are subject to similar exclusion.[96] Science is a dynamic enterprise with new discoveries supplanting and replacing old orthodoxies all the time. Science should be a matter of truth, not majority opinion.

Circular Reasoning

Circular Reasoning is simply the process of assuming your conclusion and using the conclusion to prove itself. It is less commonly know as Begging the Question.[97] In its simplest form, circular reasoning looks something like this:

Premise: I'm the best author you'll read this year.

Conclusion: You're going to enjoy reading my book because I'm the best author out there.

I've already decided how wonderful I am but provide no evidence for my conclusion other than rewording what I've already decided is true. Of course, self-deluded people will express things in more complex and convoluted ways so as to better fool you and themselves. A more common example of circular reasoning might look like this:

> Senator Farnsworth is too unreliable to be reelected! Throughout history, mankind, which of course includes all kinds of women, has sought to find leaders that they can trust to lead while keeping the public's interest uppermost in mind. After all, once they get to Washington, they're totally unsupervised.

> Right? This is why you should vote for me. Senator Farnsworth just can't be trusted.

Finding the circular reasoning in this example takes a little more work. Notice that the first and last sentences say essentially the same thing. While the intervening sentence sounds reasonable, the author does not provide any evidence of the Senator's untrustworthiness. We have only the author's assertion as evidence for his conclusion.

Argumentum Ad Fatigum[98]

This is a fancy Latin term which means "making the same argument over and over until everyone is won over by sheer repetition." Closely related to this is the idea of using "talking points." In argumentum ad fatigum, an argument is won not by clear exposition of known facts or through the discovery of new evidence, but through sheer repetition of your assertions. This works best if you have a number of like-minded associates employing the same tactics.

The arguments for gay marriage are of this variety. The laws being enacted to institute gay marriage are not based on new knowledge. They are based on a large number of people confidently asserting over and over that it should happen and that if you disagree you hate civil rights or gay people or something. People with no particular opinion on the subject eventually agree with it because they've heard it said that gay marriage is morally correct so often, they come to believe that it is common knowledge.

A follow up move in Argumentum Ad Fatigum is the eye roll. It happens right after someone revisits a disagreement. The AAF practitioner will roll his eyes and says, "Oh, we've been over this so many times. It's already been proven that everyone with any brains agrees with me. Why are you even bothering to bring this up?" In this manner, they hope to shame the questioner into silence without having to give a single good argument for their own position.

Straw Man

In the straw man technique, you refuse to engage with your opponent's real argument. Instead you invent some ridiculous parody of their position and proceed to bravely demolish this invented "straw man."

For instance, someone arguing against prayer in schools might insist his opponents want to "institute religious law in our classrooms" and then complain at length about the Inquisition and people being burned at the stake. He will then go on to discredit his opponents for being pro-burning-at-the-stake.

Another example would be claiming that a politician who introduces legislation to cut the military budget "wants to leave our country defenseless." Talking about the tragedies that would occur if we had no military makes for great drama, but it is hardly an honest engagement with the issue at hand.

Intermediate Response

I couldn't find an existing logical fallacy to fit this description so I constructed my own. In the intermediate response, the Questioner, Mr. Q., asks a question and the person giving the answer, Mrs. A., responds with something that sounds helpful, but does not answer the ultimate intent of the question.

For example, I will often ask my wife where the checkbook is. She will usually respond with, "It's in my purse." To the uninitiated, this sounds like a helpful answer that will get me to my ultimate goal of holding the checkbook in my hands. In reality, this answer is not very useful as my wife's purse is highly mobile and extremely variable in its location. So, the inevitable next question is, "OK, where's your purse?"

It's not clear what my wife's motives are in this exchange. It may be that she is pretty sure that <u>this time,</u> I will magically know where the purse has gotten to. It may also be, as I suspect, that she is giving me an intermediate answer in the hopes that I will go and search for it myself and save her the trouble of having to think further.

*****

This type of interchange comes up a lot in our quest for ultimate answers. For instance, Mr. Q. might ask, "Where did we come from?" Mrs. A., giving an intermediate response, could answer that we were brought here from another planet. While this is possible, it only answers the most immediate question. Mr. Q. is really trying to ask where did life and everything else come from, not just the immediate cause of life springing up on Earth, or for that matter, which hospital he was born in.

If Mr. Q. has the patience, he might persist in his questioning by asking, "OK, where did the people on that other planet come from?" Mrs. A. will probably say she doesn't know, exit the discussion, or continue giving intermediate answers until she finally responds with either God or the Big Bang. As God is by definition an ultimate cause, Mr. Q. can grapple with that answer as he sees fit. If instead, Mrs. A. answers "The Big Bang" Mr. Q., despite any misgivings he might have, may accept this answer because he can't think of what the next question might be. If Mr. Q. is really persistent, he might go on to the next question, "Where did the Big Bang come from?"

There the question sat for some time. Finally, Stephen Hawking took up the challenge and answered the question with, "Because there is a law such as gravity, the universe can and will create itself from nothing. Spontaneous creation is the reason there is something rather than nothing, why the universe exists, why we exist."[99]

This is a formidable attempt to take on an age-old question, but one which ultimately is as much an intermediate response as all of the rest. It inevitably leads to the next question, "So, where did gravity come from?"

*****

Logic is a very useful tool for discerning truth and one that is often overwhelmed by our feelings, passions, and desires. Logic is not the greatest gift we were ever given, but one that we ignore at our peril. In the next chapter, we discuss more of the joys of logic as well as some of the dangers of attempting to use logic in isolation.

Chapter 15

Case Study 2: Logic Gone Bad

"Logic! Good gracious! What rubbish!"
~E.M. Forster

For this case study, I am going to use as my source material of poor reasoning---a book on logic. This particular logic book attempts to convey truth about logical fallacies in 100 small essays. We will be looking at selections from three of these essays. I won't be using the author's name in the body of the text as besmirching a fellow author is not my goal.[100, 101] Besides, there are many places where the author shows genuine humility, and you know I have a soft spot for that. My purpose is to illustrate what bad thinking looks like even when it's trying very hard to be good thinking. To be fair, I want to point out that I am using the author's worst essays.

First, let's look at an essay that Bob, as I'm calling him, writes in an attempt to make a point about guilt by association. He begins the chapter with a quote from an English Catholic Cardinal. Bob's intent is to point out the errors in the Cardinal's thinking:

> That way lies eugenics, and we know from German history where that leads. We are already on that road: for what else is the termination of 6 million lives in the womb since the Abortion Act was introduced, and embryo selection on the basis of gender and genes?
> ~Cardinal Cormac Murphy-O'Connor[102]

Bob comments on this quote as follows:

> Given that Cardinal Cormac Murphy-O'Connor is a Roman Catholic, it comes as no surprise to find that he is against abortion. But it is still something of a shock to hear him compare the termination of foetal life with Nazi eugenics programmes, which he has done on several occasions. In the quote above he even evokes a comparison with the Holocaust with his references to '6 million lives'.
>
> The cardinal does not, however, offer very compelling arguments as to why we should see some kind of moral equivalence between eugenics and abortion (which are separate issues anyway) and Nazi atrocities. Perhaps he doesn't need to. Simply by making some kind of link between National Socialism and the practice he abhors, he succeeds in implying guilt by association: putting two things that have no necessary connection together in the hope that the bad name of one will taint the other.[103]

In just two paragraphs, Bob illustrates what many of you were yelling at this book the whole time you were reading the logic chapter. Namely, that without a moral center, the best logical skills on the planet aren't worth a hill of beans. With no sense of spiritual or even natural law, we are well and truly clueless. Bob looks much like Spock at the end of Star Trek II: The Wrath of Khan.* At the end of the movie, Spock saves the Enterprise by fixing something in a

---

* Best...Star Trek Movie...Ever.

radiation-flooded part of the Enterprise we've never heard of before. Trying to maintain his dignity, he stands, straightens his uniform and then walks toward Kirk steadily and confidently. That the radiation has blinded Spock becomes abundantly clear when he walks straight into the bulkhead with a resounding "Thonk."[104] That was the sound I heard when I read the preceding two paragraphs. Bob means well, and he's trying to provide a useful service, but his apparent amoral nature sometimes causes him to blindly wander into things without a clue as to what he is doing.

Not only does Bob not recognize the immoral nature of abortion, he's unable to imagine that anyone else might. He mistakes the cardinal's grief-filled statement for a rhetorical trick of some sort. God has put within our souls an understanding of right and wrong. When we silence that by replacing our God-given conscience with our own notions, the best that the greatest intelligence can hope for is incompetence. Bob further compounds the mess he is making by claiming that eugenics and abortion are not related. He is apparently unaware that, in the United States, at least, eugenics and abortion are directly connected. Margaret Sanger, founder of Planned Parenthood, promoted abortion largely out of a desire to limit the population of the feeble-minded and other undesired groups.[105]

Bob continues his analysis:

> The same trick can be applied to an astonishing array of beliefs and practices. The Nazis were very keen on ecology, forests, public rallies, compulsory gym classes and keep fit. If you yourself object to any of these, then slip in a mention of Nazi policy next time you want your criticisms to pack an added rhetorical punch. And if you're being bothered by a vegetarian while you're trying to enjoy your T-bone steak, just remind your critic that Hitler too eschewed meat.[106]

There's a valid point in here somewhere. But, I'm too busy noticing that Bob, one paragraph after complaining about false moral equivalencies, is now equating the pairing of vegetarians and Hitler with the pairing of killing babies and killing people. In general, distrust people who lecture on moral equivalencies when they have no solid moral foundation of their own. Lacking any objective set of rules on which to base their morality, they tend to build their idea of moral outrage on their own personal feelings at the moment.

Bob is a philosopher in his day job. When I listen to philosophers talk, there seems to be a lot of "thonking" going on.

We turn now to another of Bob's essays. This one tries to illustrate that people are uncomfortable with shades of gray and greatly prefer black or white. A worthy endeavor, but an ill-fated one. I'm honestly not trying to re-fight the abortion debate here, but this is where the errors keep showing up. Bob writes:

> The obvious reply is that what at conception starts out as a collection of cells gradually becomes a human baby. But the trouble with this is that any cut-off point would seem to be arbitrary. No wonder anti-abortionists try to clear up this unsatisfactory vagueness by insisting it is always a child, right from conception.
>
> Both these 'pro-lifers' [Why is this in quotes?] and Sawyer seem to me to be making a basic mistake, which is to think that unless there is a firm boundary between two states or concepts, there is no real distinction between them, and the best we can do is make one up.[107]

Bob is under the impression here that he is making a good point about seeing shades of gray. What he is illustrating instead is the danger of listening to "experts." I have no doubt that Bob is a kick-butt philosopher and knows his field backwards and forwards. Philosophy probably comes easy to him and he most likely trounces opponents regularly in the Logic Olympics.

The trouble with the Bobs of the world is that they often start to think that their expertise in things they're good at somehow transfers into areas outside of their field.[108] For example, you have high-caliber scientists who make confident pronouncements about how the economy and human government should work. These pronouncements look great on paper, but are unmitigated disasters when tried in real life. On a smaller scale, the stories are legendary of brilliant doctors who lost huge amounts of money on outside business deals because others defrauded them or through their own financial incompetence.

Bob's error here is one of simple ignorance of human biology. A few science courses would have made him aware that fertilization is the distinct beginning of human life because of biology, not psychological discomfort. Consider the following:

"Although life is a continuous process, fertilization ... is a critical landmark because, under ordinary circumstances, a new genetically distinct human organism is formed when the chromosomes of the male and female pronuclei blend in the oocyte."[109]

As well as this:

"Although life is a continuous process, fertilization is a critical landmark because, under ordinary circumstances, a new, genetically distinct human organism is thereby formed.... The embryo now exists as a genetic unity."[110]

And finally, Dianne Irving sums up well why fertilization is a clear starting point:

"Conception is the exact first moment from which that time forward only nutrition and a safe environment are necessary for full development. This single new cell directs its own growth from that point forward."[111]

For our next selection, we turn to Bob's essay on "Mood Music." I think he intended to warn us that marketers can entice us to buy things by inducing a positive mood in us that has nothing to do with the actual product. Instead of finding a good example of this, Bob unexpectedly goes off on a paranoid rant about the UK Conservative party instead:

> The election was fought using slogans that were on the whole correct. Where the slight of hand occurred is that, when such words and slogans are selected and put together in the right way; an overall impression is created which is distinct from that of the individual elements themselves. Each utterance, each slogan, is a single note which helps create the 'mood music' only if it is played in the right place at the right time. ... Because this is all about impression created, not statements made, it can be claimed that anyone who interprets the mood music unfavourably has simply got the wrong impression. My perceptions, it will be argued, reflect only my prejudices.
>
> However, it is no secret that the Conservatives were using the so-called 'dog whistle' technique: saying things that deliver messages only the intended audience can hear. Since this whole strategy relies on there being implicit as well as explicit messages, the claim that some things are being implied which are not actually being said can hardly be denied. The room for disagreement concerns only what those implied messages are.[112]

Yeah, that's just painful. First, look at, "My perceptions, it will be argued, reflect only my prejudices." Bob's implication is that such an argument would be dishonest somehow. Actually, that his perceptions reflect his prejudices is the whole point. It's why I'm picking on his book for crying out loud. I was too distracted by Bob's prejudices to listen to his useful arguments half the time.

In this essay the bad actor is the UK Conservative party. Throughout the book, the author's bad examples almost always involve conservatives. Part of the book even argues that believing Reganomics had something to do with the economy improving is most likely a logical fallacy. This shows a definite preference for one side of the political spectrum.

I do believe Bob is illustrating the effect of 'mood music'; only in the opposite way that he intended. In the selection above, Bob looks more like the mind-numbed victim of mood music rather than the steely-eyed investigator he imagines himself. A belief in "dog whistles" comes about through exposure to propaganda, not logical thought. If dog whistle communication was a real thing, conservatives would accuse liberals of using it.

Anyway, here we are in a book about logical fallacies and we find ourselves smack dab in a conspiracy theory. Consider, "an overall impression is created which is distinct from that of the individual elements themselves." This is paranoia. Bob is arguing that various elements of the UK Conservative party are secretly conspiring to coordinate their strategy so that the overall effect of a bunch of disparate parts form the secret message---that only certain people can hear. If this "dog whistle" is so cleverly designed, why can't I hear it, but Bob can? This isn't logic; this is the blind repetition of something he heard a loony on the telly say.

Finally, consider the penultimate sentence: "Since this whole strategy relies on there being implicit as well as explicit messages, the claim that some things are being implied which are not actually being said can hardly be denied."

Well, that's a mouthful. For those of you playing at home, the key to understanding this statement can be found in the previous chapter. If you want, take a moment and go back there and see what this brings to mind.

You're back? Good. Yes, this is our old friend, circular reasoning. Bob is assuming that a secret strategy exists. He then concludes that there are implicit messages. What is this conclusion based on? It is based on nothing but his initial assumption that there is a strategy to use implicit messages. Cir-cu-lar.

*****

In the preceding examples, we see that a gentleman who set out to write a book on impartial logic is time and again tripped up by his own left-wing notions. It needs to pointed out that if we use this as an opportunity to feel superior, we are sadly missing the point. It may well be that someone will come along and write a scathing review of my book, accurately pointing out that I have similar shortcomings. Perhaps they will show that my right-wing views have tainted my goal of helping others find truth in their lives. The message I hope to convey then is not, "Ha, ha, look at Bob." The message is, "Wait, am I Bob?"

So, in the spirit of fairness, education, and collegiality, let me finish this chapter with one of the essays on logic where Bob did a good job of discerning truth. In this following segment he discusses the logical fallacy of confirmation bias. Confirmation bias happens when you pay attention only to evidence that supports your position, while ignoring the evidence that doesn't. He illustrates this with a discussion of belief in psychics:*

> If we are inclined to believe in the supernatural, then it is easy to focus on those examples where predictions come true, or where psychics make accurate statements about the past or present. These 'confirm' our beliefs that they really do have access to a source of knowledge beyond the physical world, or at least the world as science understands it.
>
> If we do not believe in the supernatural, however, we will focus on the countless times when predictions are wrong or when psychics make mistakes. Reading the article about Jonathan Cainer, for example--setting

---

* Psychics, not physics. Physics is ok.

> aside doubts about the truth of the story--we will think that this one accurate prediction doesn't count for much, for the psychic probably also said many other things that were not true.[113]

Just today I heard the story of a courageous 16 year old boy who died from Ewing's sarcoma, an aggressive cancer. He died confident that he could glorify God in life or death. Like all of the other stories I've heard from people I've known personally, the teen's use of alternative medicine treatments did not help him. When people peddle alternative cures to cancer, you only hear about the success stories. You don't hear about the hundreds of people who receive no relief at all. When someone tells you how great their product worked for Bobbie Sue, it's wise to investigate what happened to everybody else who used it.

*****

In conclusion, logic is a wonderful servant, a terrible master, and an even worse god. Logic, like oxen, only produces useful results when it is harnessed and controlled by something greater than itself.

In this chapter we discussed just a few of the issues involved with the abortion debate. The next chapter is the most disquieting one in the book as we look at truth and the abortion controversy. It is our third and final case study, and delves deeper into how deception presents itself.

Chapter 16

Case Study 3: Abortion as a Typology of Lies

"The more you defend a lie, the angrier you become."
~Mitch Albom, *For One More Day*

For the record, a chapter dealing with abortion was not in my original or even intermediate plans for this book. I had set out to write a book that was emotionally and topically calm as I wanted it to be easily approachable for anyone. When you're writing, however, sometimes things suddenly appear as you type and you look back and ask, "Where did that come from"? This chapter flowed out from my finger tips almost without effort and it has shifted the book into some new directions.

Let's first talk about why abortion is thought of as desirable. A large number of totally true and factual arguments could be used to support having an abortion. A collection of such arguments might look something like the following section.

Reasons to Have an Abortion

If you bring your baby to term, you will suffer a large number of annoyances and troubles. For the first three months of the pregnancy, you will probably suffer morning sickness and throw up a lot. You may also be bothered intensely by certain smells. In the latter part of pregnancy you will feel overheated, especially in the summer, as the baby will be adding to your body heat. Speaking of childbirth, the process can be extremely painful and the delivery may take an entire day and sometimes more. After the child arrives there will be the inconvenience of nursing and changing hundreds, if not thousands of diapers.

That is just the physical pain and discomfort. The emotional pain is very often much worse. Knowing that you are pregnant when you didn't want the child can be both frustrating and shameful. Knowing that you are unable to adequately care for the child once it is born can leave you feeling humiliated and defeated. Sometimes there is the added shame of not knowing who the father is or having a father who has left the picture. Dealing with all of the questions and knowing stares from family, friends, and acquaintances can also be extremely uncomfortable.

Choosing to give up the baby may be extremely painful as well. Giving away your child can be gut-wrenching as there is no guarantee what sort of treatment your child will receive. If you are underage, having an abortion helps you avoid the emotional confrontations that might happen when you tell your parents you are pregnant. This sort of news might change those relationships forever, and there is no guarantee it will be for the good.

Further, you might be carrying a baby that is not the gender that you always hoped for. You may have dreamed about having a son all of your life, only to have your dreams crushed when you discover you have a daughter instead. Gender is permanent and your child will stay that way for its entire life.

Carrying a baby to term has huge financial consequences as well. You will have to spend extra money on maternity clothes that you won't be able to use after the baby is born. Also, you may have to miss work towards the end of your pregnancy. Finally, your insurance may or may not cover all the expenses of a hospital stay.

If you have an abortion instead, you can avoid the vast majority of these problems.

Every one of these reasons is totally true. They are possible consequences of choosing to carry a child to term. But, here is the thing I find fascinating. Not a single one of these reasons has ever been cited in my hearing, either publicly or privately, as a reason to support legal abortion.

I think I know why this is. These reasons are all real and true, but they sound trivial when compared to the life of a child. I can see how arguing for a right to an abortion based on the above arguments might make you look bad.

Instead of using any of the above arguments, pro-choice advocates[114] use a huge variety of lies to justify this hideous practice. The quantity, variety, and depth of the falsehoods used make the pro-choice movement of the last 40+ years an ideal study on the typology of lies. The following is a classification and analysis of the lies usually told by pro-abortion advocates.

The Kernel of Truth Lie

In this type of lie, something that is readily identifiable as true is introduced early on in the argument. A lie is then shaped around this small kernel of truth in the hope that this small bit of truth will convince the hearers that the surrounding lie is true as well.

This tactic is used in the pro-abortion argument: "It's the woman's body."

Note the apparent surface factualness here. Wherever the mother goes, the fetus goes. It stays inside her until birth after which the baby is clearly outside. On the face of it, there is an obvious connection between the woman's body and the baby. From any other viewpoint, this contention is a lie. Every single cell of the baby's body is different from every single cell of the mother's body. The DNA of the baby is different from the mother's DNA in every cell. Also, the mother and baby may have different blood types. Further, there is a protective device, the decidua, which along with other biochemical processes, shields the baby from the mother's immune system. If the baby did not have these special protective systems, the mother's immune system would correctly identify the baby as foreign to the mother's body and attack and destroy the baby.[115]

Think about this another way. Look yourself over. Are you a part of your mother's body? When you were a child were you a part of your mother's body? When you were an infant were you a part of your mother's body? How about a couple of weeks earlier when you were in her womb? Were you a part of your mother's body then? Have you ever thought of or described yourself as "no longer a part of your mother"?

The Big Lie

The Big Lie was a propaganda device used by Adolph Hitler. He described it in 1925 in his book, *Mein Kampf* where he infamously wrote:

> All this was inspired by the principle--which is quite true within itself--that in the **big lie** there is always a certain force of credibility; because the broad masses of a nation are always more easily corrupted in the deeper strata of their emotional nature than consciously or voluntarily; and thus in the primitive simplicity of their minds they more readily fall victims to the **big lie** than the small lie, since they themselves often tell small lies in little matters but would be ashamed to resort to large-scale falsehoods. It would never come into their heads to fabricate colossal untruths, and they would not believe that others could have the impudence to distort the truth so infamously. Even though the facts which prove this to be so may be brought clearly to their minds, they will still doubt and waver and will continue to think

> that there may be some other explanation. For the grossly impudent lie always leaves traces behind it, even after it has been nailed down, a fact which is known to all expert liars in this world and to all who conspire together in the art of lying.

Ironically, Hitler claimed that the Jews were the master of the big lie, although it was he himself who utilized it by blaming Germany's loss in World War I on the Jews.

The pro-choice Big Lie is: "Abortion protects women."

Pro-abortion advocates state they are working to protect women from imminent death by pushing to keep abortions legal and thus, "safe." In support of this assertion, Pro-abortion advocates often criminally overestimate the annual number of deaths from back-alley abortions, citing numbers from 5000 to 10,000. This is a part of the big lie as the actual reported number of maternal deaths from illegal abortions when Roe v. Wade was passed in 1973 was 45.

The number of maternal deaths in abortion had a peak in 1960 of approximately 300 deaths and has shown a steady decline since then. Women continue to die in proportionate numbers in "front-alley" abortions. Seventeen women died in 1977 from legal abortions.[116] Of these numbers, Bernard Nathanson, former abortion doctor and pro-abortion activist, said: "I confess that I knew the figures were totally false, and I suppose the others did too if they stopped to think of it."[117]

Pro-choice advocates will tell you that promoting the availability of abortion protects the lives of women. In reality, abortion kills women. It kills millions of women. It is the leading cause of death in women in the United States on a yearly basis. According to the CDC, the total reported female deaths in 2009 (preliminary) were 1,219,635. The CDC does not include abortions as part of the death rate total. The highest reported cause of death in women was heart disease at approximately 292,712 female deaths. A total of 784,507 abortions were performed in 2009. If half of these were female, that works out to 374,253 female deaths, an estimated total of 80,000 more female deaths due to abortion than by any other cause.

In a number of countries such as India and China, selective abortion kills unborn women in disproportionate numbers. In China in 2009, the ratio of males to female births was 119.45 to 100.[118] Most couples in China are limited to one child. For cultural reasons, male children are preferred to female children and first born females are often aborted as a son is more desired. In 2020, more than 24 million Chinese men of marriageable age may not be able to marry simply because there are not enough available women.[119] Those missing young women were killed by abortion.

The enormity of such a big lie (abortion protects women) is hard to grasp. As with Hitler's Big Lie, the lie is so vast it is hard for us to believe it could be possible. How could half of our fellow citizens possibly be so wrong on such a vital issue? Didn't our country learn once and for all from the horrible atrocities our ancestors committed against the Native Americans and Africans? Do we think that the dehumanization of the fetus that we do today is any different from the dehumanization that our ancestors practiced?

Most all of us would agree that we are much more enlightened than our ancestors. I do agree that we would not repeat these particular mistakes due to our clear memory of the recent past. But, if we are committing some new national sin, is there anything that makes us materially different from our recent ancestors? I believe we are the same sort of people our ancestors were and we are not the least bit wiser. There is nothing intrinsic to us that gives us the wisdom to discern a new evil. I submit that we need to exercise the same humility and soul-searching that led our ancestors to recognize and confront the evils of their day.

The "Look Over There" Lie

In this type of lie, a totally different issue than the one at hand is introduced as a distraction and substituted for the real issue. The only real issue in the abortion debate is whether the unborn child is a human being or not. Abortion advocates rarely attempt to win their argument by attempting to persuade us a fetus is not a human being. Instead, they attempt to win by arguing for ideas that most people already agree on and then attempting to substitute that for the real argument. The biggest of these is their argument that abortion is about the "Right to Privacy." Having a right to privacy is a very emotional issue that almost everyone would agree to. That being said, no one would argue that the right to privacy gives anyone the right to privately steal from, rape, or kill others.

If the unborn child is a human being, then the right of that human being not to be murdered supersedes another's right to murder that child in private. If the unborn child is not a human being, no appeal to privacy is necessary, as there is no reason to forbid abortion. Appealing to the right to privacy is a "Look Over There" lie. It is an irrelevant and deceitful substitution of one issue for the real one.

Another version of the "Look Over There" lie is character assassination. Instead of answering an argument, a person will attack the character of their opponent (also see "ad hominem attack" in the logic chapter). This is an easily used distraction as people have many faults, and we all seem to have a perverse fascination with exploring other people's defects while excusing our own. If real faults are insufficient for the occasion, imaginary ones can be hurled at an opponent just as easily.

Case in point, pro-choice advocates will accuse pro-life supporters of hating women. When this is not effective, they will then accuse pro-life advocates of not caring about the mothers or helping to care for the children after they are born. There is some truth in this as pro-life outreaches to pregnant women are not sufficient to meet the need. The imperfections of pro-life supporters, however, are irrelevant to the decision to abort a child.

The Semantic Lie

In the Semantic Lie, a lie is told by careful manipulation of key words. The goal in the Semantic Lie is to obscure the issue and confuse the listener by using words that refer to the same thing but which are clearly inappropriate. Minimization or exaggeration is common with this type of lie. Pro-choice activists use this tactic in many ways. When referring to their opponents, they consistently use the term "anti-abortion" or even "anti-choice" while consistently referring to themselves as "pro-choice."

Their use of terminology in reference to the unborn child is especially egregious. Pro-abortion advocates will often refer to the baby as a "fetus" as this is a more depersonalizing term than "baby" or "unborn child." Even more appallingly, they will refer to an unborn baby as "pregnancy tissue,"[120] "products of conception"[121] or even "a cluster of cells."[122]

The Shrill Morally Indignant Lie

There is one sure way to spot a child molester. A child molester will loudly, shrilly, plaintively, and in great depth and detail, explain and expound how <u>he</u> is the victim. Police, parole officers, and the people who press charges against them are evil, predatory, unreasonable, uncaring, incapable of empathy, and profoundly wrong. The sex offender has no apparent understanding that the person who is wrong, and profoundly so, is the sex offender himself. They show no understanding of the life-long trauma that they inflict on innocent children. In listening to their complaints, you would not know that any children were even involved in the pedophile's predicament. Their morally indignant lie is that <u>they</u> are the victims.[123] This is how I deduced that one of my clients was guilty of the charges against him. I could tell by the sheer depth and volume of his complaints against his accusers and his long detailed explanations of his own virtuousness.

When you hear or read the writings of pro-choice advocates you find much the same pattern. You will find pro-choice advocates claim that they are victims of misogyny. They assert that others need to, "Keep your hands off of my body." They will claim that others are attempting to force their moral beliefs on them. They will claim that nameless men want to disempower them, humiliate them, dictate to them, and want to enforce "a gambit to keep 'women in their place.'"[124] They state that "old white men ... assert control over a woman's uterus."[125] They claim that their very health is being threatened and that evil men want them to die in back-alley abortions. According to them, they are hated, maligned, and marginalized.

As in the sex offender discussion, if you did not know what the topic was, you would be totally unable to tell there was a child involved. But, it is the innocent, unborn children who are the ones truly in need of protection. Their health, future choices and lives are the ones that are threatened, and all so very often destroyed.

Arguing from the Extreme

Many, if not most, of the arguments for abortion are made in regards to about 2% of actual cases. Abortions for reasons of rape and incest amount to only 1% of all abortions.[126] Abortions done to save the life of the mother are rarer still and amount to less than 1% of all abortions.[127] However, you would not know that the percentage of abortions due to these causes was only 2% from listening to pro-abortion arguments.

This has always puzzled me. If these exceptional cases are the real reasons for their objections, why are they consistently lumped in with the other 98% of abortions? If they are really only concerned about the 2% of exceptional cases, why can't we work together on outlawing the other 98%?

Omission

Pro-choice arguments for abortion totally omit the known consequences of abortion. While a great deal of noise is made about the stress and psychological trauma of bringing a child to term, the stress and trauma of knowing that you've taken a human life is totally ignored. Post-abortive women commonly experience depression, grief, and guilt.[128] This grief and depression are especially pronounced on the birthday anniversaries of their aborted children.

The clearly documented medical risks of abortion are also totally omitted. Childbirth is a complex and time-consuming process which occurs at a natural pace. When an abortion is performed, the cervix is artificially and rapidly dilated and instruments are introduced into the cervix. This often causes scarring and other damage. Medical side effects are common, but are never mentioned by pro-abortion advocates. These side effects include the short term risk of infection[129] and the risk of suffering a perforated uterus.[130] The long term risks[131] include a tripling of the rate of sterility,[132] ectopic pregnancies,[133] intrauterine adhesions,[134] and subsequent miscarriages.[135]

Another glaring "omission" in these arguments is the baby itself. A typical argument is that "abortion should be between a woman and her doctor." There are actually three persons involved, a woman, a doctor, and the baby. It seems calling for abortion to be between "a woman, her doctor, and her baby" would not elicit anywhere near the same sympathy. The baby has been omitted. This omission is a lie.

Minimization

In minimization, events that happened are admitted to, but to a much lesser extent than is true. For example, an alcoholic might consume twenty drinks at a party but claim that he had, "only a few." Only a small part of reality is admitted to. Pro-abortion advocates use this form of deceit by referring to an unborn child by such terms as "pregnancy tissue" or "just a bunch of cells." It is true that if you squint hard enough these terms are technically correct. In a sense, even you the reader are just a bunch of cells. They do not mention that the developing child has a beating heart (at 18 days),[136] has brain waves (at 40 days),[137] has all its bodily systems present (at 2 months)[138] and breathes (amniotic fluid, at 3 months).[139] By so minimizing the value of the growing life in the mother, they promulgate a lie.

Impression Management

The pro-abortion crowd likes to take on the mantle of "choice." After all, isn't choice a good thing? What is freedom about if not the ability to choose? Invoking choice brings to mind things that we all want. We all desire the ability to choose our spouse and our career as well as our ability to choose who to vote for or where to live. What is overlooked in this argument is that there is something that always trumps the right to choose. Namely, the responsibility to do what is right.

Every day, some parents choose to beat their children. Other people choose to steal from the elderly. Still others choose to call certain people n*****s. None of these people are applauded for exercising their right to choose. That is because they have violated something much more important than the right to choose. They have violated moral absolutes. Pro-life advocates contend that abortion kills a human child. This is either true or false. If it is true, the moral imperative to not murder easily trumps the right to choose. If it is false, no such argument is necessary. The real question then is not whether we like for people to choose, but whether or not the choice to abort is an evil one.

Verbal Fascism

In Verbal Fascism, one side shrilly demands that the other side only use the terms that they approve of. It is normal for two sides to disagree on which terms best describe the object of a discussion. For example, one woman's "illegal alien" is another woman's "undocumented worker." To one side, "illegal alien" is a pejorative term, demeaning of a fellow human being. To the other, "undocumented worker" is a bit of specious fluff that attempts to obscure the basic immoral act of breaking a country's laws for personal gain.

This is a normal part of the argument process. Where this turns into verbal fascism is when someone not only disagrees with the other side's terms, but denounces the other side as morally and intellectually bankrupt for using them and demands that their own terms be used instead. In the abortion debate, the most contested terms are "baby" and "fetus." Both sides feel that their term more accurately describes what resides in the womb. The pro-abortion side, however, demands that the pro-life side use their term, "fetus" as that is the “scientific name” even though they are involved in a moral rather than a scientific discussion. For the record, the actual definition of fetus is: “a developing human from usually two months after conception to birth.[140]

All of this is astonishing. This is the coalition that prides itself on being "pro-choice." Yet, they have no tolerance whatsoever of people choosing which terms they prefer in a discussion. One would think a person's choice of words would be a highly personal one.

They also angrily reject the term "baby" because it is "not scientific." I would have more sympathy for this argument if they consistently relied on scientific evidence. The scientific evidence for personhood, however, is systematically ignored by abortion advocates.

*****

Abortion is the vilest crime perpetrated in the United States. Over 30 million babies have been aborted since the 1973 *Roe v. Wade* decision. To cover up a crime of this magnitude, a plethora of lies have been used to justify it. These lies are so multitudinous and pervasive that much can be learned about the basic fabric of lies by studying them.

Many of these lies are perpetrated by Planned Parenthood who, far from being a champion of women, is enthusiastic about abortion due to the millions of dollars they annually earn from this practice.[141]

*****

As we've seen, society at large, some segments more so than others, can be major wellsprings of deceit with the rest of us playing catch-up so as not to be overwhelmed by the waves of lies. What then of the church, that institution many of us look to for steadfastness in holding to the truth? With fear and trembling, in the next chapter I take up the task of addressing how the church can improve its recognition of, and reporting on, the truth. I do promise not to say: "everything the church does is wrong, but lucky for it I am here to correct every one of its mistakes with my perfect wisdom." Yeah, that kind of annoys me. Since truth is such an important ingredient to the church, I do wish to make some contribution toward it reflecting truth (in this case with a small "t") even better than before.

Chapter 17

Truth in the Church

"For where God built a church, there the Devil would also build a chapel."
~Martin Luther

Introductory Note

Previous chapters were designed to be approachable by persons with all faith backgrounds. This chapter is intended for persons who, by and large, have previously come to the same conclusions as the author in matters of the Christian faith. These are, roughly, that Jesus is the only Son of God and the only gateway to heaven. Further, that God is interested in talking to us, and that he often strives to do so at times and places of His choosing.

Certainly, if you don't share these convictions, you are more than welcome to read this chapter. You paid for the book, after all. I just wanted to let you know the approach and focus of this chapter was going to be a little different.

Why the Church Tries to Control Error

The history of the church is one of a continuous fight against error. I'm not talking here about your run of the mill, wrong on facts or minor interpretation errors. I am referring to major structural doctrinal errors. The most common, most pernicious, and most persistent doctrinal errors, starting from day one of the Christian faith, are the ones that deny the divinity of Jesus Christ. This began in the 1st century with the Gnostics, and has continued to resurface in different guises up to the present day. In a very small space, I will attempt to show why the divinity of Christ is a BIG DEAL.

Here is why. There is one piece of really bad news in the Bible, called sin. Sin is rebellion against God and separates us from God. As we have all freely chosen sin, we have also freely chosen hell. This is extremely bad news. You see, God is wholly just and could not leave something as evil as sin unpunished. The Old Testament is the story of the Old Covenant and the giving of the Law. The Law, while making clear to us what sin was, did not provide a permanent solution for sin.

What the Old Testament did was to prepare our hearts to long for the GOOD NEWS. The Good News, presented in the New Testament, is the solution for sin, Jesus Christ. You see, since God is totally loving, He could not stand to see us live in hopelessness, not even the self-inflicted kind. His complete and perfect love for us compelled Him to find a way to reconnect with us no matter the consequences to Himself. God being all loving, He created that way, sacrificing His son, Jesus.

There was one very key element to this substitutionary sacrifice. In order for this sacrifice to cover all the sin of humans born at all times in history, it had to be an eternal one. For the sacrifice to work, it had to be of an eternal being.

This takes us to a very important conclusion:

For our sins to be forgiven, Jesus must be divine.

Satan, the father of lies, does not want you rescued from sin. His biggest lie is that Jesus is not God. That is why, over and over throughout history, there is always *somebody* trying to convince you that Jesus is not God. The number of forms this lie has taken is enormous. They range from fear-based, to shame-based, to those based on "reason." Some are based merely on the personal insight of the teller.

Here is a very partial listing. In the Koran, Jesus is depicted as a prophet, but still just a normal man. According to the Koran, Jesus didn't die on the cross as God removed Him and replaced Him with somebody else. In the Gospel of Thomas and other Gnostic works, salvation itself is unnecessary as secret spiritual knowledge is able to save us. In most, if not all Christian-based cults, denial of Jesus' divinity is universal. This fundamental deviation from Christianity is usually not presented as something major. It is usually played off as something minor, even incidental. There are usually no clear details on why this claim is made. Here is the real reason for the deception:

If Jesus is not divine, our sins are not forgiven.

If Satan can convince us humans that Jesus is not divine, the whole point of Christianity disappears.

How to Talk to God.

Believe it or not, there are "wrong" ways to talk to God. The common denominator of these various approaches are all rooted in pride. Pride, among other things, is a misunderstanding of our relationship to God. Here are some of those twisted approaches.

The Vending Machine Approach

In the vending machine approach, God is seen as a cosmic dispenser of various earthly goodies. The "Name-it, Claim-it" approach of the 80's has been replaced with the Prosperity Gospel, a doctrine which mysteriously never becomes very popular in third-world countries.

In both of these, if you choose to believe in the right scriptures, and believe in them with the right kind of faith, with the right kind of language, then you can successfully arm-wrestle God into giving up whatever blessing or comfort you are looking for. If you can just find the right type and quantity of spiritual currency, you can get the candy bar you want to come out.

Sometimes books teaching on faith have a vending machine approach. Often the emphasis is on the believer's correctness and purity of belief in receiving healing, rather than God's desire to give it to us. I do believe that God is both able and willing to give us physical healing. I disagree that the "system" we use is the main ingredient in making this happen.

The Santa Claus Approach

In the Santa Claus approach, God is seen as this cosmically jolly fellow who just loves to hand out presents. Like the mythical Santa Claus, there are some minimal behavior guidelines but those usually only apply to people worse than you.

Besides, Santa is so eager to hand out gifts, the only real hurdle is making sure we accurately deliver the letter with our demands, (oops, I mean prayers), to Him. Once that is done, Santa Claus God is obliged to show up with the goodies. If he doesn't, then He must face our righteous wrath. Many a Christian has "broken up" with God because He didn't produce the protections or blessings they thought they were owed.

There is a good way to tell if you are using or in danger of using either of these two previous approaches. If your emphasis and excitement is on the gift rather than the Giver, you may be seeking God from the wrong motives.

G.O.D.--God on Demand

There is an uncanny similarity of outcome in non-Christian spiritual practices. Let's say you are in a Spiritualist church. Sooner or later you find yourself talking to various spirit guides. What happens when you practice past-life regression? You end up talking to some of your previous incarnations. It's been a while since it was popular, but if you practiced Eckancar long and hard enough, you eventually got the opportunity to talk to the ECK Master. How about Spirit Writing? Someone writes notes to you while you're in a trance.

What about Ouija Boards? Some entity is standing by to spell out the answers to whatever questions you ask. Séances? Spirits of the dead speak, blow horns, and tap out messages. Witchcraft? You get familiar spirits to help you out. Divination? Various and assorted spirits are standing by to answer your questions. It seems like no matter how you reach out into the spirit world, there is always someone or something dying for a good chat.

This is not just ancient history. My own father was involved in innumerable occultist practices. He didn't see them as occultic or demonic, he thought of them more as "scientific" endeavors. He pursued such things as Silva Mind Control, ESP, Edgar Cayce, etc. It didn't seem to matter what it was called. So long as it offered him power, he was for it. He proclaimed that he had the ability to heal people "with his mind." He would do this openly in his job as a public high school teacher. We three boys were exposed to these things as well and had some of them practiced on us.

Certainly, there are boundless opportunities for both fraud and self-deception in all of these practices. Examination of the Bible, personal experience, and talking and reading about other people's experiences, however, lead me to the conclusion that many of these encounters are in fact, satanic. This is true regardless of the original intentions of the seekers. I believe this is why the Bible forbids many of the aforementioned practices by name and all of them by implication.

All the preceding, of course, is the sort of error and questionable spiritual practice you should expect when you're not walking with Jesus, right? Look at the title of this section, "God on Demand." What am I talking about when I talk about Christians practicing God on Demand? They have different names, but I'm talking about methods that are designed to connect you with God in a way that enables Him (because we're so darn helpful) to do the "real work" in us. A common assumption is that somehow the millennia-old, God-given Christian practices of worship, prayer, fasting, and Christian meditation are somehow insufficient for this purpose. I am sure the practitioners of these new techniques are well-intentioned, but I wonder if they've ever wondered why our ancestors did not have the piety and holiness to discover these techniques for themselves. Let's face it; we're lost and frightened sinners. We long for the warmth and reassurance of God's felt presence. This is normal. But, if we do things blindly these yearnings can lead to us being easily fooled.

Let us look in more depth at one of these techniques, "Inner Healing." It also goes by the names of "Formational Prayer" or "Healing Care." It is touted as a way of connecting with God on a deeper level. The way it works is this: You go to a weekend or weeklong retreat to seek God's help with a deep emotional hurt or hurts. A staff member aids you and the rest of your group in connecting with God. God touches you, and you feel much better.

That's the rough overview, and it sounds innocent enough. The devil is in the details. If you go to one of these retreats, a staff member will invite you to imagine yourself in a place that you know and remember as being very comfortable, familiar, and safe. You picture it all in your mind's eye (with eyes closed of course). You experience the peace and pleasure of being in your favorite place. Then, you invite God to meet with you. Following the invitation, God shows up and you tell him about your hurt and pain. Then God talks to you and you feel better.

As I write this I, am physically trembling at the naïveté of the folks that do this. This is not even a remotely <u>new</u> Satanic lie. What I have described is one of the methods my father would use to consult with his occultist sources in the 1970s. It is the method described by Johanna Michelson in her book, "The Beautiful Side of Evil" for contacting her spirit guides when she was deeply involved in the occult. It is the exact same approach that I personally and disturbingly experienced at a Catholic retreat in the 80's. Our connection to God doesn't need the "help" of elements from occult and Eastern practices. God does not need our help to bridge the gap between us. We are forbidden to "conjure God."

What are the assumptions of this approach? The first assumption is that God could benefit from the assistance of our experience. The second assumption is that WE set up the time and place for God to meet with US. We are the holders of the conference. When participants are sent to their happy place, they are sent with the EXPECTATION that God will show up, right there, right then, in the next few minutes.

This is not the way God works. I fervently affirm that God is both capable of and willing to speak to us. But, He always does it in His own timing. Never on ours. Anyone who has spent considerable time seeking God in prayer knows that sometimes God is readily available, sometimes he shows up totally unexpectedly, and there are difficult times when He hides His face from us no matter how hard we bloody our hands beating on the gates of heaven begging him to come out. I do not presume to be able to explain why God chooses to interact with us in this way. I do know that it is thoroughly his prerogative to do so, and that I trust Him completely in this.

I find the belief that because we've found a better "technique," we can shortcut all of God's sovereignty and have Him perform the healing work at our desired pace to be the height of arrogance. God, for his own very good reasons, very often requires us to seek and yearn for Him. To try and shortcut this with our own techniques is to, at best, invite God's second best into our lives.

Now, to me, the most disturbing thing about the approach above is this:

"God" always shows up.

When people share their experiences afterwards, none of them relate an experience where they went to their happy place and nothing much really happened. To the contrary, they always talk about how "God" showed up and how great it was.

Go back to the beginning of this section. When misled people reach out into the cosmos looking for direction, the cosmos seems filled with beings eager to talk. When Christians reach out in ways that God has not approved, why do they think they will achieve different results?

Let us look at this from the perspective of "judging by the fruits" as we are instructed to do in Matthew 7:15-20. Most Christians who go through this "Inner Healing" experience will report that it was a moderately to highly positive experience for them. I'd like to tell you the true story of a client of mine who went through this experience. His name, of course, is not really Phil. That is just what we will call him for the sake of anonymity.

Phil was excited about going to an Inner Healing conference as he had a great deal of hurts. Based on my knowledge of the program at the time, I shared my misgivings about the program with Phil. Phil listened politely, but chose to go anyway.

When Phil came back, I was eager to hear his first-hand report of what happened so I could have a fuller knowledge of what took place at one of these events. Phil related to me the story of going to his happy place. "God," right on cue, appeared and shared some insights with Phil. I thought to myself at the time that the insights seemed rather trivial. But, Phil's excitement and happiness at this experience was unquestionable. He was quite elated.

If you've heard about these weekends, this is usually where the story ends. I, however, had the privilege of being in an ongoing, therapeutic relationship with Phil. Here is how the rest of the story unfolded.

About two months later, I received a panicky call from Phil who wanted to meet me as soon as possible. Phil was clearly not his usual self and was deeply distressed. I met with him as soon as I could, curious what had brought about this change.

As we got together, he gave me a few more details on the Inner Healing experience. He related that during his time there, he began to think about a previous marital infidelity. He had asked the staff member if this was something he should confess to his wife. The staff member replied that confessing it to him (the staff member) was sufficient.

I am not attempting to lay this isolated act of lay spiritual incompetence at the feet of the entire movement. I do, however, find the next events, and especially the timing of them, to be particularly frightening.

Phil related that two weeks after the conference, he met a woman in his town and in very short order, began an affair with her. Despite trying to hide his identity from this new woman, she discovered Phil's identity anyway and announced the news of their affair to Phil's wife. Phil moved out, and was, at the time of the session, estranged from his wife and children in every way one could be estranged.

Following this discovery, he was also removed from his substantial church leadership role, causing more emotional damage to hundreds of others. Doubtless, Phil was the main contributor to this disaster. But, if we are to be spiritually discerning, what can we say about the spiritual fruit of this ministry he trusted in?

How to Hear from God Correctly

God is sovereign and there is no way to give a step by step guide on hearing from God, but we can identify some general guidelines. Hearing from God is a difficult business. It's OK then, if you're not perfect at it the first time you try. God gets it.

First off, how does God talk to us? God is pretty creative, so it's hard to make a complete list. He definitely speaks to us through His word, the Bible. He also speaks to us through dreams, the advice of our friends and mentors, and through the timing of otherwise innocuous events.

We can sometimes hear Him talking inside of our head when we pray. Some people hear Him speak audibly on occasion. He speaks to us through the gifts of the Spirit. What do we do if we think God is telling us something? The

Bible directs us to test these voices (1 John 4:1-2). So, how do we test them? First of all, *God's voice will never violate God's word.* If you think that God is telling you to divorce your wife because she doesn't make you happy, you can tell from reading the Bible that it is your own evil heart you are hearing.

Secondly, God will often tell you to do things you aren't willing to do and that would not occur to you to do. After all, if you were going to do something anyway, why would He suggest it to you? This is not to say that God doesn't encourage us to do things we want do, but are afraid of. The behavior I am contesting is our predilection for blaming God for "telling" us to do things that we know are wrong, but we really, really, want to do anyway.

I'll be direct. God doesn't want you to have sex outside of marriage. Period. You don't have an exemption. You are not special. You haven't found a loophole in the Scriptures. Also, there are arguably Scriptural reasons to divorce your spouse. Being really unhappy is not one of them. Yes, I know your unhappiness is heartbreakingly different from any pain or suffering you've ever had before. The answer is still "no".

I digress. Another way to test God's word is with your own spirit. This is a difficult test as our own thoughts and emotions can often easily crowd out our spirit. There is, however, a very deep part of ourselves that knows when things are right or wrong. That same part of us recognizes his voice (John 10:4-5).

Some people say you should look for God's peace. There is such a thing, and you should look for it. Keep in mind that choosing what you already want may feel peaceful too; this is the peace of freedom from anxiety. Feeling peaceful about avoiding something unpleasant is quite different from God's peace.

When we first think we are hearing from God, there is a common impulse to follow the command immediately, lest God become angry with us. God is perfectly fine with us seeking confirmation from Him as Gideon discovered in Judges 6. After all, He knows that we are but flesh and He's not the least bit threatened by out insecurity. So, feel free to ask God to confirm what He's saying to you in another way that you will recognize.

Related to this guideline is knowing how to understand guilt. A word from God will lead to remorse. Remorse is a feeling of deep regret that leads to sorrow and eventual repentance. It contains within it the means of moving on from remorse and into forgiveness. Guilt, on the other hand, leads to condemnation and depression. There is no path of deliverance from guilt; it just endlessly gnaws on itself. Words from God lead to remorse. Words from other sources lead to guilt.

Finally, I've heard it said that "God doesn't scare you" so you should ignore what may be God's voice if it is frightening. There is some germ of truth in this, but I don't think it is very good advice. I have heard God say some really terrifying things to me and I am very joyful today that I listened to Him anyway.

Christian Self-Assuredness (The Bad Kind)

There is probably a word for it, surely someone has had this feeling and coined an appropriate term. It is a certain kind of deep special feeling of *certainty* and *specialness*. It is the knowledge that you are being faithful to a true and deeper level of conviction while the people around you are selling out. They are selling out, but you are *holding fast*. I do not know the exact word I am looking for, but it exists in that place where self-righteousness meets fanaticism.

No group of Christians has a monopoly on, or freedom from this pitfall. It might be the setting up of a nationwide conference for the sole purpose of denouncing charismatics. It might be your faith in a special revelation in a Pentecostal service. It might be a deep conviction about some secondary issue. Here are some major signs that you have fallen prey to this harmful attitude:

1) The point in question is relatively trivial in relation to the overall salvation message. Some examples include

(get ready to be offended!!): Whether the Earth is old or not old; whether the King James Version is inspired or really, really inspired; the "right" wording for water baptism; or the belief that "only my church is the right one." The Christian band, Petra aptly named this tendency, "Walking over dollars, looking for another dime."

2) It is not a point that is of primary importance to the Gospel.
3) You feel particularly accomplished and proud of holding to your position. You feel just a little bit superior because you hold this position. People of a different persuasion feel frustrated and offended when they discuss the topic with you.
4) Your insistence on this particular point could be better explained by your personal discomfort with Scripture not explaining this particular point in more detail.
5) Holding to your position requires no sacrifice on your part. It does not take you out of your comfort zone. It does not challenge either your humility or your compassion.
6) In order to maintain your position, you find it necessary to condemn large numbers of your fellow Christians as being particularly ungodly. Bonus points if you organize a conference whose sole purpose is to criticize other Christians.

There is a local radio pastor who seems to be a reasonable and God-fearing man. At least half of his radio show, however, seems to be dedicated to touting the specialness of the King James Version of the Bible and the obtuseness of those who do not recognize this specialness. I doubt that this is the best use of this pastor's considerable gifts.

If a Christian Says it, it Must be True

Obviously, we don't say this out loud. It's a common assumption though, and one of which I am often guilty. I'd like to spend a little time delving into this often automatic assumption.

Let's start by talking about what happened when we first came to Christ. Before Christ saved us from ourselves, we were spiritually blind and we could not recognize His truths as being superior to ours. We could not recognize evil, especially our own. Most of us couldn't find a particular Bible chapter in less than 5 minutes of searching. I embarrassed myself because I didn't know that Sirach was only in my Catholic Bible.

Now, what happened after we came to know Christ? We became spiritually connected with, and alive to, the Mind and Spirit of the Living God. We became both spiritually sighted and spiritually alive. None of us this happened because we were better or more special than our non-Christian friends and relatives. Neither did God love us more than them. We did, however, become decidedly *different* from those around us. There were other changes as well. The words of the Bible, previously opaque to us, became alive and understandable to us. Finally, we had a desire to learn and enjoyed more and more hearing from God through prayer and reading.

When relating to non-Christians, these differences give us a variety of advantages when discussing spiritual matters. In one evangelism class we were reminded that the point of evangelism is not to win an argument. We can do that easily. We've put in the time, the thought, the prayer, and felt God molding us further into his image. Winning an argument with someone who has not gone through these experiences is not usually difficult.

Here then, is the difficulty with this situation. Because we and the Christians around us excel at discussions of theology, faith, and God, we start to think that we should be able to do this in *all fields of knowledge*. I do not believe this to be true. God's Spirit shows us clearly our own sin. It does not, in the same way, clearly show us which wrench to use on the faucet. It does not tell us which is the best investment in the marketplace or how to overhaul an engine or design a bridge.

Nonetheless, we Christians will often trust an assertion simply because it is being made by another Christian. We will simultaneously discredit the opinion of a non-christian even if the topic does not involve God or theology. So, for example, we will believe medical claims which fly in the face of medical facts because a Christian has made them. We'll discard entire bodies of tortuously collected scientific knowledge because the collectors of it do not share our Christian experience. We'll buy nutritional and dietary supplements that have been evaluated by no one, simply because we heard about them on a Christian radio station. This is why objective evidence is very important. God's spirit makes us spiritually alive and spiritually sighted. It doesn't, however, automatically make us, or our brothers and sisters, experts in other fields of human endeavor.

PART 2

We now turn to some chapters that promise to show us truth from a different angle. I hope to share some insights into truth that I've learned in the field of counseling. You don't have to be involved in counseling, of course, for these chapters to be helpful. My hope is that these chapters will help you with separating truth from lies within yourself and in your relationships.

Chapter 18

Truth on the Counseling Couch

"Above all, don't lie to yourself. The man who lies to himself and listens to his own lie comes to a point that he cannot distinguish the truth within him, or around him, and so loses all respect for himself and for others. And having no respect he ceases to love."

~Fyodor Dostoyevsky, *The Brothers Karamazov*

These next few chapters will not use the same systematic, top-down instructional methods used in the previous chapters. Rather, it will be a compilation of some of the insights I've gathered in the course of being a counselor the last nine years. The emphasis of these psychologically focused chapters will have more of a "Here are some cool things I picked up along the way" feel. Throughout this book, I have tried to postulate principles by which truth can be teased out of a situation. The following chapters will continue to highlight how unveiling truth and rejecting lies makes everything work better.

*****

Individual counseling is a specialized form of seeking after truth. In counseling, you are seeking for the truth about yourself with the help of a therapist. What you're looking for will often be hidden deeply. This search requires both the courage to look and some sort of light source.

Natural sunlight, in addition to helping us see, has both healing and disinfecting qualities. An increasingly popular practice in third-world countries is to purify drinking water by pouring it into clear plastic bottles and placing the bottles on a metal roof. This exposure to sunlight kills the germs. I believe sunlight works in the emotional and spiritual arenas as well. Natural sunlight reveals hidden things and kills germs. The light of truth reveals the hidden things of the heart so that they can be treasured, healed, or eliminated as necessary.

In my counseling work, I am inspired by Ephesians 5:11-14 (NIV): "Have nothing to do with the fruitless deeds of darkness, but rather expose them. For it is shameful even to mention what the disobedient do in secret. But everything exposed by the light becomes visible, for it is light that makes everything visible. This is why it is said: 'Wake up, O sleeper, rise from the dead, and Christ will shine on you.'"

I also find Matthew 5:15 (NIV) helpful: "Neither do people light a lamp and put it under a bowl. Instead they put it on its stand, and it gives light to everyone in the house." The light of truth is useful for all causes of emotional problems. According to Ron, there are four causal factors of mental disorders: pain, lies, biology, and free will. We shall look at each of these in turn.

Pain

Emotional pain comes in many forms. We have all suffered the agony of rejection or humiliation. Some of us have experienced the misery of not having any friends to reject us in the first place. Many of us know the especially intense pain of being rejected by a lover. Few things hurt more than the message: "Now that I know you deeply and intimately, I'm too disgusted to be around you."

"Trauma" is the clinical term for extreme pain. Ordinary pain serves the very useful function of warning us that something is wrong.[142] Trauma, however, overwhelms the pain sensors and causes lasting damage. This is true of both physical trauma and psychological trauma. Psychological trauma is caused by overwhelming events such as the unexpected death of a loved one, rape, witnessing extreme violence, or suffering a brutal injury. Events in which you feel helpless or that catch you by total surprise are particularly harmful. Trauma often requires specialized psychological treatment.

Recovering from trauma often involves dealing with the pain that we shoved aside because we were too young, too overwhelmed, or too under-skilled to deal with it at the time. Dealing openly with that pain is a large part of recovery. Pulling it out into the light often requires help and, in the short run, can hurt a great deal. Pain is an unpleasant reality, but keeping it on the inside keeps truth hidden away.

Lies

While pain plays an offensive, obvious, and overt role in causing mental illness, lies are hidden, sneaky, and covert. Lies are like acid poured on your soul. They corrode your will and your sense of reality. You need to remove lies and replace them with truth. In individual counseling I use cognitive/behavioral interventions extensively. I typically use David Burns' *Feeling Good Handbook* as a resource.[143] It's not an explicitly Christian book, but I find it to be a very effective one. The essence of cognitive psychology, as espoused by Burns and interpreted by me, is to identify the lies in your heart, soul, and mind and replace them with truth.

Here is an example of how cognitive psychology would approach a problem with depression. Cognitive psychology might help you to identify that you tell yourself the lie "I'm an idiot" ten times a day. If we do a little math, that works out to 70 lies a week, 304 lies a month, and 3650 lies a year. That's just one thought. Now multiply out all of the other lies you believe and the end result is depression.

For another example, suppose you tell yourself the lie that you must do everything possible to control your husband's drinking because it's your responsibility somehow. Tell yourself this lie ten times a day. Add to this several other worrisome lies about things you have no real control over. Multiply these lies out, and the end result is anxiety. Effective therapy replaces these lies with statements that are true.

Proverbs 22:10 (NIV) says, "Drive out the mocker and out goes strife; quarrels and insults are ended." This is biblically true for a community. It is also true for an individual. Stop mocking yourself, and strife ceases.

Biology

The role that biology takes in mental health is something of a wild card. For many individuals, biology is the predominant factor in their disorder. They truly do have "a brain illness." A brain illness is something that occurs irrespective of the patient's attitudes or behavior and is rooted in chemical imbalances in the brain. There are, of course, shades of gray in all this and plenty of overlap with other factors. In almost all mental illness there is usually some degree of biological influence, however small. Generally speaking, behavioral health issues colloquially called "psychotic" have a much higher biological basis than those known as "neurotic."

Being a counselor, I am naturally more inclined to favor treatments that do not emphasize drugs. I say naturally, because it is illegal for me to prescribe them and I am only secondarily trained in their usage. I have a strong preference for therapy where it is appropriate.

Let me illustrate this with a patient we'll call Larry. When we take a PET scan of Larry's head, it clearly shows that Larry has a depressed brain. Next, the doctor gives

Larry some Prozac. He stops feeling depressed and our PET scan verifies that Larry does indeed have a verifiable change in his brain chemistry. A medication, Prozac, has produced a beneficial change in brain chemistry.

Now let's see what happens to Larry's depressed brother, Alfonso. Alfonso has decided to see a therapist. For his treatment, Alfonso takes no medications and instead uses cognitive-behavioral therapy to confront his negative thoughts and combat his counter-productive behaviors. As a result of this talk therapy, Alfonso stops feeling depressed. So, Alfonso now feels better, just like Larry. What do you think Alfonso's brain scan shows? Remarkably, Alfonso's post-treatment PET scan is now identical to Larry's; they both now have normal brains. In Alfonso, we brought about a change in the hardware of his brain merely by using the "software" of thinking and talking. Not only that, studies show that the therapy will continue to work after the therapy sessions are over, while the drugs will stop working very quickly after the patient stops taking them.[144]

Psychiatrists, on the other hand, will quite naturally favor pharmaceutical interventions. Having worked with the severely mentally ill in Cleveland emergency rooms and psych units,* this makes perfect sense to me. The two most common admissions to psych units are for people who have become markedly psychotic or for people who have so much emotional anguish, they think killing themselves is a reasonable and desirable alternative. Psychiatrists know from personal experience that routinely--and by routinely I mean hundreds of times a year, the majority of these patients will be home in less than a week. Their experience is that the biggest factor in these rapid turnarounds is medication.

A common workday for a psychiatrist is to see patients in a doctor's office during the day and then to see patients in the psych ward in the evening. For these psychiatrists, the most natural thing in the world is to hand a prescription to the next patient they see. Don't get the wrong idea, psychiatrists are very smart and very well educated. They

---

* Yes, I've had a lot of different jobs.

know about the usefulness of therapy as well as I do. With their experience, however, prescribing medications comes much more naturally to them.

For diseases like schizophrenia, drugs are a necessity. I can't talk a man into not hearing voices. For very severe depression, drugs are critical for knocking down the brain chemicals that are driving the patient to suicide.

What makes me sad is talking to a woman who has been taking Prozac for 20 years. I know that if she has been taking her meds that faithfully, then she has the discipline to confront and defeat her negative thoughts. Drugs are effective at treating symptoms, but don't reveal truth.

Now, *please* don't go and tell your psychiatrist that Ron said not to take your meds. Any changes in medication should be done only with your doctor's approval. While you're at the doctor's office though, you may want to ask how they feel about supportive therapy to go with your medications. Any doctor with a shred of self-esteem will not be threatened by a respectful question. Actually, most doctors will be excited to see you taking a more active role in your own care.

Free Will

Interwoven among all of the causal factors of mental illness is the element of free will. Researchers as well as more ordinary folk have long marveled at how two children brought up in the same horrific environments can turn out completely different. It's free will that produces these paradoxical results.

Free will is what allows us to choose being better over being bitter. Free will is what allows an addict to ask for help when he is lost in the grip of an addiction. Free will is what allows a person to say "no" to that drug when it's offered to them in the first place. Free will is what allows us to say "yes" to God and obey His commandments.

Sometimes biology seems to make our free will shrink. How much free will does a schizophrenic have? They can't just choose to stop hallucinating, can they? No, not anymore than you can choose to stop having a cold. But, they can choose whether or not to take their medicines despite the unpleasant side effects. I've worked with schizophrenics who were on their meds and ones who were off them, and I can assure you there is a world of difference. What makes this difference? The power of a simple decision that costs a minute a day. This illustrates how a very small decision to embrace truth can change our lives radically for the good. Free will is what allows us to choose truth.

The Role of the Individual in Individual Counseling

While in a narrow sense I am discussing how to get the most out of therapy, I am also trying to identify principles for the larger audience to use in becoming more whole, emotionally and psychologically. Believe it or not, the first necessity in self-growth is to admit that you are a part of the problem. I have no doubt that others contributed to your mess, but you did as well, and you are the only one that is going to get you out of it. The person that hurt you is worried about their own heartaches and will not be coming back to help you. Sorry.

This is a painful process. We all secretly believe we're well above average. To seriously accept that we're wrong 50% of the time, rather than the 5% we're willing to admit to, is a serious blow to our ego. Nevertheless, it is crucial that you be able to admit you have made a mess of your life in your thoughts, words, and deeds.

You can only make so much progress working things out in your own head, as our thoughts are naturally geared to making us feel justified. You need another person (or persons) that you can talk to so you can see things from a different perspective and in a more useful light. This will happen when you hear yourself speaking to them out loud, as well as when you receive feedback from others. The person you pick to help you should:

1) Be able to keep your secrets confidential.

2) Have some measure of wisdom. If you're not sure what this looks like, pick someone with some life experience.
3) Be able to give feedback that is neither too passive nor abusive.
4) Have some degree of objectivity on your issues. Spouses are wonderful people to bounce things off of, but you need someone who can give you advice without a conflict of interest. Spouses are sometimes tempted to give you the answer that best works for them.

You've already seen the word repeatedly in this book, but the key to getting better is *humility*. The most natural thing in the world is to become defensive. After all, you know yourself and your motives better than anybody else. After all, you are around yourself *all the time*. Even if someone gives you exceptional feedback, you can always find a detail or two to pick out which your "accuser" has gotten wrong. When you are defensive, the most natural thing to do is focus on the parts of the feedback that are wrong. Your brain will tell you that these small mistakes obviously invalidate *everything that person has to say*.

If this defensive tactic doesn't work, you can focus on the faults of the person critiquing you. Unless you're working with a professional, you probably know the person giving you negative feedback rather well. Since it is someone you know well, you can accurately diagnose all sorts of hypocrisy and foolishness in your confidant. What is difficult, but infinitely more productive, is to be able to consider their information without becoming defensive and feeling the need to justify yourself. Taking on the spirit of true humility will do you more good than all the defensiveness in the world.

Later, when you are feeling calm, "Take the fish and throw away the bones" of the feedback you have been given. Specifically thank your friend or confidant for the parts you found useful. This will help lock the feedback in and encourage your friend, who is after all, working for free.

Don't be discouraged if it takes you a while to be able to accept feedback gracefully. It would take an extraordinary person to immediately acknowledge their faults when confronted with them. We humans are just not wired that way.

Anxiety[145]

Anxiety can be a very painful and difficult illness to overcome. Entire books have been written on anxiety, but I will try and summarize some of the most important points. Most of the time you are anxious because there is something you are afraid of confronting. Through repetition, you have learned to find comfort by avoiding the thing you are afraid of. This avoidance eventually becomes a cage. While it provides you some short-term comfort, the anxiety never goes away.

Here is how to overcome this kind of anxiety. You must recklessly, and I do mean recklessly, confront your fears. If it doesn't feel reckless, it's not working. Think of the most awful possible fear-inducing situation you can think of. Now go do it. Okay, okay--there are some caveats. Don't do anything that seriously threatens you with physical harm. Also, please don't do anything illegal or morally wrong. That would just replace one problem with another.

Recklessness is the attitude that will get you out of your anxiety prison. Staying "safe" is both killing you and making your anxiety worse. A prerequisite to feeling better is to first feel unsafe. There is no other way to experientially "discover" that you can be perfectly fine even when you feel afraid. You will probably want to do this with the active guidance and support of a good therapist. A therapist will have an objective view of which situations are actually dangerous and which ones only feel that way. Make sure that you select a therapist you can thoroughly trust, as there will be times that you will need to trust their judgment over your own. Also, make sure your therapist is not too "nice" as they will be tempted to let up on you when it is crucial that you stay uncomfortable. Friends are not a good choice for this role as they are not trained in this and will probably let you off the hook too soon.

Let me illustrate this approach with a story from a conference I attended. Our workshop leader, Dr. David Burns, recounted how he worked with an elderly lady named Estelle.* Estelle was terrified of going out into public, a fear which hampered her life significantly. She feared that she would "go crazy" and embarrass herself in front of crowds of people.

Dr. Burns spent many sessions with her building empathy and trust. Finally, it was time for Estelle to confront her fears. "What," Dr. Burns asked, "would it look like if you went crazy?" Estelle had a ready answer for this: "I would roll on the ground and flail my arms around and scream gibberish." "Well," he replied, "today is the day for us to test that out. I want you to try as hard as you can to go crazy."

Estelle was not excited about this to say the least, but after some more urging and reassurances, Estelle finally sat down on the floor and proceeded to try and go crazy. She didn't try very hard initially. At first she only leaned back and flopped her hands around a little. Dr. Burns was unimpressed and urged her, politely but firmly, to try harder. Slowly Estelle worked herself up to the challenge, screaming louder, pumping her arms, and rolling around on the floor to boot. After about a half hour of this, she had had enough. "Well," she said, "I've tried as hard as I can to go crazy, and I just can't do it." Estelle finished her therapy shortly thereafter. Years of suffering with anxiety had finally been broken by a half-hour of focused confrontation. Truth had won through.[146]

Addictions

If you're addicted to a substance, you need to give up on the idea of "reasonable use." Once an addiction has overtaken your life you <u>cannot</u> go back to social drinking or the occasional use of your substance of choice. The ruts are too deep, the pathways in your brain are too firmly

---

* In case you forgot, we're not using real names.

established, and your habits are too firmly entrenched. You can't stand partway down in a hole; if you go back to the hole, you will fall all the way to the bottom.

Also, when you are working to overcome an addiction, you need to be an active participant in a group, doing it alone doesn't work. You'll hate working in a group at first. But, if it isn't uncomfortable, it isn't working. It's just as natural to hate being in Alcoholics Anonymous and the like as it is to hate having a light shined into your eyes after you've been sleeping. When you were using, you often used in secret and under a protective coating of lies. You told yourself and everyone around you that you could handle it yourself. If that were true, you would have done so by now. In a group setting, all of those lies are dragged out into the light to die from exposure.

You'll think of all sorts of reasons why you have terminally unique circumstances and AA won't work for you. Face it, you are not unique and all of those excuses have already been given. Go to the group meetings anyway, they work.

If you're on good terms with God, or even if you're not, ask Him this question when you are tempted to use: "God, what hole in my life am I trying to fill with this substance that I should be filling with You?" Ask Him this question every time you're tempted. This prayer isn't changing Him, it's changing you.

Emotional Reasoning

There are ten widely recognized cognitive distortions in cognitive psychology[147] Cognitive distortions are thought patterns that destroy the clarity and perception of our experiences. While all ten are worthy of study, the cognitive distortion of Emotional Reasoning merits special scrutiny.[148] In my estimation, this one cognitive distortion causes more misery and chaos than any of the others. This is true for both the individual and society at large.

When you use Emotional Reasoning, the truth of something is decided not on available evidence, but on how strongly you feel about it. The stronger you feel that something is true, the truer you believe it must be. Truth is held hostage to volatile emotional states.

If you are falling prey to emotional reasoning, you may decide for instance, that George doesn't like you because you feel his dislike so strongly. You'll put your energy into finding ways to avoid or get even with George rather than using that energy to see if there is any evidence to back up your feelings.

Some of my clients suffer from a very acute form of emotional reasoning. Having grown up in dysfunctional households, they will repeatedly choose dysfunctional boyfriends or girlfriends. I'll ask them why they picked the people they did. "He makes me feel so wonderful," they'll say. I'll then point out that this seems to be a very bad strategy considering their results. They'll reply that their strategy isn't bad; it's just that they have "bad luck." This is a very difficult tendency to fight. One client admitted early on that she knew she was doing this and was embarrassed about it because she prided herself on being terminally unique. Despite her conscious realization of her behavior, she continued to pick boyfriends on the same basis as before.

The pull of emotional reasoning can be very strong due to the element of fantasy. In our fantasy life, our new romantic attachment will truly fulfill us and make us feel loved at a deep and wonderful level. I remember another client of mine who could not let the fantasy die with her ex-boyfriend, even though he had cheated on her not once, not twice, but three times. Questioning our fantasy by looking at stark facts kills the elation and enjoyment that our fantasy brings us.

In our culture we are told to "follow your heart," trusting that it will lead us to happiness and contentment due to our heart's inherent goodness and wisdom. The Bible offers very different advice. It states, "The heart is deceitful above all things and beyond cure. Who can understand it?" (Jeremiah 17:9, NIV). Following our heart leads to emotional ruin. Dysfunctional backgrounds give us hearts that lead us back into the dysfunction. Greedy and selfish hearts lead us into financial ruin.

Consider what happened with the victims of Bernie Madoff. Bernie was very skilled at arousing strong feelings of both trust and excitement in his clients. The excitement of oversized financial gain often led people to trust in Bernie far too much. Reality turned out to be very different from those feelings and total personal losses were in the billions.

I remember a very long time ago watching a financial show where the special guest was asked to recommend an investment. The guest, whose name I honestly have no recollection of, stated that he thought natural gas was a great place to put your money. He went on to say that he was excited about natural gas because it was "a wonder fuel." For all I know, natural gas is a very wonderful, wonder fuel. That is not a good reason to invest in it. It might be a highly overvalued wonder fuel whose price is ready to drop like a rock.

Emotional reasoning is very seductive. We really want to put our trust in values that make us feel good about ourselves. We find these highly preferable to values that make us feel bad about our poor behavior. I remember reading about a gentleman who was expounding upon why recycling was a key part of his value system. I recycle too as I hate wasting things, but I felt sad reading this. Picking things you already enjoy to be your core spiritual values doesn't seem particularly ennobling. Adopting values that are right, irrespective of your feelings, has a great deal more potential to change you for the better as a person. Conversely, avoiding good values because they make you feel bad or guilty is another destructive outcome of emotional reasoning.

Psychological Defense Mechanisms

In getting to the truth about yourself, it is important to understand your own defense mechanisms. Defense mechanisms are devices we use to protect ourselves from unpleasant truths. Becoming aware of these defenses helps us lower them so that harsh reality can come in, an important step in becoming all that God has created us to be. Here are the more important defense mechanisms.

1. Denial

Denial is the refusal to accept the blatantly obvious facts of life. We do it very well in childhood and some people remain skilled at it well into adulthood. Denial is not always avoidable. When people receive horrible news, denial is not only normal, it is the first stage of grieving.

Your own denial can be hard to detect. Here is a very good rule that has served me well in my life: If you think everyone around you is crazy, you're the one who's crazy.

2. Regression

Regression is reverting to an earlier stage of development when you have run out of other useful options. It is a way to hide. Older children or teenagers may go back to an earlier stage, becoming clingy, using baby talk, or wetting the bed. An adult may regress to behaving like a teenager or, in extreme cases, roll up into a fetal position. It's another of our imaginative adaptations to stress.

3. Dissociation

Dissociation occurs when a person "disconnects" from reality. Driving to work and suddenly realizing you don't know where you are for a moment is a very mild form of this. In extreme cases, dissociation can take the form of a *fugue state* where a person wanders away from the stress in their life to start a life with a new identity and a new career in a different town. Dissociation is common in rape and other trauma. Victims of trauma often describe being able to look down on themselves during the traumatic event. This made it possible for them to not feel what was happening to them psychically and emotionally.

4. Compartmentalization

More often practiced by men, compartmentalization creates a mental separation between bad behaviors and good behaviors. For instance, a man might behave appropriately and morally at home, but be a total cad at work. This is because he has separated the parts of himself into "home behaviors" and "work behaviors." The value systems practiced in different settings may be completely contradictory.

5. Projection

Projection occurs when people are unable to accept their own appalling thoughts, attitudes, or behaviors. It is too much of a blow to their ego to accept that they think such terrible things, so the person "projects" those thoughts or feelings onto some innocent second person. They can then express their disdain and hatred for those things by roundly criticizing this second person. There is a common saying that summarizes projection well: "The things we hate the most about others are the very things we hate about ourselves."

6. Reaction Formation

Reaction Formation is a little complicated. In this defense mechanism, a person has an unacceptable thought or impulse. As it is too disgusting to deal with, the person handles this anxiety by behaving *in the exact opposite way*. For example, a child molester may behave in a Victorian fashion in public, upbraiding others for dressing loosely and wearing heavy makeup. Alternately, a habitual adulterer might loudly denounce others for getting divorced.

7. Repression

Repression is one of the more moderate defense mechanisms. Repression is the unconscious blocking of unacceptable thoughts, feelings and impulses. When asked, a person using repression honestly cannot tell you those things they have purposely forgotten. It is common in children who have been abused by caregivers. It is also frequently occurs in marriage, when one spouse conveniently "forgets" troubling news.

8. Displacement

Displacement is the redirection of feelings from a person who it would be unsafe to express them (e.g. a boss) to a safer target instead (e.g., a dog or spouse). This is usually used in combination with rationalization (below), and the displacer actually believes that the dog or spouse really does deserve the mistreatment. A distinct category of displacement, *transference*, happens frequently in therapy. A patient may find themselves angry with a therapist when, for example, the therapist reminds them of their rejecting father.

9. Rationalization

Rationalization is the use of reasoning or excuses to explain away or even glorify pathetic behavior. Or, as D.Q. McInerny says, "Rationalization is reasoning in the service of falsehood."[149] For example, a mugger may justify his robbery on the grounds that the victim "had it coming to him" or that he is helping "redistribute the wealth." After all, he reasons, IRS agents collect a healthy salary redistributing wealth while the mugger is performing the same service for free.

This is a very common defense mechanism that we all have used at some point. I remember a breakdown in my own rationalizations when I was 16. When my mom would ask me to do something, I always had a ready response as to why her request was too hard, unnecessary, or downright crazy. One day I suddenly had a vision of reality no less miraculous than the one Paul experienced on the road to Damascus. In one blindingly clear moment, my defenses shattered and I said to myself, "You're not refusing to do it because it's too hard, you're refusing to do it because you don't want to."

10. Intellectualization

Intellectualization is the overemphasis on thinking when confronted with an unacceptable impulse, situation or behavior. Rather than deal with difficult and overwhelming emotions, people will use intellectualization to distance themselves from the unpleasantness. For instance, a person who has been rejected by a loved one might focus on the correct setting for a breakup rather on their feelings about being dumped. In extreme cases, they might focus on their ex's poor grammar rather than the content of the Dear John letter they just received.

*****

To discern truth in others and society at large, it is necessary to first know when you are lying to yourself. Whether you are in individual counseling or just thinking on your couch, humility and courage are needed to fearlessly face the truth of your own behavior. This is certainly hard enough. To do something more challenging, but even more worthwhile, let us now turn to the next chapter as we find ways to discern truth in our marriages.

Chapter 19

Truth on the Counseling Couch: Marriage

"There is nothing nobler or more admirable than when two people who see eye to eye keep house as man and wife, confounding their enemies and delighting their friends."

~Homer[150]

I set out to be a jack of all trades general counselor, but interest and circumstance has led me to an emphasis on marriage counseling. Our society tells us that marital problems are due to circumstance and bad luck. We're all just victims of each other.

I've found it's due to selfishness and misunderstanding. An unpleasant reality, but one we can do something about. I hope you enjoy reading about my marital discoveries as much as I've enjoyed discovering them.

*****

I usually start my marital sessions with the following introduction:

> I'd like to give you my standard speech up front, while I don't know you very well. It works better that way. I don't want anyone to think I'm picking on them for something they said or did.
>
> Sometimes one or both spouses want to spend some time reviewing the evidence as to why the other spouse is "the bad one." While I need to know the issues you have with your spouse, I'd rather skip the whole process of picking the bad one. I have several reasons for this. First off, it takes up a lot of time that you're paying good money for. After all, you've been married for years and you both have lots of evidence you could bring up and sorting through it all would take hours and hours.
>
> Secondly, if I did listen to all the evidence and declare one of you to be the bad one, that wouldn't get us anywhere. The bad one wouldn't cooperate because they would resent being called the bad one and figure that I hadn't taken enough time to listen to their good evidence. On the other hand, the good one wouldn't cooperate either, because they would think: 'Hey, I'm the good one. I don't need to do any work.'

Sometimes I find that the speech isn't necessary, but we humans have an uncanny ability to find the flaws in others, while being clueless about our own shortcomings. The parable about seeing the speck in other's eyes, but not noticing the log in our own, is nowhere truer than in marriage. I am greatly relieved when both spouses come, as I can hear both sides of the story. Frankly, I don't learn very much by hearing either the wife or the husband describing their own behavior. They can describe their spouse's poor behavior quite accurately, but appear clueless about their own.

It sometimes happens that I never see the couple again after the first session and I often suspect this speech is the cause of that. Many people come to counseling with me fixing their spouse as their only plan. When that plan is frustrated, they head elsewhere. For the ones who stick with it, the speech is a good introduction to the idea of working on their own problems as a primary, rather than a secondary goal. It's also a good introduction to:

The Story of the Scales

According to Ron, marriages are much like a set of scales.

Marriages have a living, breathing dynamic balance, like a set of scales with equal weight on both sides. In the movies, there is often a really, really, bad spouse and a long-suffering good spouse. In real life, this is very rare. According to me, people tend to marry people of both equal attractiveness and equal dysfunction. Granted, they each may have very different types of dysfunction. For instance, one spouse might have very poor behavior, such as being an alcoholic, and the other spouse's dysfunction might be their willingness to excuse and put up with that very poor behavior.

The typical response to noticing you are in a poorly functioning marriage is to try and reach across and shove the other half of the scale (the other person) up. For purposes of this analogy, "up" is the direction of more healthy functioning. These attempts to improve your spouse might lead to some short-term changes, but they quickly evaporate as soon as the pressure is off or when your spouse no longer fears your punishment. Sometimes your spouse will make some surface changes in response to the pressure, but below the surface, bitterness begins to develop. When we "make" people change, the results are often just a different form of brokenness.

The good news is that marriages hate imbalance. People, *particularly the person on the relatively lower part of the scale*, find an imbalance in the marriage intolerable. This (healthy) imbalance is actually fairly easy to achieve. The key is to stop putting your energy into moving the other side of the scale up and put that energy into addressing, improving, and fixing your own issues. This will move your side of the scale up. In this way you can achieve an imbalance in the marriage without any cooperation from your spouse at all. The sheer awkwardness of this imbalance is what provides the fuel for your spouse to change. Though your spouse will probably not express it in words, they will feel this new weirdness profoundly.

Let us talk about a practical, if minor, example. Think about the last time you and your spouse were totally at odds. How did you resolve it? Chances are that one of you leaned in toward the other by either apologizing or softening your message somehow. When that happens, it is very easy for the other one to respond in love. That is the kind of response you would never achieve through loudly insisting that they think the way you want them to.

If the whole scales discussion doesn't work for you, here is another perspective on this from the Bible. In Mark 10:8 (NIV), the Bible says of marriage: “and the two will become one flesh. So they are no longer two but one.” If you and your spouse are truly one flesh, how can anything be entirely the other one's problem? Let’s look at another

Biblical example. In 1 Peter 3:1-2 (NIV) it is written: "Wives, in the same way be submissive to your husbands so, if any of them do not believe the word, they may be won over without words by the behavior of their wives, when they see the purity and reverence of your lives." These verses can raise a whole lot of other questions, but for our purposes we'll concentrate on how this ties in with working on your own stuff.

Note that the Bible doesn't recommend that the wife point out the husband's faults in a way he can clearly understand or that she scold him more forcefully so she can break through his defenses. It directs her simply to change her own behavior and character, *in order to*, give her husband an opportunity to change for the better.

So, does this work in real life? Consider the actual examples of some couples with serious problems, alcoholic men and their wives. Several studies have been conducted with the wives of alcoholics.[151,152,153] Actively alcoholic husbands rarely agree to come in for counseling. For this reason it's much easier to set up studies with the wives of alcoholics as they are often fairly motivated. The counselors in these studies did not teach the wives new and improved methods for changing their alcoholic husbands. They focused on teaching the wives how to effectively respond to their husbands through changing their own behavior. These changes included stopping nagging, discontinuing codependent behaviors, and no longer taking emotional ownership of the drinking. While the results were not entirely clear-cut, the overall trend was that wives who worked on their own stuff not only changed their own behavior, but their husband's drinking as well. The alcoholic husbands began to drink less without being lectured and *without being involved in therapy*.

As I said, the most effective approach for a spouse to bring a marriage into balance is to improve themselves so that the marriage can reach a new dynamic balance. There is a caveat to all of this. Another "solution" your spouse might have to restore the balance is to tear you back down to your previous position. They might do this by verbally assaulting you, demeaning you, or by other methods. Be forewarned that this might happen. If it does, stay the course and don't be discouraged. Keep them uncomfortable with your Biblical behavior.

Male-Female Differences

A great quantity of the stressors in marriage comes from an under-appreciation of some of the basic differences between men and women. One of the reasons for the success of the book, "Men are from Mars, Women are from Venus,"[154] was the use author's brilliant device of instructing the reader to think of their spouse as coming from a different planet entirely. When viewed from this perspective, our spouses make a lot more sense. I hope to make a few meager additions to understanding the differences between these two fine species.

First I have an offering for the wives. This one sentence alone may save you years of heartache. It is this:

HE DOESN'T KNOW!!!

Many a marriage is in an emotional deadlock with the caring but deeply frustrated husband asking his deeply wounded wife what she needs of him. Her response is the deeply feared: "YOU SHOULD KNOW!" He'll state that he doesn't know and will ask the question a different way, to which he will get the same, albeit differently worded answer, "IF YOU LOVED ME, YOU WOULD KNOW!" This deadlock can go on for years with both spouses convinced of the basic justice of their position.

Let's see if I can help untangle this mess. First, let me speak to the husbands. If we're honest, we men like to think of our wives, and women in general, as being more emotional than us and consequently, less rational. When our wives say something we don't understand, it's pretty easy for us to conclude it's some sort of emotional problem.

Wrong answer, men. If you take the time to consider your wife's insistence that you should know, *based on her viewpoint and experience*, her position actually makes a great deal of sense. Let me explain. For all of her life, your wife has been surrounded by other women. These mothers and aunts and sisters and cousins and teachers and friends and coworkers all have a very special ability we weren't even aware of. These women and girls all have the ability to know what other people emotionally need *without anyone telling them*. I am not making this up. They do it all the time. It's one of the reasons we like being around them so much.

Your wife has had a steady stream of experiences with other women where her emotional needs were readily understood and cared for. Yes, there have been a few times when other women ignored your wife's emotional needs. But, they were not ignored on those occasions because other women didn't understand your wife's needs. To the contrary, they were ignored out of spite or indifference.

So, here she is married to you, and desiring to be close to you, and assuming that you want the same. Not only that, you are supposed to be the person *who loves her the most*. Since she is supposed to be the most important person in your life, your wife assumes that you will be very focused on her emotional needs. Since she has already had the experience of dozens of people being able to tell what those needs are, your explanation that you have no clue what they could possibly be is simply not credible to her. Her logical conclusion, based on experience, is that your professed ignorance of what she needs is the product of malice.

*****

OK wives, let me talk to you for a second. Think of his ignorance as a disability. Do you get mad at your husband because he can't help you give birth? The part of your husband's brain that you use to know what other people need doesn't function. I suspect your husband uses it to store baseball stats. It's like a cheap kitchen appliance that was made in China. It only works the first few months and then stops completely.

Please listen to me and turn your frustration into something positive. Take the energy you're getting from your husband's apparent cruelty and use it to explain to him slowly and carefully what it is you need in words. Speak to him slowly and distinctly as if English were his second language. English isn't his second language, but "female" certainly is.

Be confident that at some level he does care. Here is a secret that I have learned from watching dozens of couples in therapy. Wives have a handicap as well. The vast majority of husbands that come to me for marital counseling are *nuts about their wives*. These aren't ordinary husbands. These are husbands that are very angry and frustrated with their wives. But, underneath of that is a husband who cares profoundly about his wife. I can usually pick up on this pretty quickly. When I ask the husbands about it they readily agree as if I had asked them if they need oxygen to breathe. Of course, they love their wives. *Everyone* knows that. The vast majority of the wives that I see in therapy, however, are unable to see it. It's as if they couldn't see a book six inches from their face.

Husbands, you have to do your part next. Actively try to understand your wonderful wife. Persistently attempt to do as she asks and take her requests seriously. Don't make her responsible for having to remind you. If she tells you that washing the dishes with the blue dishtowel is essential to her happiness, grab the blue dishtowel and just accept it. Sheesh.

On the other side of the coin from "You Should Know" is the husband's phrase, usually muttered under his breath:

YOU'RE ILLOGICAL!!

I remember well the first car my wife and I almost bought together. I always wanted a marriage where we would work together as a team. Actually, I was pretty young and imagined we could be sort of a spy team and even tried to convince her to learn a secret code that we could share. She didn't seem very enthused by this idea.

Anyway, I remember trying extraordinarily hard to pool our talents, expertise, and intellect toward the goal of purchasing the right used car. We had only been married about a year, and money was in short supply. My wife was still in med school and I was delivering pizzas for Dominos to support us. Since, relative to our financial position, this car purchase was going to consume a great deal of our finances, we both put a lot of time and effort into the decision.

We consulted closely on our mutual criteria for the car we would buy. We mutually agreed on which car brands were "in" and which were "out". We had strategy sessions after each test drive to discuss, not only what we thought about the car, but whether we both felt comfortable with the salesman in his affect, demeanor, and character. We repeated this process many times.

Finally, I thought, the day had arrived. We had found a car with the right price. It was an acceptable brand, had acceptable fuel mileage, and had a good life expectancy. We both felt comfortable with the dealer. We had test driven it and I had checked it out mechanically as best I could with my limited expertise and found no problems. Every item on the checklist had been ticked off. Check, check, and check. I was a happy man, as not only had we accomplished our important goal, but we had achieved it TOGETHER and in unity. Ah, the giddiness of youthful idealism.

As a final conversation, one that I thought would be a mere formality; I asked my wife if we were ready to buy the car. To my shock she quickly replied, “No.”

“Why," I insisted, “Didn’t we agree that it has all the things we’re looking for in a car?”

“Yes," she said.

“So what’s wrong with it?" I asked, my voice rising.

“I don’t like the color.”

I did not respond well.

I suspected that perhaps this was some hateful scheme she had hatched to ruin my life in retaliation for some unknown wrong I had perpetrated. I could find no logical or even vaguely logical reason why a car being white made it unusable. After I had calmed down (this took some time), I tried again, and probably with not much gentleness, to see if my wife could explain this clearly irrational behavior.

"Well," she said, tears forming in her eyes, "You want us to spend all this money on this car and I don't even *like* it"!

I had to admit, she had me there. It's not the sort of thing I would really care about, but it made perfect sense. Why would you pay all that money for something you didn't like? I had never really considered this. Women have a very different type of logic, but it *is* logic. The next time that your lady does something inexplicable, consider the possibility that she has different criteria than yours.

What Men and Women Want

In Ephesians 5:33 (NIV) it is written: "However, each one of you also must love his wife as he loves himself, and the wife must respect her husband."

Note that in this instruction the husbands and wives are instructed to do *different* things. This is because men and women are *different*. It's not just a 2000 year old idea. In a well-respected study, it was found that a clear majority of women would rather be disrespected than unloved. Also by a very clear majority, men reported they would much, much rather be unloved than disrespected.[155]

So, if you are a wife with limited energy, focus that energy on respecting your husband. Find something you respect in him and tell him about it. Husbands, by the same token, you will be amazed how much better your marriage is when you concentrate on how to best love your wives. This is a very important concept and whole books have been written on it. I'm going to refer you to two books in my endnotes. One goes into much greater detail on love and respect[156] and the other gives some insightful and somewhat surprising instructions on how to love your spouse.[157]

Since those two books have already been written and written well, let's return to my own observations on what men and women want that I've gleaned from watching couples in therapy. So without further ado, we will now discuss:

What Men Want

First of all, men want *calm*. Sure, sometimes they like loud noises and mayhem, but usually when they are the ones causing it. Otherwise, they like calm, especially the emotional sort. Let me explain why that is. First of all, men's brains handle conflict differently from women. Angry emotional conflict, for men, is an extremely uncomfortable proposition. When our anger is stirred up we think less clearly, and thinking is how we solve problems. We find that frustrating.

Secondly, and generally speaking, men have a limited capacity for handling emotions. They're like the carburetors in older cars or lawnmowers. They are very easily *flooded*. If you put in the right amount of fuel, the engine runs fine. But, too much gasoline in the carburetor overwhelms the engine. The car doesn't start at all and just sits there. Silent.

Men are just like this. They can handle negative emotions in small doses. If, however, you feed them a large amount of negative emotion or a large variety of different emotions all at once, then your man will appear to be totally emotionless. He will stare into space as if he isn't listening to you at all. When this happens, you will feel intensely hurt because you want him to share in your emotions. Please understand ladies, your husband is not disconnecting from you out of dislike. Your man is simply overwhelmed and will need some time to process.

Furthermore, stress and anger in men leads ultimately to rage, and a lot faster than it does in women. When men feel rage, two things eventually happen: hurting people and breaking things. In wartime, this tendency comes in pretty handy. In fact, we're so good at it that historically, 99+% of the people involved in the breaking and killing department of warfare have been men.

But, we men know that both of these solutions are vastly destructive in a marital context, and we wish to avoid them at all cost. This leaves us with very uncomfortable emotions that can spike very rapidly and for which we have no good outlet. We're like a car redlining while still in park. We find this situation profoundly uncomfortable and try very hard to avoid it. Were you thinking all this time that your man walks away from arguments because he doesn't like you?

Women often feel unloved and unwanted when husbands disconnect from them. It is important to remember that this separation is not an expression of disdain. There is yet another reason for this behavior. This disconnection works like a circuit breaker, stopping the flow of current before it damages something. It is a means of protecting our wives. While most men will not physically hurt their wives no matter the provocation, they are quite capable of hurting their wives with their words when they are emotionally flooded.

Men want calm.

What Men also Want

In addition to men wanting respect and calm, there is one even more important thing that men want. *They want their wives to be happy.* Men see it as a deep personal failure when their wives are not happy. This is why nagging does not work. Men do not see nagging as special, useful information. They experience it as you pointing out their shortcomings. So, the unhappier you are, the bigger of a failure your husband will feel. In counseling sessions, I've seen big husky men break down and cry because they couldn't fix their wife's unhappiness. Nothing else makes a man feel like such a complete loser.

Joe, as we'll call him, is a husband I am working with currently. His wife had no confidence he would come to counseling to work on their issues. She was overjoyed when he agreed to come in for just one session. Joe is a truck driver and immensely likable. He is also one of the most emotionally constrained men I've ever met.

Joe was so uncomfortable talking about his feelings that he asked permission to leave after only fifteen minutes. Before he left, I respectfully asked him if would consider continuing coming to counseling as I thought the prospects for his marriage would be much better if he came. Thankfully, he returned for a second session and seemed much more comfortable.

At the beginning of the third session, he asked to speak with me privately. I agreed, though a little tentatively as Joe has a few anger issues. I wondered what this private conference would be about. He admitted again that he was very uncomfortable sharing his feelings and really didn't enjoy coming to therapy. He went on to say that he was going to do it anyway *because he wanted his wife to be happy.*

This is what is in the hearts of your husbands, wives. So, the best way to make your husband miserable *is to refuse to be happy.* Conversely, one of the best ways to make him happy is to constantly tell him about the things he does right. I remember my neighbor, Pat, cheerfully commenting on her husband that, "He's 80, but he works like a 20 year old." John beamed with quiet happiness. They have been married for 60 years.

What Women Want

I remember vividly the discussion I had with an engineer and his wife. The husband, with a look of deep puzzlement and hurt, told me the following story about his wife's behavior.

"She will ask me if she looks better in the blue dress or the red one. I'll look them both over and consider the matter very carefully. *And, no matter which one I pick, it will be the wrong one.*" His tone of voice clearly implied that his wife was being manifestly unfair in asking a question to which there was no right answer. He was well and truly stuck as well as thoroughly frustrated.

Their first obstacle was that they had both married their opposite. The husband was a very logical, very steady engineer who came from a cultural background that favored seriousness and limited emotional expression. The wife, on the other hand, came from a cultural background known for its ready and forceful emotions. She expressed her feelings loudly and often.

The husband's second problem was that he didn't understand what the real question was. He was convinced that the dress question involved finding the right standard of measurements to figure out the optimal answer in regard to apparel choices. His assumptions doomed him from the start.

Well, what do you think? If you're a woman, you probably think the answer is too obvious to explain. If you're a man, the situation probably seems too bizarre to be solved. Here is what I explained to the husband. In reality, which dress he preferred was not the real question. In fact, it was the same question his wife had asked him in dozens of different contexts and which he thought were dozens of different questions. I told the befuddled engineer that the real question he was being asked each and every time was always this:

"Am I cherished?"

When his wife immediately broke into tears, I figured I was on the right track. I continued by pointing out that once you had the right question, the correct answer became fairly easy. The correct answer to the dress question was, of course, "You look marvelous in both." This is what women want above all else. No, not flattery. They want, with all of their being, to be cherished. Wives breaking into tears at the mere mention of the word "cherish" has happened repeatedly in my counseling sessions.

For those of you who don't have your dictionaries handy, here is the definition of "cherish" from dictionary.com:

cher·ish [cher-ish]

verb (used with object)

1. to hold or treat as dear; feel love for: *to cherish one's native land*

2. to care for tenderly; nurture*: to cherish a child*

3. to cling fondly or inveterately to*: to cherish a memory.*

While all of these are helpful, I am mainly using "cherish" as used in definition number two. Your wife is not a child, but much of your wife's heart responds like one.

I should point out that my evidence on this is anecdotal. This means my information comes from a relatively few number of people and was not collected in scientifically controlled conditions. Actually, most women I talk to who are not in counseling think that the more important question to them is the closely related one, "Am I loved?" Perhaps being loved is the more common question, but being cherished is the more foundational one.

*****

I've done it again; I've run out of room. Never fear, I've decided to cheat this time and just start another chapter on pretty much the same topic. So, strap in for truth in marital communication coming to you on the next page.

Chapter 20

Truth on the Counseling Couch: Communication in Marriage

"Do nothing out of selfish ambition or vain conceit, but in humility consider others better than yourselves."
~Paul of Tarsus, as recounted in Philippians 2:3 NIV

There is an important truth to discover in marriage. Namely, what the heck is your spouse thinking? To figure this out, we have to use words. Communication can be a lot of work because other people stubbornly refuse to think the way we do. You'd think that communicating with our spouse would be easy. After all, aren't you soul mates? Sadly, it doesn't work that way. Figuring out what's going on in your marriage requires some knowledge about how communication works and yes, you guessed it, more humility.

The Truth about Marital Communication

There are a few time-honored conventions in communication that are always helpful. For instance, don't say "never" or "always." When you have a complaint, use "I', instead of "you" to start your sentence. You can't go wrong with these. Here is another one: Nothing is more frustrating than not feeling heard. This happens easily, because we are very intent on our insightful response to our spouse's nonsense. This doesn't leave much of our brain to listen with. Try this instead -- every once in a while, (more often if the conversation is becoming heated), simply repeat back to your spouse what they said and ask if you heard them correctly. You will be surprised by how often they say "no" and how helpful it is to their mood when you get it right. These are all rules that apply to both men and women.

Far more damaging, but less well known, are the communication problems caused by the differences between men and women. Men and women seem very similar on the surface. They have the same number of limbs, usually speak the same language, and they both need cars and food to get around. But, trying to communicate with your spouse as you would with someone of the same gender can slowly but surely lead to destruction. Conversely, communicating with them in a way they understand and appreciate can lead to some happy surprises.

How Not to Talk to a Man

Men actually have an advantage when it comes to communication. We already know we're bad at it. We get reminded frequently. When communication goes badly, we can easily guess where the problem is--us. Women, on the other hand, have been told all their lives they're great at it. The truth is that women (or at least the ones I have seen in counseling situations) are often terrible communicators.

It is true that women are great when it comes to communicating with other women and do so with great flexibility and flair. They are terrible communicators, however, when it comes to communicating *with men*. Since women communicate with other women so well, they often assume that communicating with relatively simple creatures such as men should be a snap. So, when communication goes badly men often get the blame. Fortunately, men are relatively simple creatures. But there are a few subtle, but very important rules that need to be followed when talking to them.

One of the worst, if not the worst way to insult a man is to tell him he can't do his job. Nothing quite combines the messages of inadequacy and disrespect as telling a man he is incompetent. Men know that if they tell another man this, a fistfight is sure to follow. Men will happily insult each other's personal appearance, hygiene and intelligence loudly and in profanity-laced terms and receive laughter in return. They know instinctively, however, not to insult a man's job performance.

Women are often unaware of this landmine. Without knowing they are doing so, they will question their husband's competence as a father, husband, and provider. It usually isn't worded harshly or with that intent. But, every piece of advice, second-guessing, and constructive criticism sends an unwitting message to their man. Namely, that the husband is contemptible, stupid, irresponsible, and incompetent. Women do not understand that this is what men hear. Their intention, of course, is not to make their man feel neutered and shamed. They married the guy because they saw something great and wanted to help him become something even better.

Here is the right way to help your man. Before trying to correct him or give him your opinion consider this: A man figures that if he has a question, he is perfectly capable of asking it. Prior to volunteering your opinion, you should first ask your man, "Would you like some help with this?" or "Can I give you some advice?" This is how we men talk to each other and how we show each other respect. Always remember when talking to men that: "Unasked for advice is unwanted advice."

Another mistake that women make when communicating with men is by raising the volume of their speech. They reasonably assume that by raising the volume, men will be able to hear them better. They think that if they state their concerns louder and with more emotion, then men will be alerted to the depth of their concerns. To the contrary, I know that if I want to start a brawl with a guy, the best way to do this is to express my opinions louder and with more emotion. This increase in tension puts the other guy in a place where I can more easily goad him into a fight. Increasing the level of emotion doesn't help solve a conflict, it creates a new one.

I've learned to tune out other men's emotional escalation. I don't want to respond in kind and end up in a fistfight over something stupid. Most men that you'd want to be around have learned the same lesson. This is why the more desperately and loudly you appeal to your man, the more he will tune you out. It's a reflex. It has nothing to do with his love for you.

How to Talk to a Man

If I want to solve a conflict with another man, I have one sentence that I say to him that will immediately set the tone for the rest of the conversation. Assuming the man's name is actually Bob, I say:

"Bob, can I talk to you for a minute?"

At this point, believe it or not, I am 90% of the way to resolving things with Bob. He is aware there is a problem and is emotionally primed to deal with it, without feeling the need to defend himself or shut down.

Let me unpack for you why this sentence is so powerful. First of all, I am asking Bob's permission, which demonstrates my respect for him as a man. Secondly, I have delivered this statement in a calm voice. By so doing, I'm demonstrating that I want to solve the problem with him in a respectful way and that my goal is not to attack him or to vent on him.

Using just one sentence is very concise. I do this on purpose and for several reasons. First of all, men love conciseness. Also, using just one sentence gives Bob a chance to prepare himself for the emotional content that will follow. While this may seem very brief, I know that this one sentence, combined with the businesslike tone of my voice, is all that Bob needs to fully appreciate the emotional seriousness of the situation. The first sentence in a conversation with a man is key. You may notice that your fights with your husband start almost immediately. This is because the very first sentence sets the tone for the whole discussion.

As the discussion continues, I will also acknowledge two things. I will confess my contributions to the problem, and I will point out that I know that Bob's contributions to the problem were well-intentioned. I'll focus on the problem and how we can fix it. If I need to discuss my feelings about Bob's behavior, I'll make sure I use the word "I" and not spend more than a sentence or two on it. Take note that if I had only hinted at what I wanted, or asked Bob in an indirect way to have a discussion, he would most likely have ignored me and gone on his way. We men don't usually understand indirectness, so a straightforward approach is required.

Granted, while this exact sentence works great for me with my group of friends and my culture, it might not work in yours. If you try this sentence and get poor results, there is still a very simple way to find that powerful sentence that you need to best resolve things with your man. Simply ask your boyfriend or husband, "What would you like me to say when I want to discuss a problem with you?" Whatever he tells you should be what you say exactly. Resist the urge to improve on his suggestion, as your improvement will invariably make things worse.

While this approach will greatly assist you in being heard by your man, it will not always instill the motivation you are hoping to provide. Motivating a man cannot be done by focusing on your goals and motives. You need to look at the situation from your man's point of view. Your man does not want to be your employee. Your man certainly does not want to be reminded of yet another way he has fallen short. He's also not looking for more work. He probably doesn't care if the house looks closer to perfect as men are generally content with "good enough." It is true that he does not want you to be upset, but repeatedly appealing to this will eventually lead to resentment. What he *does* want is the opportunity to be your hero. As I mentioned in the last chapter, men are *crazy* about their wives. Being your hero is the way we most like to show this.

To hear that we are so crazy about you might sound odd, as we men often refuse to be helpful. This lack of helpfulness usually happens for one of three reasons. The first reason is selfishness. Enough said. Secondly, we may not understand the connection between our behavior and your happiness. Thirdly, and most distressingly, we may have come to believe that our behavior has no effect on your happiness. If we honestly thought that doing what you asked would make you happy, we would do it. We refuse to be helpful or are slow to act because we're convinced it won't make any difference. When we meet one of your requests and it is followed by a curt acknowledgement and then a second angry request, we "learn" that our effort doesn't contribute to our goal and is a waste of time. This stand off is very destructive to a marriage.

That's enough of what not to do, here is what to do. Let's say that you don't have the energy to vacuum and having the carpets covered with cat hair really stresses you out. Begin your request with some form of this statement: "If you would sweep the carpets once a week, I would feel so supported and loved. I feel so much more peaceful when the carpet is clean." By complying with this request, your husband doesn't have to feel like he is knuckling under to a demand from an authority. He is given a free choice, and he is given the gift he is longing for, the opportunity to be your hero.

Essential to this, of course, is that you are appreciative when he cooperates. Also, truth always wins out and your man can tell when you are conning him. When you tell him cleaning something will make you joyful, it has to be said in all truthfulness and not because you trying it out on him as a new technique.

How <u>Not</u> to Talk to Women

Men encounter problems talking to women for much the same sort of reasons that women have difficulty talking to men. Men usually do not appreciate that women are uniquely different from them and have not taken the time and effort to learn these differences. Even if they're informed of these differences, men will often be contemptuous of the way women interact and insist women do it our way because our way is "better." For example, men will often attempt to cheer up their wives with the same sort of coarse joking that works with other men. When this backfires, men will feel unappreciated and misunderstood. It is we men who do not understand. We need to change our initial response to these differences from one of dismissiveness to one of expectant curiosity.

Women, whatever sort of exterior they may project, are tenderhearted creatures. They prefer to be both nurturing and nurtured. This is in no way a criticism, nor should anyone see it as a weakness. It is the way God made them, and everything that God makes is good. Yes, you know some women that are hardened and so do I. What you won't meet is a woman who is truly indifferent to how you treat her. Hardened women develop that hardness to protect the tender places inside.

So, why do coarse jokes backfire? Women instinctively seek a close nurturing relationship with their husband. When we call them names or curse at them, we stomp on the tenderest parts of their soul. When they look to us for protection and nurturance and receive belittlement instead, they feel negated and deeply hurt. Again, this sort of behavior usually works fine with men, but women are very different and wonderful creatures.

Both sexes are tender in different areas. Women are especially sensitive when it comes to topics in the area of "womanhood." Be especially cautious and gentle when you have a criticism in the areas of cooking, housekeeping, or mothering (not an exhaustive list). When it comes to cooking, for example, we men have no real emotional attachment to food. If we criticize it, it's usually so that our wife will know not to cook that meal in the future. As long as the cooking doesn't put us in the hospital, we don't really care all that much. We'll most likely eat it anyway.

For our wives, negative feedback on their cooking, cleaning, and child-rearing is not seen as helpful data. In a way that is a total mystery to us, a criticism of these things is a rejection of our wife *as a woman*. This may seem strange, but it is not too terribly different from the way we men feel if we are criticized about our job performance.

Another area that we men should not complain about is (whispers softly), her cycle. This is an exceptionally sensitive area because--OK, I really have no idea. Despite extensive research,* I don't think I'm any wiser than when I started. Suffice it to say, that it is A RULE that you should not complain about it, or reference it, or have a facial expression that resembles you smirking about it, or you will BE SORRY. Being sensitive in this way is one of the highest forms of respect. Namely, being kind and gentle about a topic even when we don't have the faintest clue as to why.

Another way in which women are wonderful is their desire to connect with us with their words. Because they are interested in us, they will ask lots of questions. We men often mistake this for suspicion or an interrogation. We rarely appreciate this gift from our wives. It is not usually in our natures to talk this much, or at least not on the topics that women choose. The vast majority of the time, however, the more they talk to us, the more they like us.

It will take sustained, uncomfortable work, but we men <u>can</u> learn to appreciate these conversations. Even more importantly, when we learn to initiate more conversations, we will be rewarded with wives that are much more fulfilled and relaxed. Connecting with wives with our words makes them feel happy.

---

* I talked to my wife about it for ten minutes. Or maybe it just felt that long.

How to Talk to a Woman

Please indulge me in a yet another little story from my past. When I was earning my Masters degree in Counseling, one of our classes involved pretending to do therapy on our classmates. One of us would be the therapist and the other would be the client. The client would have a script as to what their problem was and the therapist and client would work through a pretend counseling session.

These therapy sessions were taped and the instructor and other class members watched them and then critiqued the skills of the therapist. I remember that in one of these sessions I was the therapist and my good buddy Kevin was the client. I don't remember Kevin's exact script but it had to do with him having marital trouble because he was a jerk. Since we already knew each other pretty well, we dove right in and had an animated conversation about his pretend problems.

I was surprised from the feedback from one of the ladies in the group. Michelle said to the class, "As I was watching you talk, I thought the two of you were going to come to blows." I suppose Kevin had annoyed me at some point and vice-versa, but we were never in danger of rolling around on the floor pummeling each other. I had no idea that anyone would think our animated conversation about his pretend marital problems would sound violent or even argumentative. I merely thought of it as "lively." But, even in a contrived conversation with someone with whom I had no ill will, there was still a part of Nicole's brain that believed there was physical danger.

That brings us to the application to marital communication. No matter how long we know our wives, they will still, to one extent or another, interpret our level of aggressiveness by female standards rather than by male standards. Our wives will often interpret our "normal" ways of communicating with our excited voices, shoulder punching, and vigorous arm movements as very frightening. Usually we men understand that women are delicate creatures and we try to tone it down accordingly. It is often not enough, however, because we are toning it down, *but to our male standards.*

Our wives may still think we're yelling when we think we're talking because they are judging by their female point of view. Even putting our hands on our hips or crossing our arms to emphasize a point can feel menacing to our wives. Take a moment the next time you see a group of women interacting to notice the subtle but distinct differences from how men talk to each other.

Women rarely speak loudly and directly at each other. If they do, other women will rush in to calm down and "fix" the situation. Women are more likely to throw out an idea for general comment "to see what people think about it." This is their way of being polite and not forcing their opinions and ideas on others. We men often find this feminine indirectness confusing and maddening. It is, however, normal *for them* and is not a conscious attempt to infuriate us.

In conclusion, when your wife mistakenly thinks that you are yelling at her and being angry, try to think of it from her point of view and not just from the point of view of your intentions. If what you are doing makes her afraid she won't be able to hear your opinion or your good intentions.

Here is one other thought on how women communicate differently. If a man were to say, "I don't want to go to the store," then 98% of the time it means, "I don't want to go to the store." The other 2% of the time, the man would be lying for some reason. If a woman says, "I don't want to go to the store," it could mean any number of things. It could mean one of the two things it might mean for a man or, it could mean: "I don't know if I really want to go, so I'm throwing out the idea to see what you think about it, at which point I might change my mind."

It could also mean, "I don't want to go and I'm hoping that you will volunteer to go for me." Another possible interpretation is, "I want to go, but I want you to offer to go with me so that then it will be your idea, in case it turns out to be a bad one." For men, saying one thing when we mean the opposite would not occur to us.

For women, this type of communication is not so much "normal" as "common." Among women, it may not even be particularly admired, especially in its more extreme forms. It's somewhat like men who attempt to control others with angry demands. We men don't admire those guys, but there is a part of us that wishes we could get away with acting like that.

Talking to a Man: Less is More. Talking to a Woman: More is About Right

It is said that men are big picture people and women are detail oriented. So, women might spend 20 minutes recounting a 30 minute phone conversation, while a man could reduce it down to two sentences. Women are certainly more detail oriented, but I think that is only part of the reason for differences in male-female communication.

Believe it or not, women are more adept at communication in general, but men are more adept at communicating in short bursts. In fact, we men actually enjoy talking that way. My roommate in college and I delighted in being able to communicate a wealth of meaning in just a few words. Being able to communicate this briefly was only possible because we knew each other so well. The smaller the number of words we used, the closer we felt. The shortness of our conversations was evidence of our closeness as friends.

Think about the movies men like. War movies, happily, always have lots of explosions. But, before the shooting starts there is---The Approach Scene. When the good guys are sneaking up on the enemy, they rely on very few words, often using only hand signals. When personal danger is the highest, the number of words is the fewest. This sequence doesn't happen in every guy movie just to set up the next sequence. Watching this type of interaction is part of the emotional impact for male viewers. We enjoy it.

For purposes of further illustrating the concept of more words versus fewer, I would like to recount a scene from Lethal Weapon 2. In this scene, Martin Riggs is about to yank Roger Murtaugh off of the toilet bomb he's sitting on, and into the relative safety of the nearby cast iron tub; a difficult maneuver in the best of times. It is made even more difficult by the fact that Murtaugh's legs have frozen up from sitting on the toilet for ten hours. While the liquid nitrogen will delay the explosion, neither one of them might survive.

This then, is a typical situation in which men might have a deeply emotional conversation.

Just before the fateful moment they speak:

Murtaugh: "Martin..."
Riggs: "What"...(long pause). Hey, I know, I know."

And there you have it... deep male communication.

I'm being a little bit farcical, but I'd like to expand this exchange to illustrate just how much content is packed into these seven words. Here is the same conversation translated into female:

Murtaugh: "Riggs, I don't know if either one of us will live through this. Before we jump, I just wanted to let you know everything you've come to mean to me. When you first started as my partner, I thought you were a royal pain in the butt who was going to make me miserable. Instead you've become a part of my family, even though I'm black and you're white. I've lost track of the number of times you've saved my life and here you are trying to save my life again at the risk of you own."

Riggs: "I feel the same way, Roger. When I first joined the force, I was desperately suicidal and on several occasions put my own gun in my mouth because of all the pain I felt. Thanks to your friendship, I've managed to overcome that. I not only owe you my life but I also feel deeply loved and accepted by both you and your wonderful family. My life would not have any purpose if it hadn't been for you. It's not necessary for you to tell me how you feel in words, because I have experienced it by living it with you."

As I've said, male communication is very compact. We're good at it and we enjoy it that way. The shortness of our communication does not make us inferior. We can often read a great deal out of small nuances and non-verbal cues. It does, however, make us quite different from women and that is where the difficulty comes in. At the beginning of a romantic relationship, men do talk more. This is both because they know they are supposed to, and also because they know they haven't developed enough familiarity with their girlfriends to be able to communicate compactly with them yet.

Then the couples get married and the problems begin. Men start talking less. Wives, perceiving some separation, attempt to connect with their husbands by talking to them more. The husbands talk with them at first, but then seem to lose interest. This makes the wives feel even more separated. Wishing to fix the apparent widening gap between them, women talk to their husbands in ever greater detail. The men interpret all of this talking as evidence that they are <u>not</u> close to their wives. Stung and confused by the evidence of an apparent widening gap between them, men back off and try to figure out what went wrong. This cycle continues with the wife ever more desperately trying to connect and the husband ever more desperately trying to get away in order to create some space that they can be close in.

For us men, learning to listen at length can be difficult. The place to start is by developing the understanding that your wife wanting to talk to you is a great thing. It shows she cares about you and thinks of you as a place to find shared happiness. Yes, men, changing how we listen is a natural part of married growth. We tend to have a natural expectation that our wives can adjust to our "normal," but we have a responsibility to change as well.

Conversely, wives need to be aware of the concise way in which we talk. I can recall a few occasions when I really wanted to talk to my wife and looked forward to talking to her all day. She would come home, and I would tell her my highly emotional news and what I thought about it. I would pour out my heart and then I would be deeply hurt when she didn't respond. Here is the problem. I would use a grand total of two sentences. I was thinking I had come up with a very clear and concise communication of my deepest feelings. She didn't respond, because in her mind, I was just introducing the topic. She was waiting patiently for me to get to the rest of it.

*****

It is the most natural thing in the world for us to judge others based upon what we would do or say. When the person we are judging is radically different from us, things can fall apart rapidly. It takes a conscious effort, and also some frustrating practice, but looking at things from our spouse's point of view can relieve the inevitable tension considerably.

PART 3

And here we reach the final chapter. In this short chapter I present some principles for life. Some are new and some are summaries of what you've already seen. This last section can be used for quotable quotes in your sparkling dinner conversations, pearls of wisdom to live by, or even for autosignatures.

Chapter 21

Principles to Live By

"It is easier to fight for one's principles, than to live up to them."
~Alfred Adler

In this chapter I present 29 principles that help us find truth. Some of these are recaps of earlier discussions while others stand on their own. If I were a huckster, I suppose I could have made this into a fancy poster; sold separately.

Principle 1: Avoid Expectation Bias.
Don't confuse personal desire with actual fact. Do you think it is true because you want it to be true or because the evidence shows it to be true?

Principle 2: Follow the Money.
Are the people trying to convince you of something going to make money if they succeed? Are they up front with their financial interests? Do they stand to gain emotionally? Do they stand to gain power if they can convince you? Does

examining which way the money flows help explain a confusing situation?

Principle 3: Judge Things by Their Fruits.

What happens to people who do something questionable? Are they better off emotionally and psychologically? What effect does it have on the people around them? What happens to their behavior, integrity, and overall well-being? Does it profit them at the expense of others?

Principle 4: Examine Past and Present Results.

Has this failed every time it was tried before? Is the proposed change a critical and necessary change or is it just rearranging deck chairs? Is there any reason it will work now when it hasn't in the past?

Principle 5: What Would Jesus Do?

It's not just a bracelet.

Principle 6: Would You Do it if Your Mother was in the Room?

Principle 7: What Would You Say if You Saw Someone Else Doing it?

Principle 8: Does it Make Sense in a Different Context?

For instance, if you're an Obama fan, would President Obama's behavior still be ok if George Bush were doing it? Now suppose you're a Bush fan. If Obama did everything the way George Bush did, would you now be an Obama fan? If your feelings change depending on who is doing what, you're probably not judging based on objective principles. While we're discussing principles, figure out what your core principles *are*. Take some serious time to do this. If you don't have any core principles, your decisions will be under other people's control. Your choices will merely reflect who is the best at swaying your emotions. As the saying goes, "If you don't stand for something, you'll fall for anything."

Principle 9: Does it Line up with the Bible?

Principle 10: Use Your Emotions Wisely.

God gave us our emotions, and he made them for our good. Emotions serve a very important purpose in decision-making. They alert us to which issues and situations require our serious attention. Once a decision has been made to act, our emotions provide us with the energy to maintain our commitment. Emotions are not good for being the basis of our decisions. Facts and principles give us fixed points on which to frame our lives. Emotions can change like the wind.

Principle 11: If it Sounds too Good to be True, it Probably is.

Principle 12: Always Trust Your Instincts, but not Blindly.

When your instincts tell you something is fishy, it probably is. Always investigate further when your Spidey-sense goes off. Don't let other people's opinions, greed, fear, or anything else stop you from following up on your instincts.

The opposite error is to be so impressed with your intuition that you always follow it. Sometimes your intuition is not responding to a real problem, but to something that happened in second grade. While you're following up to see if your intuition is correct, don't forget to check and see if it's wrong.

Principle 13: If Someone is Faithful in Small Things they will be Faithful in Large Ones.

This applies to unfaithfulness as well. Is the person you're working with been known to hide things? If so, they are probably hiding other things you don't know about. Do they talk down other people behind their backs? Then guess who they talk about when you're not in the room.

Principle 14: Beware of the Accomplished Critic.

If they spend more time criticizing the other guy than talking about their own ideas, chances are their ideas aren't that great. This applies to people trying to sell you things as well.

Principle 15: Are They Arguing the Actual Issue?

Or are they talking about some other issue that everyone agrees on and pretending the two issues are related somehow? Let's say the topic is law enforcement. Are they discussing the pros and cons of increasing or decreasing police powers? Or, are they just stating that whatever they disagree with is socialist or racist?

Principle 16: Note Responsibility.

Pay attention to whether the person you're working with takes responsibility for what they do, especially the small things. If it's never <u>their</u> problem, they have no motivation to fix it.

Principle 17: Be Wary of Guilt by Association.

If "they" are trying to convince you that someone else is guilty by association, ask yourself this: Can the amount of guilt they are trying to assign to their target be reasonably explained by that association? Casual connections to shady people don't instantaneously taint people.

Principle 18: Take Careful Note of Praise.

If people tell you you're more wonderful than you seem to deserve, one of two things is happening. One, if everyone seems to do this, you have low self-esteem. Two, if only a few people do it, you're being flattered. Be on your guard with these people.

In my early twenties, I struck up a conversation with a stranger I ran into at a job fair in the Cleveland IX Center. He complimented me profusely on how I carried myself and asked if I had attended a Dale Carnegie Course or something. We exchanged info and a month later we had the following phone conversation. I feel obliged to point out that I don't usually think this well on my feet. Here it is to the best of my memory:

Me: Hello!
Stranger: Hey there, remember me, we met at the IX Center.
Me: Oh, yeah.
Stranger: Hey, I'm having a meeting to discuss how to get people set up in their own business and make money for themselves. I wanted you to come.
Me: That sounds interesting. What kind of business is it?
Stranger: I have a policy to not tell people what kind of business it is until they come to the meeting.
Me: Oh, well I have a policy to not work with people who won't tell me what their business is.
Stranger: <click>

Principle 19: Scrutinize People that are GREAT.

There are three types of people that will always tell you they are doing wonderfully: optimists, salesman, and alcoholics, in reverse order.

Principle 20: Be Wary Trusting Victims.

Don't trust important things to people that always tell you they are victims. Serial victims, by definition, are not responsible.

Principle 21: Use Point of View Creatively.

Let me illustrate what I mean. Doctors are required to inform you of your treatment options. This is great when you have a clear preference. Very often, however, you don't have a clear preference and don't have the right questions to learn what you need to know. Here is a great question to ask the doctor. "If it were you (or your family member) what would you do"? This has never failed to give me a clearer idea of what my choices are as well as what the doctor is thinking.

Principle 22: Be Right. Be Happy. Pick One.

In relationships, you will discover that your significant other does many things "wrong." They might wash the dishes the wrong way, they might clean the house the wrong way, or they might interact the wrong way socially. They will stubbornly believe that there is some justification for the stupid way they do things.

At this point you have a choice. You may, if you wish, loudly correct your wayward Significant Other until they grudgingly comply. You are right after all, and it is only proper that they follow <u>the rules</u>. There is one downside to this. You will be totally miserable. You will still be right, but you will be horribly miserable.

Or, you can embrace the wacky way your Significant Other behaves, focus on the things that attracted them to you in the first place, and have a wonderful time with your defective lover. And be happy.

Principle 23: When You Think Everyone Around You is Crazy, You're the One that's Crazy.

Why do multiple people tell you you're arrogant? They must not be as smart as you.

Principle 24: Beware of Lovers of Modernity.

Some people will dismiss ideas simply because they are not "modern" or "sophisticated" or "scientific." For instance, many people will dismiss any discussion of the importance of the family as antiquated and give it no further thought. Whether an idea is old or new is beside the point. What matters is if it is true or not.

Principle 25: If You Have to Say "The Science is Settled," it's Not Settled.

Principle 26: Atheism is Not a Rational Position.

If you declare, "There is no God," then logically, you have to admit that every single thought you've ever had, including the thought "There is no God" results from nothing but an accumulation of random circumstances. It means that every single one of your thoughts and ideas are totally devoid of any significance or meaning. If that's really your position, why should I listen to you?

Principle 27: Trust Sad Atheists more than Happy Ones.

I can trust a man who tells me he thinks he is the product of random circumstance. I can't trust one who tells me he's excited about it. If a man is excited about atheism, he either doesn't understand, or refuses to embrace, the full implications of his atheism. A man who is excited about atheism is a man who thinks he has found a big club he can use to smack something he doesn't like.

Principle 28: If you're Receiving way more Anger than you've Earned, It's not about You.

Sometimes you will be shocked at how angry a friend or significant other suddenly becomes with you. The first question to ask yourself, of course, is whether you are blind to just how big of a jerk you're being. If the clear answer is, "Not a very big jerk." then don't develop a guilt complex over it. People very often make mountains out of molehills because it reminds them of something very painful that someone else did to them.

Principle 29: Envy Kills. Literally.

In 2001 our family was feeling desperate and looking for legal and emotional support from a local lawyer. The lawyer almost immediately launched into a tirade about how unfair it was that Alex Rodriguez had just signed a ten year $252 million dollar contract. Our initial suspicion was that this was a ploy to make the lawyer's fee seem much smaller by comparison. That may have been the case, but I suspect he was honestly offended that someone would have the nerve to make so much more than him. This is called envy. The lawyer's envy wasn't helping him any, let alone us. It certainly had no effect on A-Rod.

When envy about economic inequality is elevated to a governing philosophy it is called communism. In its heyday, communism took solid root in poorer countries where there was plenty of opportunity for such envy. There were some short-lived feelings of personal satisfaction when the rich were systematically bankrupted. Inevitably, however, everyone else became poorer as well. But it was fair. To the world's sorrow, one of the byproducts of all of this fairness was the deaths of tens of millions.[158]

Consider this; if you're reading this book, you're probably economically better off than 90% of the earth's population. Do you feel a burning need to go Haiti and apologize for your good fortune? Why do you think that Bill Gates is going to feel any differently? Do the world a favor. Use the energy you're putting into envying those more fortunate, and put that energy into being charitable towards those less fortunate.

ENDNOTES

[1] William Morris, ed., *The American Heritage Dictionary of the English Language. New College Edition* (Boston: Houghton Mifflin Company, 1980).

[2] Additional criteria are:
B. The individual is at least age 18 years.
C. There is evidence of Conduct Disorder with onset before age 15 years.
D. The occurrence of antisocial behavior is not exclusively during the course of Schizophrenia or a Manic Episode.

[3] Jean Kinney, *Loosening the Grip* (Boston: McGraw Hill, 2003), 23.

[4] Aaron Cooper, "Study: 22 million Americans use illegal Drugs," *CNN Health*, last modified August 9, 2011, accessed March 25, 2014, http://thechart.blogs.cnn.com/2011/09/08/study-22-million-americans-use-illegal-drugs-3/.

[5] Jean Kinney, *Loosening the Grip* (Boston: McGraw Hill, 2003), 23.

[6] Dr. John Townsend, *Boundaries with Teens: When to Say Yes, How to Say No* 8(Chicago: Zondervan, 2006), 187-190.

[7] A good starter book is: Josh McDowell, *Evidence that Demands a Verdict.*

[8] "Chicago Tylenol Murders," *Wikipedia*, accessed March 25, 2014, http://en.wikipedia.org/wiki/Chicago_Tylenol_murders.

---

[9] Rachael Bell, "The Tylenol Terrorist," *Crime Library*, accessed March 25, 2014, http://www.crimelibrary.com/terrorists_spies/terrorists/tylenol_murders/index.html.

[10] Tyler Durden, "The Cost of Government Regulation: $1.75 Trillion," *Zerohedge*, last modified 07 22, 2012, http://www.zerohedge.com/news/cost-government-regulation-175-trillion.

[11] I'm not sure, but I believe the book was: Richard Ryckman. *Theories of Personality*. (Belmont: Wadsworth Thomson Learning, 1979).

[12] R. Andrew Muller, "A New Rental Policy for Ontario," *The Fair Rental Policy Association*, last modified October 28, 1986, http://www.frpo.org/documents/Muller-ANewRentalPolicyForOntario.pdf.

[13] "Keynesian Economics," *Wikipedia*, accessed March 27, 2014, http://en.wikipedia.org/wiki/Keynesian_economics.

[14] And as I'm further along in the book and I'm working on the references today on March, 27th, 2014, the national debt is over 17.5 trillion dollars.

[15] "Federal Revenue Estimates vs. Actual Federal Revenue for Fiscal Year 2012," *US Government Revenue*, accessed September 22, 2012, http://www.usgovernmentrevenue.com/federal_budget_estimate_vs_actual_2012.

[16] "Laffer Curve," *Wikipedia*, accessed September 22, 2012, http://en.wikipedia.org/wiki/Laffer_curve.

[17] "Revenue Act of 1964," *Wikipedia*, accessed September 22, 2012, http://en.wikipedia.org/wiki/Revenue_act_of_1964.

[18] Mike Patton, "Do Tax Cuts Increase Government Revenues?" *Forbes*, last modified October 15, 2012, http://www.forbes.com/sites/mikepatton/2012/10/15/do-tax-cuts-increase-government-revenue/.

[19] Douglas W. Matheson, Richard L. Bruce, and Kenneth L. Beauchamp, *3rd Edition Experimental Psychology: Research, Design and Analysis* (New York: Holt, Rinehart and Winston, 1978), 8.

[20] On that note, here is one of my favorite haikus:
Yesterday, it worked.
Today it is not working.
Windows is like that.

[21] Douglas W. Matheson, Richard L. Bruce, Kenneth L. Beauchamp, *3rd Edition Experimental Psychology: Research, Design and Analysis*. (New York: Holt, Rinehart and Winston, 1978), 9.

[22] Ibid., 12.

[23] "Climate Change Improvements Needed to Clarify National Priorities and Better Align Them with Federal Funding Decisions." *GAO*, last modified June 20, 2011, http://www.gao.gov/assets/320/318556.pdf.

[24] "Cold Fusion," *Wikipedia*, accessed March 27, 2014, http://en.wikipedia.org/wiki/Cold_fusion.

[25] "Saccharin," *Wikipedia*, accessed March 27, 2014, http://en.wikipedia.org/wiki/Saccharin.

[26] Jonathan M., "NCSE's Eugenie Scott Reassures Scotland: There's No Scientific Controversy on Evolution or Climate Change," *Evolution News*, last modified September 23, 2011, http://www.evolutionnews.org/2011/09/ncses_eugenie_sco

tt_reassures051171.html.

[27] "Lucy (Australopithecus)," *Wikipedia*, accessed February 19, 2014, http://en.wikipedia.org/wiki/Lucy_(Australopithecus).

[28] "Punctuated Equilibrium," *Wikipedia*, accessed February 19, 2014, http://en.wikipedia.org/wiki/Punctuated_equilibrium.

[29] Dr. Don Batten, "Punctuated Equilibrium: come of age?" *Creation.com*, accessed February 19, 2014, http://creation.com/punctuated-equilibrium-come-of-age.

[30] "Evolution 101, More on Punctuated Equilibrium," *Berkeley*, accessed February 19, 2014, http://evolution.berkeley.edu/evosite/evo101/VIIA1bPunctuated.shtml.

[31] Dr. Don Batten, "Punctuated Equilibrium: come of age?" *Creation.com*, accessed February 19, 2014, http://creation.com/punctuated-equilibrium-come-of-age.

[32] "Falsifiability," *Wikipedia*, accessed February 19, 2014, http://en.wikipedia.org/wiki/Falsifiability.

[33] Alexander Light, "9 Scientific facts Prove that the 'Theory of Evolution' is False," *Humans are Free*, last modified December 9, 2013, http://humansarefree.com/2013/12/9-scienctific-facts-prove-theory-of.html.

[34] "Physics; Second Law of Thermodynamics," *About.com*, accessed February 20, 2014, http://physics.about.com/od/thermodynamics/a/lawthermo_4.htm.

[35] Richard Deem, "Genesis Clearly Teaches that the Days Were NOT 24 Hours," *Godandscience.org*, last modified December 30, 2005,

http://www.godandscience.org/youngearth/genesis.html.

[36] Dr. Roger C Wiens, "Radiometric Dating: A Christian Perspective," *The American Scientific Affiliation,* last modified 2002, http://www.asa3.org/ASA/resources/wiens.html.

[37] Ibid.

[38] Ibid.

[39] Ibid.

[40] B.A. Robinson, "Indicators of a 4.5 billion-year-old Earth, with rebuttals based on creation science," *Religious Tolerance.org*, last modified August 25, 2008, http://www.religioustolerance.org/oldearth.htm.

[41] Dr. Roger C Wiens, "Radiometric Dating: A Christian Perspective," *The American Scientific Affiliation,* last modified 2002, http://www.asa3.org/ASA/resources/wiens.html.

[42] "How are astronomers able to measure how far away a star is?" How Stuff Works, accessed February 20, 2014, http://science.howstuffworks.com/question224.htm.

[43] "Does Evolution Contradict the Bible?" *Bibleinfo.com,* accessed May 2, 2014, http://www.bibleinfo.com/en/questions/can-evolution-and-creation-go-together.

[44] J. Hebert, "Rethinking Carbon-14 Dating: What Does It Really Tell Us about the Age of the Earth?" *Institute for Creation Research*, last modified 2013, accessed May 2, 2014, http://www.icr.org/article/rethinking-carbon-14-dating-what-does/.

[45] Patrick Zukeran, "Archaeology and the Old Testament," *Probe Ministries*, last modified 2000, accessed April 1, 2014, http://www.probe.org/site/c.fdKEIMNsEoG/b.4955427/k.3D58/Archaeology_and_the_Old_Testament.htm.

[46] Katie Couric, "One on One with Sarah Palin," *CBS News*, last modified September 24, 2008, http://www.cbsnews.com/news/one-on-one-with-sarah-palin/.

[47] Ibid.

[48] "Exclusive: Palin on Foreign Policy," *CBS Evening News*, last modified September 9, 2008, http://www.cbsnews.com/news/exclusive-palin-on-foreign-policy/.

[49] "Transcript: Palin and McCain Interview, Katie Couric," *Clips and Comments*, last modified September 30, 2008, http://www.cbsnews.com/news/transcript-palin-and-mccain-interview/.

[50] Katie Couric, CBS Evening News, "CBS Exclusive: Gov. Sarah Palin," https://www.youtube.com/watch?v=-ZVh_u5RyiU (October 31, 2008) accessed May 6, 2014.

[51] "Media Bias 101. What Journalists Really Think--and what the Public Thinks about them," *Media Research Center*, last modified May 6, 2014, http://www.mrc.org/media-bias-101/media-bias-101-what-journalists-really-think-and-what-public-thinks-about-them.

[52] Ibid.

[53] Harry Stein, *I Can't Believe I'm Sitting next to a Republican* (New York: Encounter Books, 2009), 61.

[54] Warner Todd Houston, "The top 50 Liberal Media Bias Examples. (#36)," *Western Journalism*, last modified December 10, 2011. http://www.westernjournalism.com/top-50-examples-liberal-media-bias/8/.

[55] Cindy Loose, "Promise Keepers Headed for the Mall; Men's Christian Group Plans Oct. 4 Rally," *The Washington Post*, February 5, 1997.

[56] Derek Hunter, "Rise of the Unaccomplished," Townhall, last modified January 9, 2014, http://townhall.com/columnists/derekhunter/2014/01/09/rise-of-the-unaccomplished-n1773591.

[57] The Marietta Times did print a much more evenhanded and informative story the next day, 8/19/1996. We made the top of the front page.

[58] Bruce Watson, "Really want to Influence Politicians? Stop Donating to Campaigns," *Daily Finance*, last Modified November 3rd, 2011, http://www.dailyfinance.com/2011/11/03/really-want-to-influence-politicians-stop-donating-to-campaigns/.

[59] Edward Koch, *Politics* (New York: Simon & Schuster, 1985), 17-31.

[60] The book, *City for Sale*, alleges that Ed Koch's level of corruption went quite a bit deeper. A discussion of this is well beyond the scope of this book.

[61] Edward Koch, *Politics* (New York: Simon & Schuster, 1985), 29.

[62] Stephanie Condon, "Why is Congress a Millionaire's Club?" *CBS News*, last modified June 30, 2011, accessed May 1, 2014, http://www.cbsnews.com/news/why-is-congress-a-millionaires-club/.

63 Jim Drinkard, "House Democrats to Hear from Three actresses on Plight of Farmers," *Daily News*, last modified May 1, 1985, http://www.apnewsarchive.com/1985/House-Democrats-to-Hear-From-Three-Actresses-on-Plight-of-Farmers/id-ae77d37758ed0fa69d4d19e30c8d4cf9.

64 Andrew Ferguson, "Bubble on the Potomac," *TIME*, last modified May 28, 2012, accessed May 1, 2014, http://content.time.com/time/magazine/article/0,9171,2115062,00.html.

65 "Revenue Act of 1964," *Wikipedia*, accessed April 17, 2014, http://en.wikipedia.org/wiki/Revenue_Act_of_1964 .

66 John Tozzi, "Doctors Order More Lab Tests When They Own the Labs," *Business Week*, last modified July 16, 2013, http://www.businessweek.com/articles/2013-07-16/doctors-order-more-lab-tests-when-they-own-the-labs. Of course, defensive medicine, the practice of ordering more tests to protect the medical practice from lawsuits, also plays a role in how many tests are ordered.

67 Sarnoff Mednick, Jerry Higgins, and Jack Kirschenbaum, *Psychology: Explorations in Behavior and Experience* (New York: John Wiley & Sons, 1975), 487-492.

68 Ibid.

69 This is described in the book of Mark, chapter six, verse seven.

70 "Narzos, "How to beat a lie detector," *Everything2.com*, last modified September 24, 2000, http://everything2.com/title/How+to+beat+a+lie+detector.

71 Mark McClish, *I Know you are Lying: Detecting Deception through Statement Analysis* (Winterville:

PoliceEmployment.com, 2001), 19.

[72] Ibid., 19.

[73] Ibid., 65.

[74] Ibid., 65-67.

[75] Ibid., 69.

[76] Ibid., 69.

[77] Ibid., 79.

[78] Ibid., 43.

[79] Ibid., 43.

[80] Ibid., 47.

[81] Ibid., 51.

[82] Ibid., 200.

[83]Mike Rivero, "Bill Clinton's Known Lies." *whatreallyhappened.com*, accessed March 18, 2014, https://whatreallyhappened.com/RANCHO/POLITICS/LIES.html.

[84] Mark McClish, *I Know you are Lying: Detecting Deception through Statement Analysis* (Winterville: PoliceEmployment.com, 2001), 19.

[85] Ibid., 100.

[86] My editor tells me that when he was in school these were called "telegraph" games. Not that he's old or anything.

[87] John Cook, "CO2 lags temperature--what does it mean?" *Skeptical Science*, accessed April 15, 2014, http://www.skepticalscience.com/co2-lags-temperature.htm.

[88] D. Q. McInerny, *Being Logical* (New York: Random House, 2004), 97.

[89] Josh Clark,; "How Occam's Razor Works," *How Stuff Works*, accessed May 8, 2014, http://science.howstuffworks.com/innovation/scientific-experiments/occams-razor.htm.

[90] "Occam's Razor," *Wikipedia*, accessed May 8, 2014, http://en.wikipedia.org/wiki/Occam's_razor.

[91] "Hanlon's Razor," *Wikipedia*, accessed May 8, 2014, http://en.wikipedia.org/wiki/Hanlon's_razor.

[92] Patrick J. Kiger, "10 Things that Don't Disprove Global Warming," *How Stuff Works*, accessed 4/11/14, http://science.howstuffworks.com/environmental/green-science/10-things-dont-disprove-global-warming.htm.

[93] Ibid.

[94] Formal logicians would more narrowly apply this term to personal attacks which were factual, but irrelevant (i.e. "Yeah, a Jew would argue against sharia law"). Ad hominem has come to be more loosely applied to any attack on a person's character, true or otherwise, which distract from the argument. This is the sense in which I use it here.

[95] "Peer review," *Wikipedia*, accessed May 8, 2014, http://en.wikipedia.org/wiki/Peer_review.

[96] Ibid.

[97] Begging the Question has more commonly come to mean "raising the question" as in "Snowy Weather Begs the Question: To Shovel or Snow Blow?" Traditionally, begging the question has referred to circular reasoning.

[98] Julian Baggini, *The Duck that Won the Lottery* (Chatham: Granta Books, 2008), 147-149.

[99] Michael Holden, "God did not create the universe, says Hawking," *Reuters*, last modified February 9, 2010, accessed April 30, 2014, http://www.reuters.com/article/2010/09/02/us-britain-hawking-idUSTRE6811FN20100902.

[100] Of course, I have to reference the book in order to quote from it. The book cited is:

[101] Julian Baggini, *The Duck that Won the Lottery* (Chatham: Granta Books, 2008).

[102] Ibid., 82.

[103] Ibid., 82.

[104] It didn't occur to me until after I wrote this that Spock is the epitome of a character who relies solely on logic. Fascinating.

[105] Pastor Clenard Childress Jr., "The Truth about MARGARET SANGER," *Black Genocide*, accessed May 13, 2014, http://www.blackgenocide.org/sanger.html.

[106] Ibid., 83.

[107] Ibid., 58.

[108] Yes, I'm writing about things outside of my field of expertise as well. I have tried to be as diffident as I could in this book, but I definitely run the risk of having to eat my

own words at some point.

[109] Ronan O'Rahilly and Fabiola Mueller, (*Human Embryology and Teratology, 3rd edition.* New York: Wiley-Liss, 2001), 8.

[110] Ibid., 8,29.

[111] Dianne Irving, "When Do Human Beings Begin? 'Scientific' Myths, and Scientific Facts," *International Journal of Sociology and Social Policy* 19:3 (February 1999): 4:22-36.

[112] Julian Baggini, *The Duck that Won the Lottery* (Chatham: Granta Books, 2008), 63-65.

[113] Ibid., 17.

[114] At Dictionary.com, "pro-abortion" is listed as an adjective of pro-choice. It can be argued that "pro-choice" refers to a more passive support of abortion focusing on women's rights, while "pro-abortion" is a more aggressive level of support, actively pressing for its use and expansion. In this chapter I use the two terms interchangeably, referring to persons who spend their time and money on actively defending and promoting the practice of abortion. I readily acknowledge that most persons describing themselves as pro-choice do not engage in many or most of the activities described in this chapter. My comments are intended to be applied to the most ardent and hardened supporters of abortion.

[115] NYU Langone Medical Center, "Pregnancy: Why mother's immune system does not reject developing fetus as foreign tissue," *Science Daily*, accessed May 2, 2014, www.sciencedaily.com/releases/2012/06/120607142244.htm.

[116] Dr. J.C. Willke and Mrs. J.C. Willke, *Abortion: Questions & Answers.* (Cincinnati: Hayes Publishing Company, 1985), 164.

[117] Ibid., 164.

[118] Simon Rabinovitch, "China takes baby steps in narrowing gender imbalance," *Reuters*, Last modified 6/3/2010, http://www.reuters.com/article/2010/06/03/us-china-sex-imbalance-idUSTRE65236520100603.

[119] Ibid.

[120] "Choosing to Have an Abortion," *Teen Health Source,* accessed May 1, 2014, http://teenhealthsource.com/pregnancy-2/details-abortion/.

[121] Nancy Flanders, "Former director speaks of Planned Parenthood's lies, and watching a fetus fight for his life," *Human Rights News*, last modified March 7, 2012, http://liveactionnews.org/former-director-speaks-of-planned-parenthoods-lies-and-watching-a-fetus-fight-for-his-life/.

[122] "Experiences at the Clinic," *Silent No More Awareness Campaign*, Last modified 2010, accessed May 1, 2014, http://www.silentnomoreawareness.org/plannedparenthood/.

[123] Eric Leberg. *Understanding Child Molesters, Taking Charge* (Thousand Oaks: Sage Publications, 1997).

[124] "Know the Facts," *MIT Pro-Choice*, accessed May 1, 2014, http://web.mit.edu/pro-choice/www/reasons.html.

[125] Ibid.

[126] Tamar Lewin, "Rape and Incest: Just 1% of All Abortions," *New York Times,* last modified October 13, 1989, http://www.nytimes.com/1989/10/13/us/rape-and-incest-just-1-of-all-abortions.html.

[127] "Fact #8: Less than 1% of all abortions are performed to save the life of the mother," *Abortion Facts,* last modified 2014, accessed May 1, 2014, http://www.abortionfacts.com/facts/8.

[128] Dr. J.C. Willke and Mrs. J.C. Willke, *Abortion: Questions & Answers.* (Cincinnati: Hayes Publishing Company, 1985), 121-131.

[129] Ibid., 90-92.

[130] Ibid., 95.

[131] Abortion has been shown to be a risk factor for breast cancer in some studies. As these results are still being verified, I do not include them here.

[132] Dr. J.C. Willke and Mrs. J.C. Willke, *Abortion: Questions & Answers.* (Cincinnati: Hayes Publishing Company, 1985), 103.

[133] Ibid., 104.

[134] Ibid., 105.

[135] Ibid. 105-106.

[136] Ibid., 44.

[137] Ibid., 55.

[138] Ibid. 47.

[139] Ibid., 48-49.

[140] "Fetus," *Merriam-Webster*, accessed May 1, 2014, http://www.merriam-webster.com/dictionary/fetus.

[141] Rachael Larimore, "The Most Meaningless Abortion Statistic Ever," *Slate*, last modified May 7, 2014, http://www.slate.com/blogs/xx_factor/2013/05/07/_3_percent_of_planned_parenthood_s_services_are_abortion_but_what_about.html.

[142] For those readers who don't already know, leprosy is one of the most feared diseases in third world countries. It is caused, not by some internal rot, but from the inability of the leper to feel pain. Without pain, the leper unintentionally and repeatedly damages his hands and feet. Normally, when you accidentally touch a hot stove, the gift of pain allows to you to quickly pull your hand away. Absent this blessing, lepers accumulate multiple grievous injuries.

[143] David D. Burns M.D., *Feeling Good: The New Mood Therapy* (New York: Quill, 2000).

[144] Ibid., 13-17.

[145] Some good Scriptures for Anxiety are: Scriptures = (Anxiety: Philippians 4:6-7, 1 Peter 5:6-8, Psalm 55:22, Proverbs 12:25, and John 14:27. Some good scriptures for depression are: Deuteronomy 31:8, Psalm 34:17, Psalm 3:3, Psalm 42:11, 1 Peter 4:12-13, and Isaiah 41:10.

[146] David Burns, *Scared Stiff* workshop held March 13-14, 2013 in Cleveland, Ohio. Hosted by the Institute for the Advancement of Human Behavior.

[147] David D. Burns M.D., *Feeling Good: The New Mood Therapy* (New York: Quill, 2000), 42-43.

---

[148] The other nine are: All-or-Nothing Thinking, Overgeneralization, Mental Filter, Disqualifying the Positive, Jumping to Conclusion, Magnification or Minimization, Should Statements, Labeling and Mislabeling, and Personalization.

[149] D. Q. McInerny, *Being Logical* (New York: Random House, 2004), 29.

[150] One of my reviewers thought this was a much better quote:
"One of these days, Alice. POW! Straight to the moon!"
~Ralph Kramden

[151] B. Farid, M. el Sherbin, and D. Raistrick, "Cognitive group therapy for wives of alcoholics-A pilot study," *Drug and Alcohol Dependency* 4 (July 17, 1986): 349-358.

[152] Joan E. Dittrich and Milton A. Trapold, "Wives of Alcoholics: A treatment program and outcome study," *Paper presented at the Annual Meeting of the Southeastern Psychological Association, Augusta, GA*, March 23-26, 1983.

[153] Marianne R. Yoshioka, Edwin J. Thomas, and Richard D. Ager. "Nagging and Other Drinking Control Efforts of Spouses of Uncooperative Alcohol Abusers: Assessment and Modification," *Journal of Substance Abuse* 4, (1992): 309-318.

[154] John Gray PhD., *Men are from Mars, Women are from Venus* (New York: Harper Collins), 1992.

[155] John Gottman, *Why Marriages Succeed or Fail* (New York: Simon & Schuster, 1994), 61.

[156] Emerson Eggerichs, *Love & Respect: The Love She Most Desires; The Respect He Desperately Needs* (Nashville: Thomas Nelson, Inc., 2004).

[157] Gary Chapman, *The Five Love Languages*. (Chicago: Northfield Publishers, 1995).

[158] Numerically, the largest loss of life was in Communist China and the Soviet Union. Proportionally large losses of life also occurred in Cambodia and Vietnam, and is still occurring today in North Korea.